THE MESSIANIC MESSAGE:

Predictions, Patterns, and the Presence of Jesus in the Old Testament

R. REED LESSING

ANDREW E. STEINMANN

ENDORSEMENTS

Too often, the messianic message of the New Testament is sundered from the Old Testament witness, as if the latter has very little to do with the former. Steinmann and Lessing show in this accessible work that the expectation of the Messiah permeates the Old Testament. The good news of Jesus Christ is not limited to the New Testament but is the message of the entire Bible.

> —**Tom Schreiner,** James Buchanan Harrison professor of New Testament interpretation and professor of biblical theology (1997), associate dean of the school of theology, The Southern Baptist Theological Seminary

Lessing and Steinmann call us to read the Old Testament in the same way as the evangelists Matthew, Mark, Luke, and John, who saw in Jesus the fulfillment of all that the Lord had promised the Messiah would do and be. Even better, *The Messianic Message* captures Jesus' own teaching that when we examine Genesis through Malachi, we will find life because they testify of Jesus, the Messiah. This gem of a book will be a blessing to the Church for years to come.

> —**Kevin S. Golden,** PhD; associate professor of exegetical theology, Concordia Seminary, St. Louis

As an Old Testament professor, the most frequent question asked of me is "How should I read the Old Testament so I can see Jesus?" Steinmann and Lessing have provided a good and accessible volume that provides an introduction into reading all Scripture with an eye on Jesus. Both pastors and laity will benefit as the Testaments, Old and New, are connected together in one story while revealing their one purpose.

> —**Dr. Jeffrey H. Pulse,** Dr. Dean O. Wenthe professor of Old Testament theology, Concordia Theological Seminary, Fort Wayne

When the resurrected Jesus appeared to His disciples, He did two things. First, He reminded them that He was the fulfillment of everything written about Him in the OT. Second, He opened their minds to read the Scriptures with this central truth in mind. Since that day, God's people have delighted in reading the OT in the light of Jesus. We love to see the shadows, patterns, and prophecies that enrich our understanding of who Jesus is and what He has done for us. In *The Messianic Message*, Steinmann and Lessing have added a valuable book to this rich reading legacy. The authors have done a great service to Christian readers who may not know how wonderfully the OT witnesses to our Lord or may have forgotten what that looks like. This book promises to be a blessing to all who read it.

—**Timothy E. Saleska,** Gustav and Sophie Butterbach professor of exegetical theology, Concordia Seminary, St. Louis

Jesus claimed that the Old Testament Scriptures testify of Him (John 5:39). We are shown how they, in fact, do so in this thorough yet highly readable book by two eminent Old Testament scholars. This long-needed volume details how Jesus, the Messiah, is foretold and foreshadowed from Genesis to Malachi. Every Christian will profit from reading how the first three-quarters of the Bible presents the messianic promise. This book is the most accessible resource I know of that displays Christ as the central message of the Old Testament.

—**David Peter,** professor of practical theology and dean of faculty, Concordia Seminary, St. Louis

Steinmann and Lessing have produced an excellent resource for pastors, students, and laypeople. Their book is comprehensive in its scope and clear in its explanations. A student recently asked me about where he could go to find out about the messianic prophecies of the Old Testament. *The Messianic Message* will now be on my recommended list.

—**Walter Maier III,** professor of exegetical theology, Concordia Theological Seminary, Fort Wayne

Steinmann and Lessing offer a comprehensive nontechnical presentation of the Bible's messianic message, summarizing its New Testament presentation before tracing its development through the Old Testament. In their book-by-book analysis of the OT, they helpfully distinguish between three types of messianic revelation: predictions, patterns (correspondences between events, people, institutions), and presence (the Lord's Messenger, divine glory), thereby taking a maximalist approach to the subject without lapsing into a Jesus-on-every-page interpretive mode. The result is a reader-friendly guide to the central theme of Scripture in its forward (OT) and backward (NT) look, undergirded by the authors' assertion of its divinely inspired unity.

—**Richard Schultz,** Blanchard professor of Old Testament, Wheaton College

THE MESSIANIC MESSAGE:

Predictions, Patterns, and the Presence of Jesus in the Old Testament

R. REED LESSING AND ANDREW E. STEINMANN

Published by Concordia Publishing House

3558 S. Jefferson Avenue, St. Louis, MO 63118-3968

1-800-325-3040 • cph.org

Manufactured in the United States of America

2 3 4 5 6 7 8 9 10 32 31 30 29 28 27 26 25 24

TABLE OF CONTENTS

FOREWORD

As educational models have evolved in North America, science and technology programs have understandably been accented. A mostly unintended consequence of such a focus is less and less exposure to history and literature. This development has made a beneficial and informed reading of the Bible, and especially of the Old Testament, more challenging.

Andrew Steinmann and Reed Lessing have written a splendid and substantive invitation to a fresh reading of the Old Testament by inviting the reader to behold and benefit from its messianic center. This entry point to reading the Old Testament bears rich fruit for multiple reasons. First, Jesus taught the apostles about His character and mission by expounding the Old Testament. The apostles, in turn, proclaimed the meaning of His person in categories and texts from the Old Testament. Jesus is to be understood as the Second Adam, Lamb of God, Suffering Servant, Prophet, Priest, King, and so on. This volume aptly links these categories by focusing on each portion of the Old Testament, from Genesis to second temple texts. While some contemporary portrayals place Jesus in alien semantic fields and make Him into a marginal peasant, a consummate therapist, or an extraordinary leader, Lessing and Steinmann honor and share the claims of the Old Testament—the proper setting to understand the historical Jesus. Second, not only the richness of these messianic interpretations but also the Christological inferences bring the entire Bible into a single story with Jesus at the center.

The hermeneutical suggestion that "Jesus' life is Israel's history reduced to one" comes through clearly in this study. Lastly, this volume describes the realities of Jesus' life in a manner that invites prayer and reflection on the depth of the Father's love in sending Jesus to take our flesh at a particular place and time. God's redemptive purpose, at the heart of the Old Testament, is fulfilled in the life, death, resurrection, and ascension of Jesus.

The attentive reader, by God's grace, will be drawn to a fuller understanding of Jesus as well as of the blessed and Holy Trinity.

Dr. Dean O. Wenthe
Professor of Old Testament
President Emeritus
Concordia Theological Seminary
Fort Wayne, Indiana

ABBREVIATIONS

Gn . . . . . . Genesis

Ex . . . . . . .Exodus

Lv . . . . . . Leviticus

Nu . . . . . .Numbers

Dt . . . .
Deuteronomy

Jsh. . . . . . .Joshua

Jgs. . . . . . .Judges

Ru . . . . Ruth

1Sm . . . . . 1 Samuel

2Sm. . . . . 2 Samuel

1Ki . . . . . . .1 Kings

2Ki. . . . . . .2 Kings

1Ch . . . .
1 Chronicles

2Ch . . . .
2 Chronicles

Ezr. . . . . . . .Ezra

Ne . . . . . Nehemiah

Est. . . . . . . Esther

Jb. . . . . .Job

Ps . . . . . . .Psalms

Pr . . . . . .Proverbs

Ec . . . .
Ecclesiastes

Sg . . . .
Song of Solomon

Is . . . . Isaiah

Jer . . . . . .Jeremiah

Lm. . . . .
Lamentations

Ezk . . . . . .Ezekiel

Dn . . . . Daniel

Hos . . . . . . Hosea

Jl . . . . .Joel

Am. . . . . . . Amos

Ob . . . . . . Obadiah

Jnh . . . . . . Jonah

Mi . . . . Micah

Na . . . . . . Nahum

Hab . . . . .Habakkuk

Zep . . . . Zephaniah

Hg . . . . Haggai

Zec . . . . Zechariah

Mal . . . . . Malachi

Mt . . . . . . Matthew

Mk. . . . . . . Mark

Lk . . . . Luke

Jn. . . . . John

Ac . . . . Acts

Rm. . . . . . Romans

1Co . . . .
1 Corinthians

2Co . . . .
2 Corinthians

Gal. . . . . . Galatians

Eph . . . . Ephesians

Php . . . . Philippians

Col. . . . . Colossians

1Th . . . .
1 Thessalonians

2Th . . . .
2 Thessalonians

1Tm . . . . 1 Timothy

2Tm. . . . 2 Timothy

Ti . . . . Titus

Phm . . . . Philemon

Heb . . . . . Hebrews

Jas. . . . . . . James

1Pt. . . . . . . 1 Peter

2Pt. . . . . . . 2 Peter

1Jn. . . . . . . 1 John

2Jn . . . . . . 2 John

3Jn . . . . . . 3 John

Jude . . . . . Jude

Rv . . . . . Revelation

PREFACE

"Sir, we wish to see Jesus" (Jn 12:21). That is what some visiting Greeks asked Philip while they were in Jerusalem for Passover. They wanted to see Jesus.

There were a lot of people who wanted to see Jesus. Magi traveled for hundreds of miles. Shepherds left their sheep. Fishermen abandoned their boats. Zacchaeus climbed a tree. These people took decisive action. They had to see Jesus.

JESUS

People have given more adoration to Jesus, more attention to Jesus, and more devotion to Jesus than any other person who has ever lived. People have analyzed, debated, scrutinized, and sifted through every recorded word Jesus ever said. After two thousand years, there is never a minute that millions of people are not reading and studying about Jesus.

Think about it. Here is a person who lived on the margins of the Roman Empire two millennia ago, yet His birth divides the centuries—BC and AD. BC, before Christ, and AD (anno Domini, the year of our Lord), after Christ.

CHRIST

When we hear the term *Christ*, we sometimes misunderstand it. Christ is not Jesus' last name. Christ is a title. It is the Greek translation of the Hebrew word *Messiah*, which means "anointed one." With only four exceptions (out of 130 occurrences in the Old Testament), the verb *anoint* refers to a ritual when oil is used to inaugurate or dedicate someone or something. To be anointed means to be designated, set apart, consecrated, appointed, and elected by God as an object or person for divine service.

Although others were anointed, specifically priests[1] and prophets,[2] the focus of the Old Testament is on anointed kings. And then the spotlight shines on one final, end-time messianic king—Jesus. Jesus is Israel's ultimate, definitive, and supreme Anointed One. He is the Messiah. God the Father selected His Son, Jesus, to do what Old Testament–anointed kings, priest, and prophets failed to do—usher in the kingdom of God. Israel's messianic hope, then, is central to the Bible's message. Jesus, the Christ, stands at the heart of the biblical revelation.

Since it would have been difficult—if not impossible—for non-Aramaic speakers during the time following Jesus' ministry to understand the term *Messiah*, the word appears only twice in the New Testament (Jn 1:41; 4:25). Compare that with the more common Greek title *Christ*, which occurs 529 times.[3] Jesus Christ, then, is another way of saying Jesus, the Messiah.

A broader understanding of the Messiah derives from John the Baptist's question "Are You the one who is to come?" (Mt 11:3; Lk 7:19). Connecting the Old Testament messianic hope with the idea of a "coming one"—just like John the Baptist—enables us to broaden this study to include a number of passages that promise an end-time deliverer who will restore all things—though He is not always called "the Messiah."

To see Jesus as the promised Messiah is to take a deep dive into the Old Testament—thirty-nine books chock-full of drama and action, poetry and praise. Be honest, though. When you hear the words *Old*

1 E.g., Lv 4:3, 5, 16; 6:22.

2 1Ki 19:16; 1Ch 16:22; Ps 105:15; Is 61:1.

3 "G5547 - christos - Strong's Greek Lexicon (ESV)." Blue Letter Bible. https://www.blueletterbible.org/lexicon/g5547/esv/mgnt/0-1/.

Testament, what is your initial reaction? "Oh no! Not a lecture again on the Hittites and Jebusites." "This will be all Law with no Gospel." "There's no benefit in learning about Jeremiah, Jehoshaphat, Jonah, or Josiah."

We understand these feelings. At one time, that is what we thought about the Old Testament. After all, when we first are exposed to the Old Testament, whether as children or adults, it is largely though Bible narratives—stories about creation, the tower of Babel, Abraham, Moses, David, or Nehemiah. When we encounter the Old Testament in this way, it can seem simply to be a prelude to the New Testament or nothing more than interesting historical background material with a few poems (Psalms), some wise sayings (Proverbs), and the writings of some stern prophets of doom who directed their message at the unfaithful among the people of Israel. For us, as with many Christians, the significant section of the Bible began in Matthew—and not even Matthew 1:1 but Matthew 1:18. After all, that Gospel's first seventeen verses are just a list of Old Testament names. Therefore, many conclude that the Christian faith begins with the birth of Jesus.

Is it any wonder that we have all looked at the Old Testament and summarized it with one word: *irrelevant*? Some of us have been confused by the complexity of Israel's history and quickly shoved it aside. Others have been overwhelmed by the Old Testament's long lists, bloody wars, and strange things like Methuselah's longevity, the Urim and Thummim, and Isaiah going barefoot and naked for three years. Besides, the Old Testament is one huge failure—Israel could never get on the straight-and-narrow path, so why spend time reading about one disaster after another?

That is why it is tempting to reduce the story of the Old Testament to Adam and Eve—of every person sinning and needing a Savior. Genesis 4 through Malachi, then, is not necessary—not once you know about the fall into sin and the promise that God will make things right again.

Then there are the Church's creeds. After both the Apostles' and Nicene Creeds state that God made the heavens and the earth, they jump straight to Jesus. If the creeds do not mention anything in the rest of the Old Testament, then why should we bother with it?

Furthermore, Jesus frequently rebukes the Jews. They had wrong ideas about God, the Gentiles, salvation—you name it, and they did not understand it. And their Bible was the Old Testament, right? Case closed. There is no need for it.

To the contrary! There is an indispensable need for Israel's Scriptures. The books from Genesis to Malachi are like beautiful stained glass windows with different shapes and colors. They portray a wonderful portrait of the world's most important figure: Jesus, the Messiah and Savior of the world. Our primary reason for writing this book is to help you see Jesus in the Old Testament so that your relationship with Him deepens and your knowledge of God's Word increases. Then you will see what the New Testament sees—that Israel's Scriptures not only speak of the Messiah but also identify Jesus as the Christ.

Thus, the Messiah did not appear unannounced. His cross and empty tomb are declared in advance throughout the pages of Israel's sacred texts. After rebuking Cleopas and his companion on the road to Emmaus for their slowness to learn, Jesus opened the Scriptures—the Old Testament—for them (Lk 24:27). He will do the same for you.

We invite you to see Jesus.

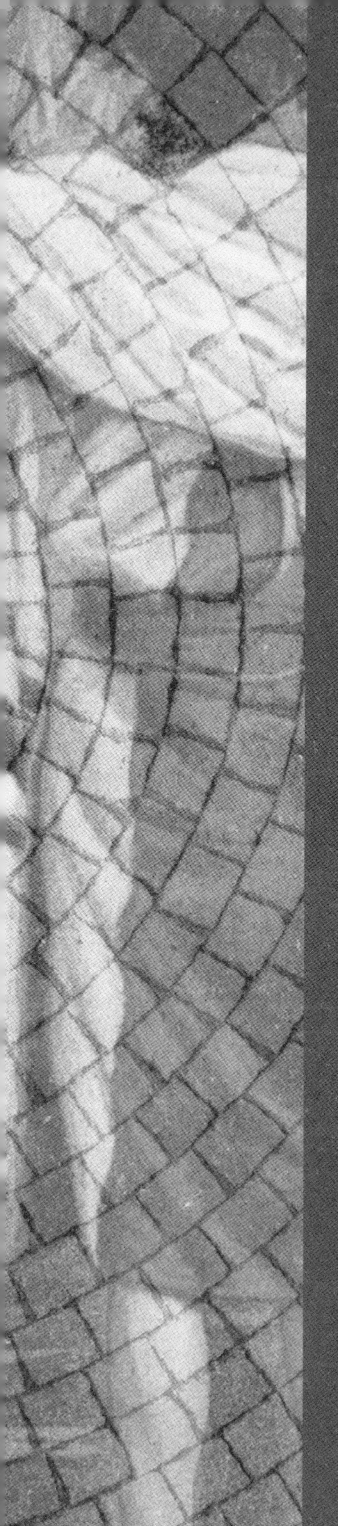

CHAPTER 1

THE MESSIANIC EMPHASIS OF THE NEW TESTAMENT

In 1866, Katherine Hankey wrote the lyrics of the song "I Love to Tell the Story." The well-known refrain added by William G. Fisher in 1869 includes these words:

> I love to tell the story, 'Twill be my theme in glory,
>
> To tell the old, old story Of Jesus and His love.

Where does the old, old story begin? In the Jerusalem temple, with the angel's message to Zechariah about John the Baptist? In Nazareth, with Gabriel's announcement to Mary? In Bethlehem, with Christ's birth? Matthew says that the story begins with Abraham (Mt 1:1). Mark writes that it begins with Isaiah (Mk 1:1–2). Luke tells us that the story begins with Adam (Lk 3:38). John says it commences with the creation of the world (Jn 1:1).

With great clarity, the four Gospel writers announce that the old, old story of the Messiah and His love begins in the Old Testament. This is the consistent belief throughout the rest of the New Testament. That is why, before we survey the Old Testament, we want to demonstrate that the authors from Matthew through the Book of Revelation read Israel's sacred texts messianically.

The first half of this chapter consists of how the New Testament speaks of the Messiah. We analyze the four Gospels, the Book of Acts, Paul's writings, and Revelation. Then, in the second half, we ask this question: What interpretive tools did these New Testament authors use to see the Messiah so clearly in the Old Testament?

MATTHEW

Matthew begins his Gospel by summarizing the Old Testament with a genealogical list of names, using three sets of fourteens—or six sevens (Mt 1:1–17). Biblical stories usually have complete sets of sevens. A story with six sevens is not a complete story. There must be another seven. Matthew's story lacks an ending. That is his point. The Messiah brings the Old Testament story to completion. He is the seventh seven. Jesus ushers in the final stage in God's plan of salvation. Matthew, therefore, begins his Gospel by stating that the Old Testament is headed toward a goal. Though Israel's history is checkered and often tragic, full of faithlessness and failures, there is symmetry and purpose to it. The promised Messiah holds it all together.

Jesus, then, is Israel's end-time Messiah, who fulfills and completes the Old Testament. Matthew hammers his point home throughout his Gospel by citing ten specific Old Testament promises, writing "so that what was spoken by the prophets might be fulfilled" (Mt 2:23, et al). He also cites the Old Testament an additional fifty times and alludes to it more than two hundred fifty times.

There is more. In Greek, the first two words in Matthew's Gospel are *biblos geneseōs*—literally "the book of origins" but often translated along the lines of "the book of the genealogy" (Mt 1:1). However, because the same phrase that can be translated as "the book of the origins" appears in Genesis 5:1—a verse that cites Adam and creation—it is better to set the story of Jesus as originating in the Old Testament. This is the whole point of Matthew's Gospel. The Messiah comes to complete what God started, to renew what had become old, and to perfect and bring to fulfillment everything God planned and promised from Genesis to Malachi. Jesus says as much.

> Jesus said to them, "Truly, I say to you, in the new world [also translated: *in the renewal of things*], when the Son of Man will sit on His glorious throne, you who have followed Me will also sit on twelve thrones, judging the twelve tribes of Israel." (Mt 19:28)

When the Messiah says "the renewal of things," the "things" refer to the Old Testament—beginning with the account of creation in the Book of Genesis. Jesus had a script. It was the entire Old Testament.

MARK

Mark begins and leads his Gospel to its pivotal point with the confession that Jesus is the Messiah—like Matthew, making his Gospel a messianic Gospel (Mk 1:1; 15:32). Designating Jesus as the Messiah is not a secondary theme for Mark. It comprises the foundational framework in which he presents Jesus.

Several times, Jesus forbids His followers to tell others that He is the Messiah—when He cleanses a leper (Mk 1:43–44), raises Jairus's daughter (Mk 5:43), restores a man's hearing and speaking (Mk 7:36), praises Peter's confession (Mk 8:30), and debriefs His disciples after His transfiguration (Mk 9:9). Why be silent? Because the Savior's messianic calling was radically different from other messianic narratives circulating in first-century Palestine. None of them taught about a *crucified* Messiah.

For example, the Psalms of Salomon, Jewish hymns composed about 50 BC, reflect the following messianic ideas. The Messiah will do these things:

1. Defeat the foreign nations who occupy Judah and Jerusalem
2. Judge the nations of the earth
3. Bring these nations to serve him
4. Rule Israel in wisdom and righteousness
5. Remove all foreigners from Israel
6. Purge the land of unrighteous Israelites
7. Eliminate all oppression
8. Gather a holy people[4]

Other Palestinian movements awaited a Messiah with supernatural power (e.g., 1 Enoch 37–71), while at Qumran (the Dead Sea community), people envisioned two messiahs—one priestly and another kingly.[5] Philo, a leading Jewish thinker of the day, held out hope for a Messiah who would conquer the nations.[6] Jewish writings at this time give the Messiah several titles, such as "Son of David," "Son of God," "the Prophet," "Elect One," "Prince," "Scepter," "Star," "Chosen One," and "Coming One." None of them, however, come close to "Suffering Servant" or "the Crucified One."

That is why Mark leaves no doubt that the cross is the Messiah's destiny. Five times in his Passion narrative, the evangelist connects

---

4 For more on this, see "Psalms of Salomon" in *New English Translation of the Septuagint* (Oxford University Press, 2009), http://ccat.sas.upenn.edu/nets/edition/31-pssal-nets.pdf.

5 For further reading, see 1QS 9.11; and 1QSa 2.17–22 in Joseph A. Fitzmyer, *A Guide to the Dead Sea Scrolls and Related Literature* (Grand Rapids, MI: Eerdmans, 2008).

6 For further reading from Philo on the theology and prophetic office of Moses, see *On the Life of Moses* 1.290–291, http://www.earlychristianwritings.com/Yonge/book24.html.

Jesus with the title "King of the Jews." Pilate asks Jesus if He is this king (Mk 15:2), then asks the crowd if they want him to release "the King of the Jews" (Mk 15:9). Roman soldiers also call Him by the title (Mk 15:18), and it is posted on the sign above His head (Mk 15:26). The chief priests and the scribes mock Him as well, using the title "the King of Israel" (Mk 15:32), and the criminals crucified with Jesus revile Him (Mk 15:32). Do you see the irony? The Messiah's archenemies call Him the Messiah. The Crucified One—for friend and foe alike—is the God-ordained Messiah of the world.

LUKE

Like Matthew, Luke highlights Jesus' Davidic origins. In his first chapter, the third evangelist mentions David three times (Lk 1:27, 32, 69). Luke cements this connection in his second chapter, where he accents Joseph's ties to the house of David (Lk 2:4), thus indicating that Jesus is the Messiah (Lk 2:11). Importantly, Luke 2:11 also connects the title of *Messiah* with *Lord* (cf. Ac 2:36). *The Messiah is God incarnate*. He is also God's Son—a messianic title the Father bestows upon Him at His Baptism (Lk 3:22; cf. Ps 2:7).

After affirming His messianic mission while the devil tempts Him to deny it (Lk 4:1–13), Jesus cites Isaiah 61:1–2 while preaching at a synagogue in His hometown of Nazareth. "The Spirit of the Lord is upon Me, because He has anointed Me" (Lk 4:18).

At the end of his Gospel, Luke furthers our understanding of the Messiah. Two times after His resurrection, Jesus declares that He is the central message of the Old Testament (Lk 24:25–27, 44–45). In both encounters, Jesus uses the word *all* (Lk 24:25, 27, 44). The entire Old Testament—not merely a dozen-or-so proof passages—points to Jesus as the goal of Israel's messianic hope.

JOHN

Just as Matthew, Mark, and Luke highlight Simon Peter's declaration regarding Jesus—"You are the Christ [*Messiah*], the Son of the living God"[7]—John's goal is also for people to believe that "Jesus is the Christ" (Jn 20:31). In fact, the fourth evangelist employs the term *Christ* seventeen times in his Gospel. He even uses the Hebrew word *Messiah* twice (Jn 1:41; 4:25) instead of the Greek equivalent *Christ*.

But what about John 1:17? It does not seem to invite a messianic reading of the Old Testament. The verse sounds much more like Israel's Scriptures only consist of Law: "For the law was given through Moses; grace and truth came through Jesus Christ."

Some clarifications are in order. First, John's use of *law* in this verse does not mean the Ten Commandments. Instead, it implies the Pentateuch—the first five books in the Old Testament written by Moses. Second, there is no *but* after the word *Moses*. John is not making a contrast. The Pentateuch, as well as grace and truth, are God's gifts. Third, the Pentateuch "was given." It is a divine gift, while even more so are grace and truth in Jesus.

The relationship between the Testaments, therefore, is not one of contradiction but of completion. Supplying grace has become super-abounding grace (Jn 1:16). In fact, later in his Gospel, John quotes Jesus as saying, "For if you believed Moses, you would believe Me; for he wrote of Me" (Jn 5:46). Do you need more clarification? Then consider this: "Philip found Nathanael and said to him, 'We have found Him of whom Moses in the Law and also the prophets wrote'" (Jn 1:45). Here is the point: Genesis through Malachi bear witness to Jesus (Jn 5:39).

---

7 Mt 16:16; see also Mk 8:29; Lk 9:20.

The Samaritan woman calls Jesus the Messiah (Jn 4:26, 29). This is followed by a debate over whether Jesus is the Messiah.[8] Jewish authorities attempt to silence the discussion (Jn 9:22). It all comes to a head on Good Friday.

Pilate questions Jesus. He asks, "Are You the King of the Jews?" (Jn 18:33). *King* means one thing to the Jews—the Messiah. It means something else to the Romans—a military ruler. The chief priests want to confuse Pilate into thinking that Jesus is a military leader, and thus a threat to Rome. It does not work because Jesus tells Pilate, "My kingdom is not of this world" (Jn 18:36). The Roman governor has Jesus scourged just short of death. Pilate hopes that now everyone will just go home.

But the crowd is not satisfied. They want more. They want the Messiah killed. So the Jews play their trump card. They say to Pilate, "If you release this man, you are not Caesar's friend" (Jn 19:12). Pilate knows exactly what they mean. At the time, Caesar—the King, Tiberius—was sick, suspicious, and often violent. He would not like getting news about a riot in Judea, especially when Pilate was appointed there only because of family connections. This is blackmail, pure and simple. And it works. If the choice had been between Jesus and the Jews, Pilate would have let Jesus go. But that is not how the Jewish leaders frame the issue. It is a choice between Jesus and Rome.

Pilate asks, "Shall I crucify your King?" (Jn 19:15). This Messiah is not the military type, looking for a battle. No. This Messiah is the suffering and bleeding type, looking for us. The chief priests answer Pilate, "We have no king but Caesar" (Jn 19:15). A Jewish riot would end Pilate's political career. He caves in. Pilate orders the Messiah to be crucified.

---

8 Jn 7:26–27, 31, 41–42; 10:24–25; 12:34.

THE BOOK OF ACTS

Just like the four Gospels, the foundational message in the Book of Acts is that Jesus is the long-awaited Messiah. For instance, on Pentecost, Peter proclaims that Jesus is now enthroned as the Messiah at God's right hand (Ac 2:34–36). Fisherman-turned-preacher Peter uses Psalm 110:1, a text Jesus also employs to announce that as David's son He is also David's Lord.[9]

Like his message on Pentecost, while preaching in Solomon's Colonnade after healing a lame man, Peter says that this miracle happened in the name of Jesus, God's Messiah (Ac 3:18). Peter goes on to say that Jesus is the prophet Moses predicted—in fact, all the prophets foresaw the Messiah's day (Ac 3:17–24). When Peter subsequently defends the lame man's healing before the Jewish Council (the Sanhedrin), he quotes from these messianic words in Psalm 118:22: "The stone that the builders rejected has become the cornerstone" (see Ac 4:11). Peter's confessions in Acts 2–4 are echoed throughout the rest of the Book of Acts.[10] The Jesus story is a messianic story.

The longest sermon in Acts reaches its pinnacle when Stephen declares that Old Testament prophets announced the Messiah's advent—Jesus, the Righteous One (Ac 7:52). In Paul's first speech in Acts, in Pisidian Antioch, he argues that Jesus is the Messiah, basing his case upon the fact that Jesus is a descendant of David (Ac 13:22–23). The apostle goes on in Acts 13:33 to reference Psalm 2:7: "You are My Son; today I have begotten You." Paul follows the same strategy while in Thessalonica (Ac 17:1–3), arguing from the Old Testament that the Messiah had to suffer and rise from the dead. Christians in the Book of Acts do not set aside the Old Testament. They announce its completion.

9 Mt 22:41–45; Mk 12:35–37; Lk 20:41–44.

10 E.g., Ac 5:42; 9:22; 17:3; 18:5, 28.

Here is part of Paul's defense when he was on trial before the Roman governor Felix: "But this I confess to you, that according to the Way, which they call a sect, I worship the God of our fathers, believing everything laid down by the Law and written in the Prophets" (Ac 24:14). Later, stating his case to another Roman leader, Festus, Paul asserts, "To this day I have had the help that comes from God, and so I stand here testifying both to small and great, saying nothing but what the prophets and Moses said would come to pass" (Ac 26:22). The apostle summarizes "the prophets and Moses"—our Old Testament—by announcing that the Messiah must suffer, rise from the dead, and be a light to Israel and the nations (Ac 26:23). No wonder Luke writes that followers of Jesus in Syrian Antioch were called "Christians."[11] The Church was (and still is) a messianic movement.

PAUL'S LETTERS

The confession that Jesus is the Messiah permeates the New Testament, but these same writings reveal that the title was only applied to Jesus in a consistent way after His death, resurrection, and ascension. For instance, *Christ* appears only seven times in Mark's account of the life of Jesus but sixty-five times in Paul's Letter to the Church at Rome. Jesus Himself largely avoided the designation because it had developed misleading connotations. Many Jews of His day longed for a Messiah who would exercise political and military control from Jerusalem.

That was Paul's definition of Messiah. On the road to Damascus, though, his definition changed—radically. The resurrected and glorified Messiah appeared to Paul, thus vindicating His suffering on the

11 Ac 11:26; cf. Ac 26:28; 1Pt 4:16.

cross for the sin of the world. This became the theme of Paul's first sermons, preached in several Damascus synagogues (Ac 9:20–22): the crucified Messiah has triumphed over death and the grave. The apostle went on to make this message the centerpiece of his writings, employing the term *Christ* (*Messiah*) 270 times from Romans to Philemon.

Romans 15:19 summarizes this message: it is "the gospel of Christ." Moreover, Romans 1:2–4 and 15:12 create a set of messianic brackets composed at the beginning and ending of Romans. In the middle, Paul sums up God's gifts to Israel with these words: "To them [Old Testament Israel] belong the patriarchs, and from their race, according to the flesh, is the Messiah" (Rm 9:5, authors' translation). The Messiah is God's ultimate gift for His people.

And this Messiah was crucified—a stumbling block for Jews and folly to Gentiles (1Co 1:23)—but deeply rooted in the Old Testament. "For I delivered to you as of first importance what I also received: that Christ died for our sins in accordance with the Scriptures" (1Co 15:3). Note that Paul says that Jesus' death was according to the Scriptures. Why does the apostle Paul state things so broadly? What books, chapters, and verses specifically state that the Messiah would die and be raised? The answer: there are too many Old Testament texts for Paul to list!

For instance, note the apostle's appropriation of messianic psalms to Jesus.[12] The messianic age has arrived. We are now living in the last days (Rm 13:12; 1Co 10:11). To be "in Christ" is to participate in the coming of the Messiah's kingdom (2Co 5:17).

But what about Galatians 3–4? At first glance, Paul appears to teach that the Old Testament is Law-based and filled with moralists,

12 Rm 11:9/Ps 68:23–24; Rm 15:3/Ps 68:10; Rm 15:9/Ps 18:50; Rm 15:11/Ps 117:1; 2Co 4:13–14/Ps 116:10.

ritualists, and legalists. Paul's argument, however, is not between the Old Testament and New Testament. It is between the right understanding and the wrong understanding of the Old Testament. Old Testament Israelites are not Paul's enemies. Judaizing legalists in Galatia are.

Similarly, 2 Corinthians 3:6–18 looks like the Old Testament "kills" and is both "the ministry of death" and "the ministry of condemnation." Here, however, Paul is not describing the entirety of the Old Testament. Instead, his focus is upon what is "carved in letters on stone" (2Co 3:7)—that is, the Ten Commandments. The Ten Commandments bring death and condemnation. When God's revelation at Sinai is taken out of its grace-based context (Ex 20:1–2), when we try to achieve a relationship with God by what we do, divine mandates kill and condemn. Just like in Galatians 3–4, in 2 Corinthians 3, Paul is not belittling the Old Testament. He is pointing out a Jewish misreading that had no place for a gracious Messiah.

THE BOOK OF REVELATION

In the Book of Revelation, John employs the term *Christ* for Jesus in 1:1, 2, 5; 11:15; 12:10; 20:4, and 6—for a total of seven appearances. Given the importance of the number 7 in Revelation, John presents Jesus as the world's perfect Messiah. Additionally, Revelation 12:10 employs the expression "the authority of His Christ," thus alluding to Psalm 2:8–9—a key messianic psalm. Psalm 2:9 is applied to Jesus again in Revelation 19:15, which includes the phrase "He will rule them with a rod of iron."

The beast in Revelation also has authority.[13] His comes from brute force; the Messiah's comes from His shed blood and empty

13 Rv 13:4–5, 7, 12; cf. 17:12–13.

tomb. Alive on the third day, Jesus sits upon the throne, along with His Father.[14] John's visions, then, in chapters 4–21, are framed by the Messiah's victory and exaltation. He is the Lion from the tribe of Judah and the Root of David who has triumphed (Rv 5:5).

SEEING THE MESSIAH IN THE OLD TESTAMENT

How did these New Testament authors so vividly see the Messiah in the Old Testament? What interpretive tools did they use? Where did they get the idea that the Old Testament is a unified collection of writings revealing God's plan of salvation for all people through His crucified and risen Messiah? Inspired by the Holy Spirit, these writers read Israel's Scriptures looking for messianic predictions and patterns, along with the Messiah's presence.

MESSIANIC PREDICTIONS

Perhaps you are familiar with the expression "winged words." Some words take flight and travel great distances. Old Testament messianic predictions are like that—they travel through vast amounts of time and history, finally to land upon the Messiah.

This is what Peter says: "Concerning this salvation, the prophets who prophesied about the grace that was to be yours searched and inquired carefully, inquiring what person or time the Spirit of the Messiah in them was indicating when he predicted the sufferings of the Messiah and the subsequent glories" (1Pt 1:10–11, authors' translation). Old Testament writers studied. They searched. They inquired. Then they made messianic predictions. We can group their predictions about the Messiah into several categories—the Messiah's first advent, His ministry, Holy Week events, and His second advent.

---

14 Rv 3:21; 22:1, 3.

THE MESSIAH'S FIRST ADVENT

Several Old Testament prophets predicted the Messiah's coming. Amos peers into the future, using the categories that made the most sense to him, revolving around a rebuilt Davidic city (Am 9:11). Isaiah speaks about a shoot from Jesse's stump (Is 11:1), while Jeremiah sees a new David who is "a righteous Sprout, a King who will reign wisely and do what is just and right in the land" (Jer 23:5, authors' translation). Micah envisions a new David coming from Bethlehem who will be "ruler in Israel, whose coming forth is from of old, from ancient days" (Mi 5:2), while Ezekiel declares that in the coming age God will set over His people "one shepherd, My servant David" (Ezk 34:23; cf. 37:24–25).

This hope that David's line would be restored is not confined to these prophets from the Southern Kingdom. When David lamented the deaths of Saul and Jonathan (2Sm 1:11–27) and made a covenant with the North (2Sm 5:1–3), he endeared himself to the Northern Kingdom as well. When David returned to Jerusalem after Absalom's revolt, the North expressed a greater claim upon him than the people of Judah (2Sm 19:43). Hence, even the Northern prophet Hosea promises a return to Davidic splendor (Hos 1:11; 3:5).

THE MESSIAH'S MINISTRY

After the Messiah emerged victorious in the wilderness over Satan, He began His public ministry, making His headquarters in Capernaum—the ancient territory of the northern tribes of Zebulun and Naphtali—thus fulfilling this prophecy:

> In the latter time He has made glorious the way of the sea, the land beyond the Jordan, Galilee of the nations. The people who walked in darkness have seen a great light; those who dwelt in a land of deep darkness, on them has light shone. (Is 9:1–2; cf. Mt 4:13–16)

When John the Baptist was in prison, he sent messengers to Jesus, asking, "Are You the one who is to come, or shall we look for another?" (Mt 11:3). The Savior's answer references Isaiah 35:5–6: "The blind receive their sight and the lame walk, lepers are cleansed and the deaf hear, and the dead are raised up, and the poor have good news preached to them" (Mt 11:5).

HOLY WEEK EVENTS

Sometimes we approach the New Testament as though it fills in the blanks left by Old Testament prophecies. This is not always the case. Old Testament passages like Genesis 3:15 (the Messiah's battle with Satan) and Psalm 22:14 ("My heart is like wax; it is melted within My breast") give us insights into Good Friday that the four Gospel writers do not. Then there is Isaiah 52:13–53:12, a section that sheds more insight on the Messiah's suffering and death than any other place in the Bible.

The temple cleansing—predicted in Isaiah 56:7—is expanded in the Synoptic Gospels.[15] And to describe Palm Sunday, both Matthew 21:5 and John 12:15 quote from Zechariah 9:9, filling out the contours of that momentous day.

THE MESSIAH'S SECOND ADVENT

Daniel calls the Messiah "Son of Man"—a title that the New Testament employs for Jesus eighty-eight times—and predicts His return upon the clouds (Dn 7:13). At Jesus' second coming, the Ancient of Days (who is God the Father) will give the Messiah an eternal kingdom and all people will worship Him (Dn 7:14). At that time, the dead will be raised—some to everlasting contempt and others to everlasting life (Dn 12:1–3). Death will be defeated; indeed, it will be swallowed up forever (Is 25:6–9). David's prediction of the

15 Mt 21:13; Mk 11:17; Lk 19:46.

Messiah will finally come to pass: "The Lord says to my Lord: 'Sit at My right hand, until I make Your enemies Your footstool'" (Ps 110:1). At long last, when the Messiah returns, He will crush the enemy's head (Gn 3:15). Satan will not only be defeated; he will also be destroyed in a lake of fire (Rv 20:10).

MESSIANIC PATTERNS

Messianic predictions are only understandable when considering future fulfillment. For instance, Zechariah 12:10 states, "They look on Me, on Him whom they have pierced." This makes sense only if it describes the Messiah pierced by a Roman soldier on Good Friday (Jn 19:34). On the other hand, messianic patterns do not need a future reference for us to understand them. For instance, when Moses writes about a Passover lamb's blood saving Israelites from the angel of death, we know what he means. There is salvation in the blood of the lamb (Ex 12:13). The promise of protecting blood, though, sets a pattern that is repeated in Israel's worship life (as detailed in the Book of Leviticus) and reaches its fulfillment when Jesus dies through the horror of crucifixion (Jn 1:29).

Messianic predictions and patterns, however, have several features in common. Both spring from the belief that the Old Testament is a forward-looking collection of books that focus on the Messiah. And both believe that the gracious and sovereign work of God will bring about creation's renewal and restoration.

DEFINING MESSIANIC PATTERNS

We can compare a messianic pattern to a stone that is dropped in the middle of a pond, creating a ripple effect—small waves move out from the center and land upon the bank. From a biblical standpoint, these waves include people (e.g., Adam, Moses, and Aaron), events (e.g., creation and the exodus), and institutions (e.g., the tabernacle and temple). Messianic patterns parallel and find deeper realization in Jesus. The past sets the stage for the future.

Patterns do not only move from the Old Testament to the New. They also appear within Israel's Scriptures, with Old Testament patterns referencing other Old Testament events. Take, for example, the exodus from Egypt. It certainly foreshadows the Messiah's exodus—way out—of the tomb on Easter. That is what Jesus says in Luke 9:30–31. Yet Isaiah foresees Judean captives in Babylon marching in freedom in much the same way their ancestors came out of Egypt (Is 43:14–21).

What does this mean? New Testament authors learned how to look for patterns from their Old Testament counterparts. What God did in the past, He will do in the future—though in a greater and better way. The key ideas with messianic patterns are correspondence, continuity, heightening, and fulfillment.

EXAMPLES OF MESSIANIC PATTERNS

Jonah's three days and three nights in the big fish, this corresponds with the Messiah's death and resurrection (Mt 12:39–41; Lk 11:29–30). The queen of the South was attracted to Solomon's wisdom, while the ends of the earth will be drawn to the Messiah (Mt 12:42; Lk 11:31). Elisha miraculously fed hundreds of people with twenty loaves of bread (2Ki 4:42–44). The Messiah did that, and then some—providing bread and fish for more than 5,000 men.[16]

Let us take a more detailed look at these words from Hosea 11:1: "Out of Egypt I called My son." Moses led Israel out of Egypt, but the nation repeatedly rebelled against God and His Word. The tortuous relationship resulted in the multiple deportations to Babylon in the late seventh and early sixth century BC.

16 Mt 14:13–21; Mk 6:30–44; Lk 9:10–17; Jn 6:1–14.

Matthew tells us that Joseph, Mary, and Jesus fled to Egypt to escape King Herod's wrath. Upon leaving Egypt, after Herod's death, Matthew cites Hosea 11:1: "This was to fulfill what the Lord had spoken by the prophet, 'Out of Egypt I called My son'" (Mt 2:15).

This is a remarkable claim: Jesus, the Messiah, embodies, represents, and summarizes Israel's history. He goes where Israel went—Egypt. He stood where Israel stood—the Jordan River (Mt 3:13–17; cf. Jsh 3–4). And the Messiah encountered temptation where Israel encountered temptation—in the wilderness (Mt 4:1–11). To understand Israel's exodus from Egypt, forty-year sojourn in the wilderness, and entrance into the Promised Land is to understand the Messiah. He relived Israel's history faithfully and perfectly.

The Messiah's forty days in the wilderness (Mt 4:1–11) are worth exploring further. Consider these parallels between Israel and the Messiah. Both are called God's "son."[17] In both circumstances, God tests to prepare for a great mission (Israel, entering the Promised Land; Jesus, His public ministry). And, of course, the number *40* and the location are exact matches. Jesus even quotes from Deuteronomy 6:13, 16; and 8:3, indicating that He is recapitulating Israel's story—carrying things to their intended consummation (Mt 4:4, 7, 10).

What do these patterns imply about the Messiah? First, He is not a revolutionary. Jesus did not come to establish something new but to renew and fulfill something old—Israel's long and often-tragic history with God. Second, the Messiah is superior to the Old Testament; He is not different, but He is better and greater. Third, the Messiah ushers in the last days. He not only repeats many events, people, and institutions in the Old Testament but He also perfects them. This means that the messianic age has arrived; the end of the ages has

17 Ex 4:22; Dt 8:5; Mt 4:3, 6.

come.[18] Finally, patterns demonstrate that Jesus fulfills more than a handful of Old Testament predictions. He completes and consummates the entirety of Israel's sacred texts.

MESSIANIC PRESENCE

Through predictions and patterns, we see the Messiah in the Old Testament. We also see Him when He is present—present through the form of the Lord's Messenger and divine glory. What do we mean? The Messiah's work of salvation does not begin in Bethlehem. As the Old Testament was unfolding, Jesus was not prepping for His birth and subsequent ministry or simply practicing His lines and preparing for His bitter agony and suffering on the cross. Does it make sense to suppose Jesus was sitting on the sidelines in heaven waiting to get into the action? Not on your life!

THE LORD'S MESSENGER

It might be strange to think of Jesus as present and active before His birth in Bethlehem, but the human restrictions to time and space do not apply to Him. Long before the Messiah became flesh in Mary's womb, He was present in the world as the "angel of the Lord." The term appears fifty-seven times from Genesis 16:7 through Zechariah 12:8. This angel does not appear sporadically or occasionally. He delivers and rescues throughout the Old Testament.

We get confused because of the word *angel*. More literally, the Hebrew word denotes *messenger,* which describes what an angel does rather than what an angel consists of. Every angel is a messenger, but only the Messiah is the Messenger who is one substance with the Father.

---

18 1Co 10:11; also note Heb 1:2, "But in these *last days* He has spoken to us by His Son" (emphasis added).

The Messenger first appears to Hagar near the spring on the way to Shur after she had fled from Sarai's mistreatment (Gn 16:7). He makes a promise that only God can make: "I will surely multiply your offspring so that they cannot be numbered for multitude" (Gn 16:10). Hagar realizes that she has seen God (Gn 16:13). Later, when Hagar and Ishmael are expelled from Abraham's camp, the Messenger of God called to her and once again promised her concerning her son, "I will make him into a great nation" (Gn 21:18).

The Lord's messenger also speaks to Abraham to stop him before he sacrifices Isaac on Mount Moriah (Gn 22:11, 15). Again, this Messenger is identified as God when He says, "You have not withheld your son, your only son, from Me" (Gn 22:12) and "I will surely bless you, and I will surely multiply your offspring as the stars of heaven and as the sand that is on the seashore" (Gn 22:17).

Near the end of his life, Jacob refers to this Messenger when he blesses Joseph's sons, Ephraim and Manasseh: "The God before whom my ancestors Abraham and Isaac walked, the God who has been my shepherd all of my life to this day, the Messenger who has redeemed me from all danger: May he bless these boys" (Gn 48:15–16, authors' translation).

God's epiphany at the burning bush (Ex 3:2–6) makes clear that the Lord's Messenger and the Lord share the same attributes. The Messenger appears (Ex 3:2), the Lord speaks (Ex 3:4, 7), and then God speaks (Ex 3:6, 12, 14–15). This same Messenger then goes ahead of Israel to defeat the nation's enemies (Ex 23:20; 32:34).

The Messenger of the Lord appears several times in the Book of Judges. He admonishes Israel for its unfaithfulness when He says, "I brought you up from Egypt and brought you into the land that I swore to give to your fathers" (Jgs 2:1). Later, He appears to Samson's mother and father. On this occasion, Manoah confessed,

"We have seen God!" (Jgs 13:22). This Messenger is unlike other angelic beings in the Old Testament. He displays divine attributes, actions, and names. He is even worshiped.

Sometimes this Messenger is simply called a man. Jacob wrestles all night with a "man" (Gn 32:24). The next morning, Jacob says, "I have seen God face to face" (Gn 32:30). Joshua also has a vision from heaven that includes a man (Jsh 5:13). He is "the commander of the army of the LORD" (Jsh 5:14). This same man appears to Zechariah throughout his eight visions[19] explaining God's actions and plans for the world. Importantly, this is how John explains the role of the Messiah—the Messiah explains the Father (Jn 1:18). It follows, therefore, that anyone who sees the Messenger sees the Father (Jn 14:9).

There are several important clarifications about this Messenger. In the Old Testament, the Messenger takes the form of a man. In the New Testament, the Messenger takes the flesh of a man. From Genesis through Zechariah, the Messenger appears as a man but is not yet a part of humanity. When the Messiah becomes incarnate, He keeps His deity while becoming a real human being.

DIVINE GLORY

The Messiah is present through the Lord's Messenger. He is also present through God's display of glory. We might think that glory is something we feel. However, in the Bible, glory is something people see. It is tangible and visible. Throughout the Bible, people say, "I *saw* God's glory!"

Messianic glory first appears just after the Israelites leave Egypt and are on their way to Mount Sinai. "And as soon as Aaron spoke to the whole congregation of the people of Israel, they looked toward

19 E.g., Zec 1:8–10, 19; 2:1–3; 3:1, 5–6; 4:1, 4, 11; 5:2–3, 10; 6:4.

the wilderness, and behold, the glory of the LORD appeared in the cloud" (Ex 16:10). The Messiah's glory is revealed in, with, and under the cloud. This cloud of divine glory appears at pivotal points in the Old Testament. For instance, the cloud leads God's people out of Egypt (Ex 13:21), protects them from enemies (Ex 14:19–20), descends upon Mount Sinai (Ex 19:9), fills the tabernacle (Ex 40:34), appears over the mercy seat (Lv 16:2), and fills Solomon's temple (1Ki 8:10).

The prophet Ezekiel also speaks of messianic glory. "As I looked, behold, a stormy wind came out of the north, and a great cloud, with brightness around it, and fire flashing forth continually, and in the midst of the fire, as it were gleaming metal" (Ezk 1:4). Ezekiel goes on to liken this glory to a super-charged chariot. Four creatures are under this chariot. Each has four faces: a human, a lion, an eagle, and an ox. When this glorious presence leaves the temple, Ezekiel has another vision: "And the glory of the LORD went up from the cherub to the threshold of the house, and the house was filled with the cloud, and the court was filled with the brightness of the glory of the LORD" (Ezk 10:4). But then, in an act of extraordinary grace, divine glory returns to His new temple that Ezekiel envisions in chapters 40–48. He wondrously declares "the glory of the LORD filled the temple" (Ezk 43:5).

Divine glory never returned to the second temple, built by Zerubbabel and dedicated in 515 BC. Postexilic authors like Ezra, Zechariah, and Haggai never record an event like Exodus 40, 1 Kings 8, or Ezekiel 43 when glory—by means of a cloud—filled the tabernacle or temple.

No one knew how the promise in Ezekiel 43:5 would come to pass, how heaven would descend to earth one more time. Then, in a moment, it happened. Paul saw the glory of God in the face of the Messiah (2Co 4:6). This glory blinded Paul when he was on his way to Damascus (Ac 9:8), but soon he saw the Messiah's glory throughout the Old Testament (2Co 1:20).

The message of the New Testament, then, is singular. Divine glory is back. "And the Word became flesh and dwelt among us, and we have seen His glory, glory as of the only Son from the Father, full of grace and truth" (Jn 1:14). Indeed, the Messiah "is the radiance of the glory of God" (Heb 1:3)—no longer in a cloud but now in the flesh.

THE MESSIANIC MESSAGE: PREDICTIONS, PATTERNS, PRESENCE

What if we heard that a team of scholars had uncovered and deciphered an ancient book that recorded the history of Jesus, along with His thoughts, words, and origins? And what if this book from antiquity was accessible to us? Wouldn't we do almost anything to get our hands on this book? If we have a copy of the Old Testament, then we have this book!

And we also have interpretive tools that enable us to see the Messiah throughout Israel's Scriptures. Our look at predictions, patterns, and the Messiah's presence will give us eyes to see and ears to hear the voice of our Savior. In later chapters, we will present the messianic message without explicitly maintaining the predictions, patterns, and presence organization of the early chapters. Hopefully, by that point, you will be well equipped to classify each passage discussed into one of these three types of messianic revelation. We begin our study of the Old Testament at the beginning—the Book of Genesis.

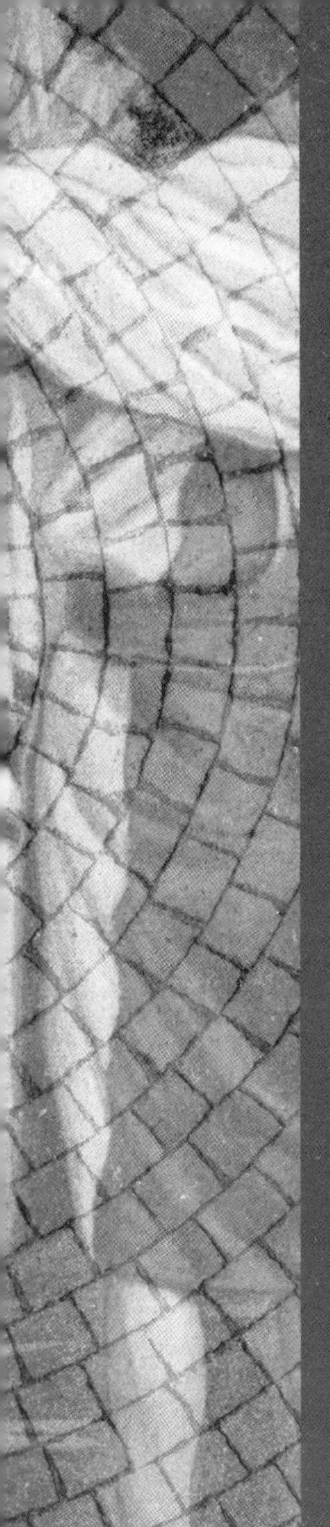

CHAPTER 2

THE MESSIANIC FOCUS IN GENESIS

The Book of Genesis is foundational to the entire Old Testament. It introduces topics that shape the rest of the books of Moses and the prophets. Among these topics are creation, God's institution of marriage, the source of the sinful inclination of all humans, and the origin of the people of Israel. Most importantly, Genesis introduces the promise of a Savior, who will deliver humanity from sin and eternal death, and it traces that promise from Adam to Jacob and then to Judah. Moreover, Moses gives the first portraits of this Messiah through appearances to His people and as He is mirrored by the lives of godly persons.

PREDICTIONS: FROM EVE TO JACOB

Perhaps the clearest Old Testament pictures of the coming Messiah are presented in direct predictions about Him. These often include indications of the Savior's identity and work. In addition, on several occasions, God spoke directly to people in Genesis. Many of these direct revelations of God gave promises about the coming Savior and what He would accomplish for our salvation. They not only reveal what the Messiah would do but also trace the human ancestry leading to the coming of Jesus in the flesh through Adam, Abraham, Isaac, and Jacob.

CRUSHING THE SERPENT'S HEAD (GENESIS 3:15)

The great human tragedy—the curse of sin that fell upon all humans through the acts of Adam and Eve—is told vividly yet quickly in just seven verses (Gn 3:1–7). However, the consequences of that first sin are portrayed in more than twice that number of verses

(Gn 3:8–24). When God confronted our first parents, He told them and the deceiving serpent of the curses that they had brought upon themselves and all creation (Gn 3:14–19).

The serpent and the woman together, apart from Adam, defied God. (Although Adam was present, he did not participate in the conversation with the serpent [see Gn 3:6].) Therefore, the curse on the deceiver began with the penalties he would suffer (Gn 3:14). However, the second part of God's address to the serpent focused on his future relationship with the woman:

> I will put hostility between you and the woman, and between your offspring and her offspring; he shall strike your head, and you shall strike his heel. (Gn 3:15, authors' translation)

While the serpent had sought an alliance with Eve in defying God's order not to eat of the tree of the knowledge of good and evil, the Lord now made them hostile to each other. This antagonism would be played out between the offspring (literally *seed* in Hebrew) of the serpent and the woman. The woman's seed is often explained as a collective singular used to denote all her descendants. This would be like how we speak of *grass seed* in English, meaning not a single seed but a mass of seed collectively. However, the context does not allow that. The following pronoun *He* is singular and points to a particular offspring of the woman who will strike the serpent's head—the Messiah (see Gal 3:16, which references a similar meaning for *seed* at Gn 22:18).[20]

20 For other instances where *seed/offspring* must be singular because it is used either with a singular verb with singular modifying adjectives or with a singular pronoun; see Gn 4:25; 21:13; 22:17 (second occurrence); 24:60; 1Sm 1:11; 2Sm 7:12; 1Ch 17:11; Is 6:13.

Thus, the curse on the serpent was also a promise to Adam and Eve that someone would come to undo the tempter's work. That coming Savior would be the Messiah, who would have to suffer ("you will strike His heel") to deliver humanity. While Adam and Eve would be sent away from Eden and its tree of life (Gn 3:24), they had the prediction of access to the tree of eternal life through a better source—the One who would come from the woman's offspring to bring everlasting life to many (Rv 2:7). It is no surprise, then, that many early Christian interpreters of Genesis 3:15 referred to it as the protoevangelium—the first Gospel.

NOAH SPEAKS OF THE FUTURE FOR HIS SONS AND THEIR DESCENDANTS (GENESIS 9:25–27)

Genesis 9:20–23 presents the only incident from the life of Noah following the great flood. In this account, we learn of Noah's vineyard, his becoming drunk from the wine from his grapes and lying nude in his tent, and his sons' reaction. Ham saw his father sleeping but did nothing to restore Noah's dignity. Instead, he gossiped about his father to his brothers. In contrast, Shem and Japheth restored their father's respectability by covering him up without looking at his nakedness.

When Noah awoke, he learned of Ham's failing to honor him, and it resulted in a curse on Ham's son Canaan, a thrice-repeated prediction that would be fulfilled in the subjugation of the Canaanites to Israel (Gn 9:25, 26, 27).

Noah also must have learned of the honorable way in which Shem and Japheth had acted, and he also prophesied about them. For Japheth, he predicted that his descendants would benefit from association with Shem ("dwell in the tents of Shem") and that Canaan would be his slave (Gn 9:26).

Most importantly, aside from the prediction that Canaan would be Shem's slave, there is no prediction about Shem's descendants (Gn 9:25). Instead, there is a blessing for Yahweh, the God of Shem. This presumes that Yahweh and Shem had a prior close relationship. Shem had *already* been chosen by God to be the ancestor of the Messiah.[21] This is borne out in Genesis 11:10–32, the second great list of names in Genesis that traces Shem's line down to Abraham, the great ancestor of the Messiah in Genesis (Mt 1:1).[22]

POSSESSING THE ENEMIES' GATES (GENESIS 22:17; 24:60)

The apex of the story of Abraham's life is the account of the sacrifice of Isaac (Gn 22:1–19). With unwavering faith, Abraham was willing to obey God's command to sacrifice the child who was to bear the messianic line, trusting that God had a solution to how a Savior could be born from a man who had been made a sacrifice on an altar (see Heb 11:17–19). After observing Abraham's faith and providing a ram as a substitute, God, in the form of the angel of the Lord, reiterated and expanded on His prior pledges to the patriarch:

> "By myself I have sworn"—a declaration of the Lord—"Because you have done this thing and have not withheld your only son, I will indeed bless you and make your offspring as numerous as the stars of the sky and the sand on the seashore. Your offspring will possess the city gates of his enemies. And all the nations of the earth will be blessed by your offspring because you have obeyed my command" (Gn 22:16–18, authors' translation).

21 See the genealogy in Lk 3:23–38, especially verse 36.

22 The first great genealogy traces the line from Adam to Noah in Gn 5.

This promise to Abraham is in three parts:

1. A blessing for Abraham—his offspring (Hebrew *seed*) will be like the stars and the sand (Gn 22:17a; see Gn 15:5).

2. Abraham's offspring (*seed*) will take possession of the gate of his enemies (Gn 22:17b).

3. All nations will be blessed by Abraham's offspring (*seed*, Gn 22:18; see Gn 12:3).

The first and third statements are repetitions of previous promises. The second is new. Key to grasping how these promises are to be understood is the proper understanding of the word *seed* in each of is occurrences. Is it a collective term referring to many offspring or is it a singular term referring to a specific seed?

Clearly, in the first part of this pledge, God is referring to a collective seed—the many offspring of Abraham will be like the many stars in the sky or the many grains of sand on the seashore. Yet there is a change signaled at the beginning of the second part that can only be seen in the Hebrew text: the verb form used signals a break, not a continuation. In this way, the attentive reader is alerted that there is a change in referent coming. Moreover, the offspring (seed) in the second part of the promise is referenced by a *singular* pronoun (*His* enemies), not a plural pronoun (*their* enemies). Unfortunately, many English versions ignore these subtle but important hints in the text and attempt to lead their readers to understand *offspring* in the second part of the promise to be collective by changing the pronoun to plural.[23] Nevertheless, it is clear from a careful examination of the

23 See English Standard Version (ESV), Christian Standard Bible (CSB), and New International Version (NIV).

Hebrew text that the offspring in the second part of this pledge to Abraham is a particular offspring—the Messiah. He will take possession of His enemies' gates. The promise then continues to speak of this offspring as blessing the nations.

The figure of speech used here—a metaphor that depicts the Messiah as capturing the gates of His enemies' city—is one of a Savior who defeats His foes. He will overcome Satan and death. This is an extension of the promise of the striking of the serpent's head at Genesis 3:15. When Jesus spoke to Peter about this, He explained that through His Church the Savior would extend His kingdom and conquer death and hades by the proclamation of the Gospel: "And I tell you, you are Peter, and on this rock I will build My church, and the gates of hell shall not prevail against it" (Mt 16:18). This claim that the Messiah's Church will prevail against the gates of hades ought to be viewed as a claim that He is the Promised Seed of Abraham. In Him the promised victory will be won. Thus, in Matthew 16:18, Jesus claims to be the one to fulfill the promise to Abraham of an offspring who will take possession of the gate of His enemies. This promise was both missional—through the Church, which holds the keys that can open the gates of heaven and hades—and focused on the final victory, when He will have subdued the last enemy: death (1Co 15:19–26).

JACOB SPEAKS OF THE FUTURE FOR HIS SONS AND THEIR DESCENDANTS (GENESIS 49:1–28)

As he lay on his deathbed, Jacob called his sons to hear what would happen to them and their descendants in the days to come. Jacob's prophecy would proceed son by son with predictions for each of the tribes of Israel. One might expect that the eldest son would receive the greatest blessing—the promise that the Messiah would come from his line. But as often happens in Genesis, the first-born son did not receive the greater promise. Reuben, Jacob's first son, was disqualified because he had committed adultery with one of his father's concubines (Gn 49:3–4; see Gn 35:22).

The next two sons in line—Simeon and Levi—were also excluded from the messianic line because of their sin. They had deceived and then brutally killed all the men of Shechem because one of those men had raped their sister Dinah (Gn 34). Their outrage and fierce anger led them to excessive acts of violence against an entire city.

Next, Jacob spoke to his fourth son, Judah, and his prominence: "Judah, your brothers shall praise you; your hand shall be on the neck of your enemies; your father's sons shall bow down before you" (Gn 49:8). To emphasize the importance of this blessing, Jacob used a threefold play on words: "Judah (*yehuda*) … praise you (*yoduka*) … your hand (*yadeka*) … ." Whereas Judah and his brothers had been bowing before Joseph,[24] Jacob now predicted that in the future the most preeminent tribe of Israel would be Judah.

Following this, Jacob introduced a new metaphor to describe Judah: "Judah is a lion's cub; from the prey, my son, you have gone up. He stooped down; he crouched as a lion and as a lioness; who dares rouse him?" (Gn 49:9). Not only would Judah as a lion be regal but also no one would dare to disturb him just as no one would intrude upon a lion with his captured prey. As we will see, this figure of the lion of Judah will become an important messianic metaphor in the rest of Scripture. It will be used again in the prophecies of Balaam (Nu 23:24; 24:9), as well as by Isaiah and Amos, who pictured Yahweh, Israel's God, coming to defend Zion like a lion.[25] Thus, Genesis 49 and Isaiah 31 offer a picture of the two natures of the

---

24 Gn 37:9–10; 42:6; 43:26.

25 Is 31:4; Am 1:2; 3:8.

coming Savior: His human nature (a man from the line of Judah) and His divine nature (the God of Israel who defends and rescues His people). These two natures of the Messiah are presented again in the New Testament, where Jesus is the Lion of the tribe of Judah and the one worthy to receive worship as God (Rv 5:5–14).

Following this, Jacob depicted Judah as royalty: "The scepter shall not depart from Judah, nor the ruler's staff from between his feet, until tribute comes to him; and to him shall be the obedience of the peoples" (Gn 49:10). The signs of kingship are bestowed upon Judah: a scepter and a leader's staff. The staff is pictured as "between his feet." Since antiquity, this reference to feet has been interpreted as a euphemism for the sexual organs. Thus, Judah is described as fathering royal leadership throughout the coming generations (Dt 33:7; Mi 5:2). Indeed, the great Old Testament king David was from the tribe of Judah, and the New Testament acknowledges Jesus as the ultimate king from Judah through David's line. He was recognized as the greater king when people called Him "Son of David,"[26] a point that the Jewish scribes could not dispute (Mk 12:35; Lk 20:41). Moreover, from Judah will come a king not simply for Israel but also for all nations, since "the obedience of the peoples" belongs to Him.[27]

The phrase translated above as "until tribute comes to him" is one of the most difficult passages to understand in the Old Testament. The Hebrew text could be simply translated as "until *Shiloh* comes." While the word *Shiloh* has been understood in various ways, it is best to understand it as one of the many descriptive names given to the Messiah in the Old Testament.[28] The name *Shiloh* most probably

---

26 Mt 1:1; 9:27; 12:23; 15:22; 20:30–31; 21:9, 15; Mk 10:47–48; Lk 18:38–39.

27 Is 9:6–7; Lk 1:31–33; Rv 11:15; see especially Gn 12:3; 18:18; 22:18; 26:4; 28:14.

28 For other such names, see Is 7:14 (Mt 1:23); 9:6; Jer 23:6; Zec 3:8.

means "rest" or "prosperous" (from the Hebrew root *šlh*). It pictures the Messiah as a man from the tribe of Judah who will bring rest and prosperity to Israel and the nations (Mt 11:28; Rv 14:13). This view of Shiloh as a name for the Messiah is confirmed from antiquity, since several early Jewish interpretations of this passage simply substitute *Messiah* for *Shiloh* when discussing this passage.[29]

The final portion of Jacob's blessing on Judah goes on to depict the lush benefits of the Messiah's reign in highly figurative terms:

> Binding his foal to the vine and his donkey's colt to the choice vine, he has washed his garments in wine and his vesture in the blood of grapes. His eyes are darker than wine, and his teeth whiter than milk. (Gn 49:11–12)

The donkey is associated in later messianic passages with the coming of the Messiah.[30] Here Judah ties his donkey to a vine, something one would not normally do since the donkey likely would eat the valuable grapevine. However, the picture is one of such great abundance brought by the Messiah that the vine is viewed inconsequential. In addition, the Messiah will wash his clothes in wine. Once again, the normally expensive wine will be as common as water, so that it can be used in this most unusual way. Finally, the Messiah's beauty is described in terms of His "eyes . . . darker than wine" and His "teeth whiter than milk." The message is clear. The messianic age will be one of great abundance (cf. Jn 10:10).

29 For further reading, see 4Q Patriarchal Blessing; Targum Onkelos; Targum Pseudo-Jonathan; Talmud, *baba Sanhedrin* 98b.

30 Zec 9:9; Mt 21:5; Jn 12:15.

PATTERNS: PEOPLE WHOSE LIVES AND ACTS POINT TO JESUS

The lives of God's people are guided by their faith. Through faith, they receive forgiveness of sins and everlasting life. By faith, they seek to live godly lives. It is in that living and in the events surrounding the lives of the godly men in Genesis that there are glimpses of the greatest and only person to live a perfect godly life, Jesus. In particular, the accounts of three men in Genesis stand out as precursors to Jesus: Noah, Melchizedek, and Joseph.

NOAH: FORETASTE OF THE MESSIAH'S SECOND COMING

Noah is introduced to readers of Genesis as a singularly righteous man of his era:

> So the LORD said, "I will blot out man whom I have created from the face of the land, man and animals and creeping things and birds of the heavens, for I am sorry that I have made them." But Noah found favor in the eyes of the LORD. These are the generations of Noah. Noah was a righteous man, blameless in his generation. Noah walked with God. (Gn 6:7–9)

Noah's well-known story tells of how this righteous man's acts rescued the lives of eight people: himself and his wife as well as his three sons and their wives (Gn 7:7; see 1 Pt 3:20). Noah constructed an ark that allowed life to be preserved through the judgment of God on humanity that was wreaked by the great flood. Only Noah and his family escaped, while the rest of humanity went about their business as if nothing were amiss, ignoring the demands of God's Law and participating in the wickedness that came to characterize human society.

This rescue of the faithful among humanity through Noah pointed forward to a much greater salvation that would be wrought by Christ, who was perfectly righteous and by whose actions many will be saved from the final judgment of God. Jesus' work will rescue all who have trusted in Him when divine wrath arrives on the Last Day. Moreover, when the Almighty Judge appears, human society will be much like society in Noah's day. Jesus noted this parallel with Noah's day:

> But concerning that day and hour no one knows, not even the angels of heaven, nor the Son, but the Father only. For as were the days of Noah, so will be the coming of the Son of Man. For as in those days before the flood they were eating and drinking, marrying and giving in marriage, until the day when Noah entered the ark, and they were unaware until the flood came and swept them all away, so will be the coming of the Son of Man. (Mt 24:36–39)

MELCHIZEDEK: PRIEST OF THE MOST HIGH GOD

One of the most mysterious figures in the entire Old Testament is Melchizedek. He is mentioned only at Genesis 14:18–20 and Psalm 110:4. Unlike Israel's priests who, according to the laws given to Moses, had to descend from Aaron, Melchizedek is presented without any lineage (see Heb 7:3). After receiving a blessing from Melchizedek, Abraham gave him one-tenth of all his spoils of war, an acknowledgment of his status as a legitimate priest of God.[31]

31 Cf. Nu 18:26; Dt 14:22–29; 2Ch 31:5–6; Ne 10:37–38; 13:12; Heb 7:2–9.

Melchizedek's interaction with Abraham pointed forward to a greater priest—Jesus—who also would not be from the line of Aaron and who would become an eternal priest.[32]

BLESSING FOR ALL NATIONS THROUGH ABRAHAM, ISAAC, AND JACOB (GENESIS 12:3; 22:18; 26:4; 28:14)

The great bulk of the Book of Genesis relates the lives of Israel's patriarchs—Abraham, Isaac, and Jacob. God gave promises to each of these men that were centered around the Messiah. There are seven elements to the patriarchal promises.

THE LORD'S SEVEN PROMISES TO THE PATRIARCHS IN GENESIS

PROMISE	ABRAHAM	ISAAC	JACOB
Progeny: Become a great nation/numerous	12:2; 13:16; 17:2; 22:17	26:4, 24	28:14; 46:3
Reputation: Have a great name	12:2		
Messianic seed: Will be a blessing to the nations through his seed	12:3; 22:18	26:4	28:14

32 Ps 110:4; Heb 3:1; 4:14; 6:20.

Protection: Bless those who bless and curse those who curse; the Lord will be with him and will be his God, the God of his seed	12:3; 15:1; 17:7–8	26:24	28:15; 31:3; 46:4
Land: God will give the land of Canaan to his seed	12:17; 13:15, 17; 17:8; 22:17	26:3–4	28:13; 35:12
Influence: Father of many nations	17:5–6		35:11
Royalty: Will produce kings	17:6		35:11

These divine commitments did not simply benefit Abraham, Isaac, and Jacob; they also were intended to benefit all peoples through the Messiah. In fact, the messianic pledge is the climax of the promises given to Abraham when God first called him:

> Now the Lord said to Abram, "Go from your country and your kindred and your father's house to the land that I will show you. And I will make of you a great nation, and I will bless you and make your name great, so that you will be a blessing. I will bless those who bless you, and him who dishonors you I will curse, and in you all the families of the earth shall be blessed." (Gn 12:1–3)

Note that the final pledge is that all people will be blessed through Abraham. This is the promise that Abraham would be the ancestor of the Savior who would bring forgiveness and life to people of all nations. While the verb in this climactic commitment is passive ("shall be blessed"; see Gn 18:18; 28:14), a different verb form is used when this promise is repeated at Genesis 22:18 and 26:4. There it is better understood as "will consider themselves blessed through you." That is, peoples of the earth who receive the benefits won by Jesus, Abraham's great descendant, will esteem Abraham as their great predecessor and father in the faith (see Rm 4:16). This is how Abraham would obtain a great name.

The other commitments of progeny, protection, land, influence, and royalty all reinforce this messianic pledge. The progeny—especially the people of Israel—will produce the Messiah in human flesh. Protection from God will guard the patriarchs at times when they are threatened, and the land will provide a place for Israel to flourish as it awaits the Messiah. The royal promise of kings will foreshadow the great king, Jesus.

The repetition of many of these promises for two more generations—and especially the promise that all the earth's families would be blessed through Isaac and Jacob—demonstrates that God was constantly focused on saving not only Israel but also all the world. The story of Israel that is begun in Genesis is not a story simply about one people chosen by God; it also relates how God was working through Israel to choose many from every nation to be part of the true Israel (Eph 2:12–19; 1Pt 2:9–10).

JOSEPH: ONE MAN SUFFERS FOR THE GOOD OF MANY

Another life account in Genesis that parallels that of the Messiah is Joseph's (Gn 37, 39–50). Here we meet one of Jacob's sons whose story is as familiar as Noah's. Betrayed by his own brothers, enslaved, and imprisoned in Egypt, he was rescued by his heavenly Father's favor in providing him with the ability not only to interpret dreams but also to give wise advice to Pharaoh (Gn 41:28–40). Most importantly, Joseph, who was counted as dead by his own father (Gn 37:33–35) and his brothers (Gn 42:13), proved to be their deliverance from the life-threatening famine when they learned that he was still alive (Gn 45:25–28). Joseph was sent ahead of his family to Egypt to preserve life (Gn 45:5–8). They had meant to do him harm, but God intended their acts to benefit His people (Gn 50:19–21).

The parallels between Joseph's life and Jesus' ministry are striking: both were rejected and suffered at the hands of their own people.[33] Neither Joseph's brothers who sold him into slavery nor the Jewish authorities who condemned Jesus understood the real impact of their deeds (Jn 11:49–53; 18:14). Moreover, both Joseph and Jesus forgave those who intended them harm (Gn 50:19–22; Lk 23:34), and the deeds of both saved many (Heb 9:28). Joseph's acts, therefore, prefigure the greater salvation that was won by the Messiah. The long account of Joseph—second in length in Genesis only to that of Abraham (Gn 12:1–25:11)—was cast by Moses into a messianic pattern as he recorded how God preserved His chosen Israel from the famine that endangered their existence.

PRESENCE: THE MESSIAH'S APPEARANCES IN GENESIS

The Savior came in human flesh through His mother, Mary, and lived among us (Jn 1:14). Yet even before that time, Jesus, the Messiah, had appeared to select people. In Genesis, these appearances are not uncommon and He often—but not always—is called "the angel of the LORD" or "the angel of God." Genesis contains more of these appearances than any other book of the Old Testament.

33 Jn 1:11; Ac 2:36; 7:52.

While we often conceive of angels as created beings who do God's will, it ought to be borne in mind that the Hebrew word for *angel* simply means "messenger." This Hebrew word can refer to human messengers (Gn 32:3, 6), to God's created heavenly messengers,[34] or to God serving as His own Messenger—the Messenger of the Lord. In every instance of the mention of the Messenger of the Lord in the Old Testament, this figure is identified as God Himself.[35] Moreover, the New Testament indicates that no one has ever seen God the Father but that the Son of God—the Word that would be made flesh in Jesus—has made God known (Jn 1:18). Therefore, these appearances of God in the Old Testament ought to be viewed as manifestations of Jesus before His incarnation.

HAGAR AND THE MESSENGER OF THE LORD (GENESIS 16 AND 21)

The first mention of an appearance of the Messenger of the Lord in all of Scripture was to Sarah's slave girl Hagar, who had provided Abraham with his first son, Ishmael. When Hagar fled from Sarah because she had been mistreated, the Messenger of the Lord appeared to her and gave her a promise remarkably like the one given to Abraham when God called him: "The angel of the LORD also said to her, 'I will surely multiply your offspring so that they cannot be numbered for multitude'" (Gn 16:10). Hagar recognized this messenger as God Himself, naming Him *El-roi*, "God Sees Me," and Moses specifically identifies Him as the Lord (Gn 16:13).

Later, when Sarah insisted that Abraham send Hagar away permanently, Hagar found herself in the wilderness of Beersheba without food and water and facing death. Once again, the Messenger of God spoke to her, this time from heaven, and He renewed His promise:

34 Gn 19:1, 10, 12, 15, 17; 28:12; 32:1.

35 E.g., Gn 16:7, 13; Ex 3:2, 4.

> And God heard the voice of the boy, and the angel of God called to Hagar from heaven and said to her, "What troubles you, Hagar? Fear not, for God has heard the voice of the boy where he is. Up! Lift up the boy, and hold him fast with your hand, for I will make him into a great nation." (Gn 21:17–18)

In both cases, the reader sees a kindhearted God whose care extends beyond the chosen family of Abraham, Sarah, and Isaac to an Egyptian woman and her son. Because of His promise to Abraham (Gn 13:16), and because of His love for all people, including Hagar and Ishmael, God showed kindness and offered blessing. Here readers of Genesis see the compassionate Messiah as He intervened to save a mistreated slave woman and her son. This same Jesus would show similar compassion to the crowds who followed Him in the wilderness and needed provisions, both spiritual and physical.[36]

SARAH LAUGHS AND ABRAHAM SPEAKS BOLDLY TO THE LORD (GENESIS 18)

Genesis 18 is the account of Abraham receiving three visitors. From what is said later, it appears as if two of these visitors are angels (Gn 19:1) and the third is the Lord Himself (Gn 18:10, 22). God had promised that Abraham would father a great nation and kings through Sarah (Gn 17:15–16). With this visit, God promised Abraham that the first step to this promise—a son born to Sarah—would take place within one year. To Sarah, who was an old woman, this was laughable, but God had the power to fulfill this promise and His vow to bless all peoples through Abraham.[37]

God revealed to Abraham His plan to destroy Sodom for the

36 Mt 15:32; 20:34; Mk 6:34; 8:2.

37 Gn 18:11–15; see Gn 12:3; 18:18.

wicked acts of its citizens. When the two angels left for Sodom, Abraham was still standing before the Lord (Gn 18:22). Abraham boldly spoke to God, venturing to try the Lord's patience and pleading with God to spare the city if fifty, then forty-five, then forty, then thirty, then twenty, and finally ten righteous persons were found in the city.

This divine visitor to Abraham appears as a man. He was the Messiah before He took on human flesh. In this story of God's visit to Abraham, readers are again shown some qualities of the Messiah that become even more sharply defined in the Savior's ministry: His laser-like focus on His promise to bless all nations through Abraham[38] and His patience as a judge who withholds judgment to spare the righteous (Jn 12:47). The subsequent narrative, the rescue of Lot from Sodom before it is destroyed (Gn 19), becomes a glimpse of the Messiah's final judgment (Lk 17:28–30; 2Pt 2:7–9). At that time, He will destroy the sin-corrupted world, but His angels will gather His followers out of it (Mt 13:41–43).

JACOB'S DREAM LADDER AND THE MESSIAH'S PROMISE (GENESIS 28)

One of the best-known events in the life of Jacob is his dream of a ladder—actually, a staircase—reaching to the sky, with God's angels ascending and descending on it (Gn 28:10–22). In this dream, Jacob saw the Lord standing beside him (some English versions read "above it," i.e., above or at the top of the staircase). The Lord promised Jacob several things (Gn 28:14): possession of the land on which he was lying, many offspring, offspring that would spread out in all directions, and that all families on earth would be blessed through him and his offspring. In addition, God promised to watch over Jacob and bring him back to this land (Gn 28:15).

38 Mt 24:14; 28:18; Mk 16:15; Lk 24:46–47; Jn 3:16–17.

There are two important references to the Messiah in this dream. First, the promise that all families on earth would be blessed through Jacob and his offspring points to the great offspring of Jacob, Jesus. Second, the Lord that Jacob saw in his dream was Messiah appearing to him. In fact, Jesus referred to this when He said this to Nathanael: "Truly, truly, I say to you, you will see heaven opened, and the angels of God ascending and descending on the Son of Man" (Jn 1:51). Just as the angels were ascending and descending on the Lord as He stood at the bottom of the staircase next to Jacob, so Nathanael was to see God's angels with Jesus. As the promised Messiah, Jesus was making a statement not only about what Nathanael would see but also about the One whom Jacob saw in his dream.

JACOB'S DREAM FLOCK (GENESIS 31)

Another brief encounter with the Angel of God came in a second dream to Jacob. He recounted this dream to his wives Rachel and Leah:

> In the breeding season of the flock I lifted up my eyes and saw in a dream that the goats that mated with the flock were striped, spotted, and mottled. Then the angel of God said to me in the dream, "Jacob," and I said, "Here I am!" And He said, "Lift up your eyes and see, all the goats that mate with the flock are striped, spotted, and mottled, for I have seen all that Laban is doing to you. I am the God of Bethel, where you anointed a pillar and made a vow to Me. Now arise, go out from this land and return to the land of your kindred." (Gn 31:10–13)

Note that in this dream the Messenger of God identified Himself as "the God of Bethel." *Bethel*, meaning "house of God," was the name Jacob had given to the place where he dreamed of the staircase (see Gn 28:17–18). Here readers are assured that the Messiah is trustworthy—He always keeps His promises. He pledged that He would watch over Jacob, and here He was reminding Jacob that He had done that—the Messenger was aware of Laban's ill-treatment of Jacob and was remedying it. Thus, this brief reference to Jacob's dream reminds us that all of the Messiah's promises are unfailing. In the New Testament, Paul reminded Timothy of this:

> Therefore I endure everything for the sake of the elect, that they also may obtain the salvation that is in Christ Jesus with eternal glory. The saying is trustworthy, for: If we have died with Him, we will also live with Him; if we endure, we will also reign with Him; if we deny Him, He also will deny us; if we are faithless, *He remains faithful—for He cannot deny Himself.* (2Tm 2:10–13, emphasis added)

JACOB WRESTLES WITH THE MESSIAH (GENESIS 32)

Perhaps the second-most remembered story about Jacob is his nighttime wrestling match (Gn 32:24–32). The night before he was to meet his estranged brother, Esau, Jacob had sent gifts to his brother; sent his possessions, wives, and children across the Jabbok River; and spent the night alone (Gn 32:21–24). Very abruptly, Genesis introduces a man who began to wrestle with Jacob. Jacob's refusal to let go of the man until he received his blessing not only underscores Jacob's tenacity but also indicates that Jacob thought that this was no ordinary man, but someone who could bless him. The new name Jacob received, *Israel*, commemorated his tussle with this mysterious man that night and confirmed that he had "struggled with God" (Gn 32:28, authors' translation). Jacob recognized that this man was God, since he named that place *Peniel*, meaning "face of God" (Gn 32:30). In fact, Jacob was amazed that he had seen God—and therefore had a glimpse of God's glory—and yet lived. But to see God face to face is to see Jesus. In fact, Paul later reminded the Christians in Corinth that God had shone His light into their hearts so that they, too, could have knowledge of God's glory. Yet this comes only through seeing the face of Christ (2Co 4:6). This same man will be seen by Joshua (Jsh 5:13) and Zechariah (Zec 1:8).

GENESIS: THE FIRST OF THE MESSIANIC BOOKS IN AN ENTIRELY MESSIANIC OLD TESTAMENT

As the first and foundational book of the Old Testament, Genesis is not merely about the origin of the universe or the origin of Israel. The golden thread that is woven throughout the fabric of its text is the promise of a Messiah, an anointed Savior who was promised to rescue fallen humanity from sin, death, and the devil. As such, it points the way to how we ought to read the rest of the Old Testament: not merely as stories about the people of Israel, their kings, and their prophets but primarily as a witness to God's unfailing commitment to send the Messiah as the world's only Redeemer and Savior.

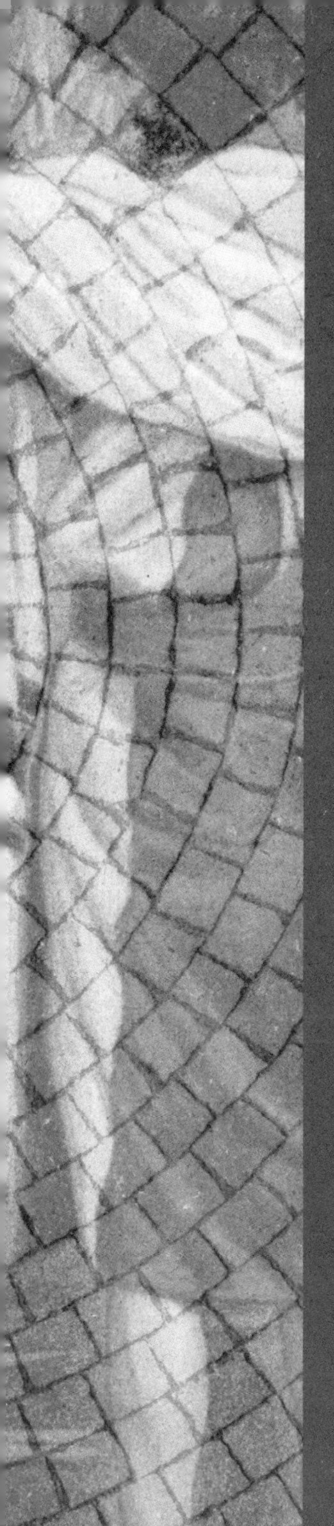

CHAPTER 3

THE MESSIANIC THRUST OF EXODUS—DEUTERONOMY

"As the twig is bent, so grows the tree" is a well-known adage. It is often applied to the rearing of children. Teach them good behavior, and they will retain that conduct into adulthood as admirable self-discipline. Allow them to behave badly and neglect disciplining them, and they will maintain the same rude, destructive, and childish habits when grown.

We might observe a similar phenomenon in the Bible. Genesis is saturated with predictions, patterns, and the presence of the Messiah. This continues into the rest of the Pentateuch not only with explicit prophecies but also through Israel's God-given religious institutions and divine encounters in the wilderness.

PREDICTIONS: A KING AND PROPHET TO COME

Jesus is not only presented as God's anointed one, the Christ, in the New Testament but He is also presented in the New Testament as having a threefold office: Prophet,[39] Priest,[40] and King.[41] It is no coincidence that in the Old Testament those three offices are associated with induction into service through anointing. All holders of these offices were in some sense anointed ones or messiahs.[42] In the Pentateuch beyond Genesis, two aspects of this threefold office—King (in Balaam's prophecy) and Prophet (foretold by Moses)—are expressly predicted of the One who was to come. The third—Priest—was already foreshadowed in Genesis (see the discussion of Melchizedek in chapter 2) and will be further depicted in the office

39 E.g., Mt 21:11; Lk 24:19.

40 E.g., Heb 3:1; 4:14; 6:20; 9:11.

41 E.g., Mt 27:37; Jn 19:19; Ac 17:7; Eph 5:5; 2Tm 4:1; 2Pt 1:11; Rv 11:15; 12:10.

42 Cf. 1Sm 24:7, 11; 26:16; 2Sm 1:14, 16, 21; 19:22; 23:1; Lm 4:20.

of Israel's high priest (see "Patterns: Tabernacle, Sacrifices, Festivals" in this chapter).

BALAAM'S ORACLES: A KING WITH A STAR AND A SCEPTER (NUMBERS 23–24)

The story of Balaam is an intriguing one filled with direct communication from God (Nu 22:9–12, 20), a talking donkey who saw the Messenger of the Lord when Balaam could not (Nu 22:22–30), and seven predictive poems from God.[43] For two of these poems, God met with Balaam and put them in Balaam's mouth (Nu 23:5, 16). One was by direct inspiration of God's Spirit (Nu 24:2). Balaam's words clearly are prophetic blessings on Israel and predictions of future persons and events.

Balaam's relationship with God appears to be muddled—he not only spoke God's word but he also called the Almighty "the Lord my God" (Nu 22:18). Yet he was eager to hire himself out as an agent to bring a curse on Israel—a curse that God turned into a blessing.[44] He stands censured for his greed in what Peter called "the way of Balaam, the son of Beor, who loved gain from wrongdoing, but was rebuked for his own transgression; a speechless donkey spoke with human voice and restrained the prophet's madness" (2Pt 2:15–16; see Nu 25:1–5). John also condemned him, writing "the teaching of Balaam, who taught Balak to put a stumbling block before the sons of Israel, so that they might eat food sacrificed to idols and practice sexual immorality" (Rv 2:14). He would be killed by the Israelites for being "the one who practiced divination" (Jsh 13:22; cf. Nu 31:8).

So, why are three full chapters of Numbers devoted to this man and his oracles? Why do his predictions merit as much or more

43 "His discourse": Nu 23:7, 18; 24:3, 15, 20, 21, 23.

44 Dt 23:4–5; Jsh 24:9–10; Ne 13:2; see Mi 6:5.

attention than the prophecies of Samuel, Nathan, and Gad (1Ch 29:29)? The answer is that Balaam saw the coming Messiah and spoke of Him at a critical juncture in Israel's history, just as they were preparing to enter the Promised Land.

Balaam's first poem concludes with a reference to God's previous promises to Abraham and Jacob, "Who can count the dust of Jacob or number the fourth part of Israel? Let me die the death of the upright, and let my end be like his!"[45] Readers who know about God's pledges to Israel's patriarch should suspect that a message about the Messiah is looming. Indeed, when Balaam speaks God's Word a second time, his final words echo Jacob's deathbed messianic prophecy, "Behold, a people! As a lioness it rises up and as a lion it lifts itself; it does not lie down until it has devoured the prey and drunk the blood of the slain" (Nu 23:24; see Gn 49:9). Here the people of Israel—not simply the tribe of Judah—are compared to a lion, as in Jacob's prophecy. The change highlights the Old Testament mission of Israel to be a people dedicated to God and from whom the world's Savior would come.

Balaam's third oracle moves even closer to the messianic promise, once again building on Genesis. In the middle of this poem, Balaam speaks of Israel's great King who will, "be higher than Agag, and His kingdom shall be exalted" (Nu 24:7). While many English versions have the name *Agag* here, there is little reason to believe that this is a prophecy about King Saul defeating the Amalekite king Agag (1Sm 15). In fact, Saul's failure to execute Agag does not result in his having an exalted kingdom but his being rejected as king by God (1Sm 15:23; see 1Sm 15:3). Instead, in many ancient versions, the name is *Gog*. These include the Samaritan Pentateuch; the Septuagint; the Greek translations associated with Aquila, Symmachus, and Theodotian;

45 Nu 23:10; see Gn 13:16; 28:14.

and one of the Dead Sea Scrolls.[46] The prophet Ezekiel would later depict "Gog, of the land of Magog, the chief prince of Meshech and Tubal" (Ezk 38:2) as the great enemy of God's people to be destroyed before the establishment of God's eternal kingdom at the end of time (Ezk 38–39; see Rv 20:8). It will be with the defeat of Gog that God's eternal kingdom, the Messiah's kingdom, will be exalted.

Ezekiel 38:17 confirms that the correct name is *Gog* in Numbers 24:7 as the prophet depicts the Lord addressing this end-time enemy and saying, "Are you he of whom I spoke in former days by My servants the prophets of Israel, who in those days prophesied for years that I would bring you against them?" Clearly, Ezekiel's words talk about Gog as the subject of prophecy "in former days." However, Gog is not mentioned anywhere else in the prophets before Ezekiel unless it is here, in the third oracle of Balaam.

Balaam went on to say of this king, "God brings *him* out of Egypt and is for *him* like the horns of the wild ox; *he* shall eat up the nations, *his* adversaries, and shall break their bones in pieces and pierce them through with *his* arrows" (Nu 24:8, emphasis added). This king will come out of Egypt and will defend his people from their enemies. Note how this king's experience parallels Israel's experience as described in Balaam's previous oracle: "God brings *them* out of Egypt and is for *them* like the horns of the wild ox" (Nu 23:22, emphasis added). The Messiah will have His exodus just as Israel did, and He will lead His people out of the slavery to sin and death, and He will give them eternal life. For more on this, read Luke 9:31, where Jesus spoke with Moses and Elijah, "who appeared in glory and spoke of His departure [Greek: *exodos*], which He was about to accomplish at Jerusalem."

46 For further reading, see 4Q27 [4QNum^{b}] f24ii in Joseph A. Fitzmyer, *A Guide to the Dead Sea Scrolls and Related Literature* (Grand Rapids, MI: Eerdmans, 2008).

Then, at the end of his oracle, Balaam says, "He crouched, he lay down like a lion and like a lioness; who will rouse him up? Blessed are those who bless you, and cursed are those who curse you" (Nu 24:9). The first part of this verse matches almost exactly the wording of the last part of Genesis 49:9, the depiction of the Messiah as the lion from the tribe of Judah (Rv 5:5). In the Hebrew text, both are six words and only one word is different in each—synonyms for *lay down*.

The second half of Numbers 24:9 matches the words of Isaac's blessing on Jacob except that the promise of a blessing is placed before the threat of a curse (Gn 27:29). God had promised to protect both Abraham and Jacob in this way. Now that promise is extended to the people of Israel and overtly connected to Israel's function as the nation from whom the Messiah would come. God would protect Israel not simply for Israel's sake but also because the salvation of all humanity was to arise from God's Old Testament people.

The most important part of Balaam's poems is the fourth oracle:

> And he took up his discourse and said, "The oracle of Balaam the son of Beor, the oracle of the man whose eye is opened, the oracle of him who hears the words of God, and knows the knowledge of the Most High, who sees the vision of the Almighty, falling down with his eyes uncovered: I see Him, but not now; I behold Him, but not near: a star shall come out of Jacob, and a scepter shall rise out of Israel; it shall crush the forehead of Moab and break down all the sons of Sheth. Edom shall be dispossessed; Seir also, his enemies, shall be dispossessed. Israel is doing valiantly. And one from Jacob shall exercise dominion and destroy the survivors of cities!" (Nu 24:15–19)

This oracle begins with words like those of the previous one (compare Nu 24:3–4 with Nu 24:15–16). Balaam claims to be relating a vision that God has given him.

The vision itself is of someone: "I see Him." Yet the person Balaam sees is "not now . . . not near" but someone to come in the distant future. This person will originate "out of Jacob . . . out of Israel." Moreover, He is presented as rising star and a scepter. The scepter, a symbol of royal authority, marks this person as a king. In addition, He is depicted as defeating the enemies of His people, symbolized by those who were hostile to Israel in antiquity: Moab, sons of Sheth and Edom, and Seir. Finally, He will establish His eternal realm: "one from Jacob shall exercise dominion."

As Israel was preparing to take its first steps on the soil of the land of Canaan, Balaam's poem looked beyond their current circumstances to the coming of the Messiah and His kingdom. They would occupy the land, but much would have to happen before their ultimate king would arise. His final oracles would mention some of these events leading up to His arrival: The Amalekites would be destroyed (Nu 24:20). The Kenites, who eventually would settle among the Israelites, would be taken into captivity by the Assyrians (Nu 24:21–22; see 2Ki 17:6–23). Ships will come from the Mediterranean—from Greece—and would raid Syria and Lebanon, but they too would be destroyed (Nu 24:23–24; see Dn 11:30).

After all these things happened, and the Greek kingdoms that had established themselves in the Near East fell to the Romans, Balaam's prophecy came to fruition:

> Now after Jesus was born in Bethlehem of Judea in the days of Herod the king, behold, wise men from the east came to Jerusalem, saying, "Where is He who has been born *king of the Jews*? For we saw *His star* when

> it rose and have come to worship Him." (Mt 2:1–2, emphasis added)

The Magi connected the star that had arisen with a king: a star and a scepter. They knew the Messiah had come, and Matthew records their trip to see Him, just as Balaam had seen Him centuries earlier.

A PROPHET LIKE MOSES (DEUTERONOMY 18:15–19)

There can be no question that Moses looms large over the entire Old Testament. He is the great prophet to God's ancient people. He led them out of slavery in Egypt and continued to lead them for forty years. Moses spoke to God face to face and was able to communicate to Israel what God had said directly to him (Ex 33:11; Dt 34:10). He gave them the Pentateuch, the foundational books of the Old Testament. Almost a millennium after his death into the latest era of the Old Testament, his writings remained at the center of Israelite faith and piety.[47] Could there ever be another Moses? As great as many of the Old Testament prophets such as Samuel, Elijah, Isaiah, and Jeremiah were, none of them was another Moses. Yet Israel continued to look for a new Moses. Why? Because Moses said they ought to.

In Deuteronomy 18, Moses demonstrated a keen awareness that when he died there would be a perceived vacuum of communication from God. Israel might be tempted to seek spiritual guidance in the same way that the people in the land of Canaan did, through occult practices (Dt 18:9–14). Yet Moses was emphatic that "the LORD your God has not allowed you to do this" (Dt 18:14). Instead, Israel was to remain steadfast and wait for God to send them another prophet like

---

47 Ezr 3:2; 6:18; 7:6; Ne 1:7, 8; 8:1, 14; 9:14; 10:29; 13:1; Mal 4:4.

Moses. In fact, Moses was quite emphatic that this coming prophet was to be heeded:

> The Lord your God will raise up for you a prophet like me from among you, from your brothers—it is to Him you shall listen—just as you desired of the Lord your God at Horeb on the day of the assembly, when you said, "Let me not hear again the voice of the Lord my God or see this great fire any more, lest I die." And the Lord said to me, "They are right in what they have spoken. I will raise up for them a prophet like you from among their brothers. And I will put My words in His mouth, and He shall speak to them all that I command Him. And whoever will not listen to My words that He shall speak in My name, I Myself will require it of him [better: *I will hold him accountable*]." (Dt 18:15–19)

Moses spoke of a particular prophet to come ("a prophet," not "prophets"; "Him," not "them"). Moreover, this prophet would come from the Israelites ("from among you"; "from your brothers," and "from their [the Israelites'] brothers"). The future prophet would be like Moses in that at Mount Horeb—Mount Sinai—Israel asked for God not to speak directly to them but through an intermediary.[48] They asked Moses to be that intermediary (Dt 5:27). Moses promised that God would send another prophet, who would also hear divine revelation directly and speak to Israel. Finally, those who refused to listen to this future prophet would be held accountable for their unbelief.

48 Dt 18:16; see Ex 20:19; Dt 5:23–26.

At the end of Deuteronomy, a later author added a final chapter that tells of Moses' death. Then he noted that in his day a prophet like Moses had not arisen:

> And there has not arisen a prophet since in Israel like Moses, whom the Lord knew face to face, none like him for all the signs and the wonders that the Lord sent him to do in the land of Egypt, to Pharaoh and to all his servants and to all his land, and for all the mighty power and all the great deeds of terror that Moses did in the sight of all Israel. (Dt 34:10–12)

This passage further defines the prophet like Moses, noting that no prophet yet had done what Moses did: Moses spoke to God face to face, had a ministry not simply to Israel but also to non-Israelites, and did manifold miracles that displayed "mighty power" and were awe-inspiring deeds. The "deeds of terror" were the plagues on Egypt.[49]

In Jesus' day, Israel had seen a procession of prophets. Some, like Elijah and Elisha, had performed great and impressive miracles.[50] Some, like Jonah and Daniel, ministered to non-Israelites. Yet, in the first century the Jewish people were still looking for a prophet like Moses, who would do all these things. When John the Baptist appeared, there were those who wondered whether he was "*the* Prophet," meaning the prophet like Moses (Jn 1:21, 25, emphasis added). John denied that he was that prophet, but he pointed to someone who was already among them (Jn 1:26–27), whom he would identify as Jesus one day later (Jn 1:29–31). On the road to Emmaus, when Jesus asked the men what they were talking about, their words convey that they thought Jesus was the prophet like

49 See Dt 4:34; 26:8; 34:12; Jer 32:21.

50 1Ki 17:1–24; 18:20–46; 2Ki 2:23–24; 4:1–44; 6:1–6.

Moses. They spoke about him as "a man who was a prophet mighty in deed and word before God and all the people."[51] Of course, Jesus would use the Scriptures to demonstrate that He was exactly that (Lk 24:27).

Moreover, after Jesus fed the five thousand, the people recognized Him as "the Prophet who is to come into the world" (Jn 6:14). Just as Moses provided food for hungry Israelites—manna in the wilderness—so Jesus gave food to a hungry crowd in the wilderness. Later, at the Festival of Tabernacles, Jesus prophesied that from those who believe in Him "out of his heart will flow rivers of living water" (Jn 7:38). This was a clear connection to Moses, who brought flowing water from a rock in the wilderness (Ex 17:6).

In fact, the Gospels are peppered with parallels between Jesus and Moses. For instance, Moses was with the Lord on Mount Sinai in the wilderness for forty days, where he "neither ate bread nor drank water."[52] Jesus fasted in the wilderness for forty days.[53] Moses brought the people God's Word from Mount Sinai. So also, Jesus brought the Word of God to His people from a mountain (Mt 5:1). As a result of speaking directly to God on Mount Sinai, Moses' face shone with the reflected glory of God (Ex 34:29, 34–35). When Jesus went up on a mountain to be transfigured, His face radiated glory as He spoke with Moses and Elijah (Mt 17:2; see Lk 9:29). The transfiguration shows us Jesus not only as one like Moses but also as even greater. Perhaps most important, there are only two prophets in all of Scripture who initiated a covenant from God: Moses and Jesus. Moses initiated Israel's covenant with God through the blood from sacrificed oxen (Ex 24:8). Jesus initiated the new and better covenant with His own blood from His sacrificed body.[54]

51 Lk 24:19; compare Dt 18:18; 34:12.

52 Ex 34:28; Dt 9:9; see also Ex 24:18.

53 Mt 4:1–2; Mk 1:12–13; Lk 4:1–2.

54 Mt 26:28; Mk 14:24; Lk 22:20; 1Co 11:25; see Jer 31:31; Heb 7:22; 12:24.

In all these things, Jesus is the prophet like Moses, and Peter would proclaim Him as that (Ac 3:22). Moreover, the Messiah is a prophet greater than Moses whose miracles and deeds only foreshadowed God's great salvation. By contrast, the Savior's acts accomplished the redemption of the world. Thus, John compared Jesus to Moses, indicating that Jesus was the prophet like Moses who nevertheless outshone Israel's great Old Testament prophet: "For from His [Jesus'] fullness we have all received, grace upon grace. For the law was given through Moses; grace and truth came through Jesus Christ" (Jn 1:16–17).

PATTERNS: TABERNACLE, SACRIFICES, FESTIVALS

THE TABERNACLE

Exodus 25–27 contains God's instructions to Moses about the construction of the tabernacle and its furnishings. The building of these items is narrated in Exodus 36–38. The tabernacle was a tent that served as a portable temple where God would live among His people Israel (Ex 25:8; 29:45, 46). The Lord's presence was evident in that His glory was seen when He came to dwell there.[55] Throughout their forty-year travels in the wilderness, the people moved the tabernacle from place to place, and wherever it was erected, God's glory was in it.[56] This served as a picture that foreshadowed the Messiah, who later would be God in the flesh, dwelling among humans, just as the tabernacle was "the tent where He [God] dwelt among mankind" (Ps 78:60).

55 Ex 14:4; 29:43; 40:34, 35; see also Lv 9:23.

56 Nu 14:10; 16:19, 42; 20:6.

In the New Testament, John notes that Jesus brought God's presence to His people: "And the Word became flesh and dwelt [literally: *pitched His tent*] among us, and we have seen His glory, glory as of the only Son from the Father, full of grace and truth" (Jn 1:14). As Jesus moved about Galilee, Perea, and Judea, the glory of God was revealed. Once again, John makes this explicit when telling of Jesus at Cana. There, Christ changed water into wine and "revealed his glory" (Jn 2:11, authors' translation).

SACRIFICES

The opening chapters of Leviticus describe the procedures that the Israelites were to follow when they offered sacrifices to God. Unlike the sacrifices of the pagan religions of antiquity, these sacrifices were not to be viewed as a means of currying favor with God. Instead, these sacrifices were gifts of God to Israel, instituted by Him as a way for them to receive His gift of forgiveness and to be reconciled to Him. They were also ways to respond appropriately with thanksgiving (Lv 7:12–15) and freewill offerings (Lv 7:16; 22:18–25). While all these sacrifices relate in some way to the work of the Messiah and their consequences in the life of believers, we will concentrate here on the sacrifices that most directly communicated to Israel aspects of the coming ministry of the promised Savior.

THE WHOLE BURNT OFFERING (LEVITICUS 1:1–17; 6:8–13)

The first sacrifice mentioned in Leviticus is the whole burnt offering. This sacrifice was perhaps the most important, since it also was the offering that was to be continually on the altar for sacrifice in the tabernacle courtyard in the form of the evening and morning sacrifices (Lv 6:8–13). Individual Israelites could bring steers, rams, male goats, doves, or pigeons to serve as this offering. As the name of this sacrifice implies, the entire animal is offered to the Lord. For all the animals except birds, there is an explicit requirement that the animal be without blemish (Lv 1:3; 1:10). This is generally true of other types of animal sacrifices—the fellowship, sin, and guilt offerings.[57] Leviticus 22:22–25 gives detail as to the types of bodily defects that disqualify animals as sacrifices. This requirement not only mandated that the Israelites offer their best animals to God but it also pointed forward to the Messiah as God's best and most precious offering, unmarred by sin (Heb 9:14). Peter compared Jesus to this offering, "like that of a lamb without blemish or spot" (1Pt 1:19).

The worshiper was to lay his hand on the head of the animal when it was presented to the Lord (Lv 1:4). Again, this was generally true for all animal sacrifices.[58] It was a sign that the worshiper's sin and guilt were being transferred to the animal, which was then "accepted for him to make atonement for him" (Lv 1:4). This pointed forward to the transfer of all human sin to the Messiah, who would atone for the world's sin.[59]

Next the blood of the slaughtered animal was to be collected and splattered on the sides of the altar (Lv 1:5, 11). In the case of a bird sacrifice, the blood was drained beside the altar (Lv 1:15). Once again, this was typical for all animal sacrifices.[60] The blood was important, since it conveyed the very life of the sacrifice that was presented to God to cleanse the worshiper from sin and reconcile him to God.[61] As with other sacrifices, this foreshadowed the power of the Messiah's blood to cleanse all sinners.[62]

---

57 Lv 3:1, 6; 4:3, 23, 28, 32; 5:15, 18.

58 Lv 3:2, 8, 13; 4:4, 24, 29, 33.

59 2Co 5:19; 1Jn 2:2; 1Pt 2:24.

60 Lv 3:2, 8, 13; 4:7, 18, 25, 30, 34; 5:9; 7:2.

61 Lv 17:11, 14; Dt 12:23.

62 Eph 2:13; Heb 9:14; 1Pt 1:18–19; Rv 1:5.

Finally, it ought to be noted that the continual whole burnt offerings of lambs each morning and evening were always burning on the altar (Nu 28:3–8). They were a sign of the ability of the Messiah's sacrifice to atone for the sin of all people for all time, just as the New Testament testifies in the words of John the Baptist concerning Jesus, "the Lamb of God, who takes away the sin of the world" (Jn 1:29).

THE SIN AND GUILT OFFERINGS (LEVITICUS 4:1–6:7; 6:24–7:10)

The sin and guilt offerings are like the burnt offerings but are specifically tied to transgressions against God's Law. The sin offering was required for intentional infractions of the Law. Because the person deliberately broke the Law, this sacrifice required the most expensive animal offering, a bull (Lv 4:3, 14). The guilt offering was for unintentional offenses and involved an animal of lesser value, a goat (Lv 4:23, 28) or a lamb (Lv 4:32).

Unlike the whole burnt offering, the entire animal for these sacrifices was not burned on the altar in the tabernacle courtyard. Only the fatty portions were.[63] Most of the animal was burned outside of Israel's camp (Lv 4:11–12). This foreshadowed Jesus, who like the sin and guilt offerings, would suffer outside the Israelite settlement, that is, outside of the city of Jerusalem (Heb 13:11–12).

Finally, note carefully that the sin and guilt offerings brought the worshipers God's forgiveness.[64] Both deliberate and inadvertent transgressions of God's Law required an atoning sacrifice. So, too, Jesus would suffer for all sins, even those that were not recognized as sins when they were committed. Many centuries after Moses, Isaiah would depict the Messiah as a guilt offering: "Yet it was the will

63 Lv 4:8–10, 19, 26, 31, 35.

64 Lv 4:20, 26, 31, 35; 5:10, 13, 16, 18; 6:7; 19:22.

of the LORD to crush Him; He has put Him to grief; when His soul makes an *offering for guilt*, He shall see His offspring; He shall prolong His days; the will of the Lord shall prosper in His hand" (Is 53:10, emphasis added). Moreover, Paul depicts Jesus as the ultimate sin offering: "For our sake He made Him to be sin who knew no sin, so that in Him we might become the righteousness of God" (2Co 5:21). Note that in Hebrew, the word for *sin* and *sin offering* are the same: *khattath*. Paul's words might be understood to say "He made Him to be a sin offering."

THE RED COW'S ASHES FOR PURIFICATION (NUMBERS 19:1–22)

One noteworthy sin offering required a red cow as the sacrificial animal. Like earlier sacrifices, the blood of the animal plays an important part in the ritual: the priest sprinkled it toward the front of the tabernacle before the rest of the animal was burned. The ashes were then collected to be used to cleanse people who were made unclean before God when they went near a human corpse. When a person touched a dead body or was in close indoor proximity to someone who had died, some of the ashes were to be placed in water. Then the water was sprinkled on the person and the dwelling to purify them. By becoming united with the red cow's ashes in the sprinkling of water, the stain of sin and death was removed.

This seemingly strange ritual pointed to another aspect of the Messiah's ministry: the conquering of death. Since the fall into sin, death has come to all humans (Rm 5:12). The curse of sin and death was reinforced through the ceremonial uncleanness that attached to all Israelites who encountered a corpse. The freedom from death's curse that was to be won by the promised Messiah was prefigured in the red cow's sacrifice that led to cleansing (cf. Heb 9:13).

In the New Testament, cleansing by water that incorporates the Messiah's death is located in Baptism. This sacrament is greater than its Old Testament counterpart in the cleansing of the water with the red cow's ashes. Paul tells us that Baptism unites us with Christ's death so that we might overcome sin and death:

> What shall we say then? Are we to continue in sin that grace may abound? By no means! How can we who died to sin still live in it? Do you not know that all of us who have been baptized into Christ Jesus were baptized into His death? We were buried therefore with Him by baptism into death, in order that, just as Christ was raised from the dead by the glory of the Father, we too might walk in newness of life. For if we have been united with Him in a death like His, we shall certainly be united with Him in a resurrection like His. We know that our old self was crucified with Him in order that the body of sin might be brought to nothing, so that we would no longer be enslaved to sin. For one who has died has been set free from sin. Now if we have died with Christ, we believe that we will also live with him. We know that Christ, being raised from the dead, will never die again; death no longer has dominion over Him. For the death He died He died to sin, once for all, but the life He lives He lives to God. So you also must consider yourselves dead to sin and alive to God in Christ Jesus. (Rm 6:1–11)

THE FELLOWSHIP OFFERING (LEVITICUS 3:1–17; 7:11–21)

The only offering that allowed worshipers to eat portions of the meat was the fellowship offering. In some English versions of the

Bible, this is called the peace offering, since the Hebrew name is *zebakh shelamim* and appears to share the same root as the Hebrew word for peace, *shalom*. Words from the root *šlm* connote variations on the concept of being whole (e.g., *peace* results from having a *whole* or *restored* relationship with someone). Thus, the name of this sacrifice most likely points to the fellowship that comes from a whole and restored relationship with God that also leads to fellowship with other believers.

This offering could be from one's cattle, sheep, or goats and, like other animal sacrifices, it must be without blemish (Lv 3:1, 6). The worshiper who offered the animal placed his hand on its head to signify that sin was being transferred to the animal (Lv 3:2, 8, 13). The animal's blood was splattered on the altar as with other sacrifices (Lv 3:2, 8, 13). All the fatty portions of the animal were burned on the altar as a sacrifice to God (Lv 3:3–5, 9–11, 14–16). The sacrifice was accompanied by offerings baked from flour and olive oil, a portion of which was given to the priest (Lv 7:12–14). The meat of the sacrifice was given to the worshiper and those who were with him to eat (Lv 7:15–16). This offering could be offered with thanksgiving (Lv 7:11–15; 22:29–30). It was also given when a vow was completed (Lv 7:16–18; 22:21–25) or as a freewill offering expressing devotion and praise to God (Lv 7:16–18; 22:21–25).

When the fellowship offering was part of a series of offerings, the peace offering was always offered last, signifying that God was now reconciled to the worshipers and, as a result, they were reconciled to one another. For instance, see Leviticus 9:8–21, which gives the sequence as the high priest's sin offering, a whole burnt offering, the people's sin offering, and afterward the fellowship offering.

This sacrifice clearly represents the promised Messiah's work of bearing the sin of others and shedding His blood for them. Yet it goes beyond this to depict the consequences of the Messiah's salvific work: restored fellowship with God, leading to peaceful fellowship among God's people. In the opening of his first letter, John mentions such fellowship though the blood of Jesus sacrificed to cleanse us from sin:

> That which was from the beginning, which we have heard, which we have seen with our eyes, which we looked upon and have touched with our hands, concerning the word of life—the life was made manifest, and we have seen it, and testify to it and proclaim to you the eternal life, which was with the Father and was made manifest to us—that which we have seen and heard we proclaim also to you, so *that you too may have fellowship with us*; and indeed *our fellowship is with the Father and with His Son Jesus Christ.* And we are writing these things so that our joy may be complete. This is the message we have heard from Him and proclaim to you, that God is light, and in Him is no darkness at all. If we say we have fellowship with Him while we walk in darkness, we lie and do not practice the truth. But if we walk in the light, as He is in the light, *we have fellowship with one another, and the blood of Jesus His Son cleanses us from all sin.* (1Jn 1:1–7, emphasis added)

FESTIVALS

Just as Christians celebrate annual festivals such as Christmas, Easter, and Pentecost, so also the ancient Israelites had several yearly feasts or festivals. These pointed to aspects of the coming Messiah and His work. We will look at four of them: Passover, the sheaf of the firstfruits, the Day of Atonement, and the Festival of Trumpets.

PASSOVER (EXODUS 12:1–28; DEUTERONOMY 16:1–8)

Perhaps the best known of the Old Testament festivals is Passover because of its connection with the exodus from Egypt. The Passover lamb was at the center of the rites performed during this festival. The Passover lambs, like all sacrifices, had to be unblemished, pointing to the Messiah's sinless nature.[65] For the first Passover, a lamb was to be taken into each Israelite home and live with the family for four days (Ex 12:3, 6), symbolizing that the coming Messiah would live among Israel before He was sacrificed. The lamb was to be sacrificed on the fourteenth day of the first month of spring at twilight, the time of the beginning of the day by Israelite reckoning (Ex 12:1, 6; Dt 16:1). Its blood was to be placed on the doorframe of the house, and God would pass over that house but not kill any firstborn human or animal in the household (Ex 12:7, 13). This prefigured the shedding of the blood of the Messiah that would save humans from eternal death.

On Thursday, April 2, AD 33, at twilight, the Passover began. Jesus ate the Passover meal with His disciples and went to the Garden of Gethsemane on the Mount of Olives, where He prayed and was arrested. After His trial before the high priest and Pilate's sentencing Him to crucifixion, He was nailed to the cross. It was Friday, April 3, but still Passover according to Jewish reckoning. He was removed from the cross before sundown. Jesus truly was the Passover lamb, sacrificed on the very day of Passover! Therefore, Paul could write, "Christ, our Passover lamb, has been sacrificed" (1Co 5:7).

THE SHEAF OF THE FIRSTFRUITS (LEVITICUS 23:9–14)

Every year when the barley harvest began in spring (late March or early April), each Israelite was to bring to a priest the first bundle

---

65 Ex 12:5; e.g., 2Co 5:21; Heb 4:15.

of his grain from the harvest—the first sheaf of barley. The first day after the first Sabbath after the Passover was designated as the day the Israelite priest would make an offering of these first sheaves of the spring barley harvest to God. This offering of the firstfruits from the land foreshadowed the Messiah as the first to rise from the dead.

On Passover, Friday, April 3, AD 33, Jesus was crucified. The next day was the Sabbath. The day after that, Sunday, April 5, was the day after the Sabbath—the day for priests to present the firstfruits to God. It was also the first Easter. Jesus rose from the dead, fulfilling "what the prophets and Moses said would come to pass: that the Christ must suffer and that, *by being the first to rise from the dead*, He would proclaim light both to our people and to the Gentiles" (Ac 26:22–23, emphasis added). The Messiah's suffering is prophesied in several places by the prophets who also predict the proclamation of the Gospel to the entire world. However, there is only one place in the Old Testament that pointed forward to the Messiah as being the first to rise from the dead: Moses' instructions concerning the offering of the sheaves of firstfruits to God in Leviticus 23. Not only was Jesus the firstfruits from the grave but He also became that by rising on the day of the offering of the firstfruits of the barley harvest! No wonder Paul would write, "Christ has been raised from the dead, *the firstfruits* of those who have fallen asleep" (1Co 15:20, emphasis added).

THE DAY OF ATONEMENT (LEVITICUS 16:1–34)

On the tenth day of the seventh month of the ancient Israelite calendar—the first month of autumn— the Israelites were to celebrate the Day of Atonement. Known in Hebrew as *Yom Kippur*, this day featured several sacrifices and was designed to be a yearly festival to atone for all the sins of Israel.

The Day of Atonement was the only day of the year when someone—namely, the high priest—could enter the tabernacle's Most Holy Place. The ark of the covenant resided in the Most Holy Place, and God appeared in a cloud over its mercy seat, a throne formed by two cherubim that were part of the ark's lid. The high priest would enter the Most Holy Place with the blood of sacrifices: a bull for his own sin and a male goat for the sins of Israel. He was to sprinkle the blood on the mercy seat.

This sprinkling of the blood on the mercy seat pointed the Israelites to a greater atonement that would be offered before God the Father and that would come though the work of the Messiah. In the New Testament this atoning for sin employs the Greek word that was used for the mercy seat: *hilastērion*, meaning "means of atonement or reconciliation." When used of the ark in the Greek Old Testament and at Hebrews 9:5, it denotes the mercy seat. In the New Testament, this word is used several times to describe the work of Christ, "whom God put forward as a propitiation [better: *atoning sacrifice* or *means of reconciliation*] by His blood, to be received by faith" (Rm 3:25, emphasis added). Twice, John described Jesus by this word:

> He is the propitiation [i.e., *atoning sacrifice* or *means of reconciliation*] for our sins, and not for ours only but also for the sins of the whole world. (1Jn 2:2)

> In this is love, not that we have loved God but that He loved us and sent His Son to be the propitiation [i.e., *atoning sacrifice* or *means of reconciliation*] for our sins. (1Jn 4:10)

Moreover, when He took on our humanity, Jesus became one of us so that He could serve as our High Priest, thereby being both priest and sacrifice. As the writer to the Hebrews notes: "Therefore He had to be made like His brothers in every respect, so that He might become a merciful and faithful high priest in the service of God, to make propitiation [i.e., *atoning sacrifice*] for the sins of the people" (Heb 2:17). Thus, the Israelite high priest and his functions on the Day of Atonement served as a picture of the coming Messiah in His priestly office.

The Day of Atonement featured a second picture of the Messiah. On that day, a second goat would be chosen to bear the sins of the people. The high priest would lay both hands on a live goat and confess all the sins of the Israelites. In this way, the goat would bear the sins of the people. Then an assistant would take the goat into the wilderness and release it there. This symbolized the Messiah's carrying away the sins of the people into the wilderness, where He would die. Thus, this goat was the *escape goat,* which in English is shortened to *scapegoat.* Like the scapegoat, Jesus, "bore our sins in His body on the tree, that we might die to sin and live to righteousness" (1Pt 2:24).

THE FESTIVAL OF TRUMPETS (LEVITICUS 23:23–25; NUMBERS 29:1–6)

At the beginning of autumn on the first day of the month, the people of Israel were to hold a sacred assembly that not only featured sacrifices but also included trumpet blasts. In antiquity trumpets were used not only for music but also in battle as the king signaled his troops. In fact, Zechariah 9:14 depicts God sounding a trumpet at the final judgment as He marches to battle to defend His people: "Then the Lord will appear over them, and His arrow will go forth like lightning; *the Lord God will sound the trumpet* and will march forth in the whirlwinds of the south" (emphasis added). This is also referenced elsewhere in Zephaniah 1:16. In addition, Isaiah 27:13 pictures

God coming with the sound of a trumpet to summon His people from exile to worship in His eternal kingdom in Jerusalem. It is no surprise, then, that in four separate passages in the New Testament, Christ's return and the resurrection of all the dead is accompanied by a trumpet blast:

- And He will send out His angels with *a loud trumpet call*, and they will gather His elect from the four winds, from one end of heaven to the other. (Mt 24:31, emphasis added)
- In a moment, in the twinkling of an eye, at the *last trumpet*. For *the trumpet will sound*, and the dead will be raised imperishable, and we shall be changed. (1Co 15:52, emphasis added)
- For the Lord Himself will descend from heaven with a cry of command, with the voice of an archangel, and with *the sound of the trumpet of God*. And the dead in Christ will rise first. (1Th 4:16, emphasis added)
- Then the seventh angel *blew his trumpet*, and there were loud voices in heaven, saying, "The kingdom of the world has become the kingdom of our Lord and of His Christ, and He shall reign forever and ever." (Rv 11:15, emphasis added)

The Festival of Trumpets served, therefore, as Israel's yearly festival commemorating the final judgment of God—the coming of the Messiah to gather His people.

PRESENCE: THE MESSENGER OF THE LORD, A FIERY CLOUD, AND A ROCK

Just as Genesis depicted times when the Messiah was present with His people, so also the rest of the Pentateuch shows Him with Israel as they came from Egypt and lived in the wilderness. We will briefly explore three of these manifestations of His presence.

THE MESSENGER OF THE LORD

The Messenger of the Lord appeared at critical junctures in Israel's history. He was God, who spoke to Moses at the burning bush (Ex 3:2).

Later, God promised to send His Messenger to lead His people into the Promised Land:

> I am sending a messenger before you to protect you on the way and bring you to the place I have prepared. Pay careful attention to him and listen to him. Do not defy him, because he will not forgive your acts of rebellion, since my name is in him. However, if you carefully obey him and do everything I say, then I will be an enemy to your enemies and a foe to your foes. For my messenger will go before you and bring you to the land of the Amorites, Hittites, Perizzites, Canaanites, Hivites, and Jebusites, and I will wipe them out. (Ex 23:20–23, authors' translation)

In this passage, we have a strong foreshowing of God the Father speaking of His Son, the relationship fully revealed in the New Testament. This Messenger was clearly God:

1. Unconditional obedience to Him was emphasized twice.
2. He possessed the power to withhold forgiveness.
3. God's name was in Him.

Even after Israel sinned by worshiping a golden calf, God promised Moses once again that His Messenger would lead Israel to the land of Canaan (Ex 32:34; 33:2). In addition, we have already seen earlier in this chapter that the Lord sent His Messenger to protect Israel by warning Balaam to be careful to speak only what God gave him to say (Nu 22:22–35).

THE CLOUD THAT LED ISRAEL

One well-known fact about Israel's exodus from Egypt and wandering in the wilderness is that they were led by a cloudy, fiery pillar.[66] Moreover, most know that this pillar was the very presence of God. In, with, and under the cloud, God Himself was present: "And the LORD went before them by day in a pillar of cloud to lead them along the way, and by night in a pillar of fire to give them light, that they might travel by day and by night" (Ex 13:21; see Nu 10:34). However, few realize that this pillar that was God was also the Messenger of God: "Then the *Messenger of God* who was going before Israel's army moved and went behind them, and *the pillar of cloud* moved from in front of them and stood behind them" (Ex 14:19, authors' translation). This was the Messiah, the Angel of God, Jesus in the form of a cloudy pillar, who led Israel out of Egypt, just as He would later lead His people out of sin and death by His crucifixion and resurrection.

66 Ex 13:21–22; 14:19, 24; 33:9–10; Nu 12:5; 14:14; Dt 31:15.

THE ROCK THAT GAVE WATER

When Israel complained about the lack of drinking water, God had Moses strike a rock from which flowed water (Ex 17:1–7). That rock would be with them forty years later, and once again God provided water from it (Nu 20:1–13; see Dt 8:15). Clearly, this was no ordinary rock.

Later, Jesus would be in Samaria where He told a woman that He was able to give her "living water" (Jn 4:10, 14). Moreover, at the fall Festival of Booths, Jesus offered water to anyone who came to Him (Jn 7:37–39). This water Jesus proffered was greater than the water from the rock in the wilderness which quenched thirst only temporarily: it was the Holy Spirit (Jn 7:39).

Thus, the rock in the wilderness was the preincarnate Messiah. His gift of water to a thirsty Israel was a precursor to the greater water that He would provide when He came in the flesh. It is no wonder, then, that Paul would tell the Corinthians, "For they [i.e., the Israelites] drank from the spiritual Rock that followed them, and the Rock was Christ" (1Co 10:4). Jesus expanded on His role as the rock that provides water to sustain life when He spoke the Samaritan woman at the well (Jn 4). In the wilderness He manifested Himself as the rock that provided water when Israel needed it. He spoke of "living water," which allowed Him to make a play on words, since "living water" was not only an idiom for constantly flowing water but also an implication that the water He spoke about brought eternal life to those who believe in Him (see Jn 7:37–38).

EXODUS–DEUTERONOMY: THE PROMISED MESSIAH PROPHESIED AND PICTURED AS LEADER OF ISRAEL

Apart from the story of the exodus from Egypt and incidents from Israel's forty years in the wilderness, the last four books of the Pentateuch are often avoided as if they contain mostly out-of-date Israelite laws and windy speeches by Moses. However, there is much to be learned in these books, especially about the Messiah. We have presented only some of the more important aspects of the messianic message in Exodus, Leviticus, Numbers, and Deuteronomy. There are many more ways that the Pentateuch is connected to Jesus: the Sabbath, the Sabbath and Jubilee Years, the furniture and rites associated with the tabernacle, and other festivals such as the Festival of Tabernacles, to name only a few. Far from being esoteric, antique laws with confusing discourses, the Pentateuch was intended to keep Israel's eyes focused on God and His promise of the coming Messiah.

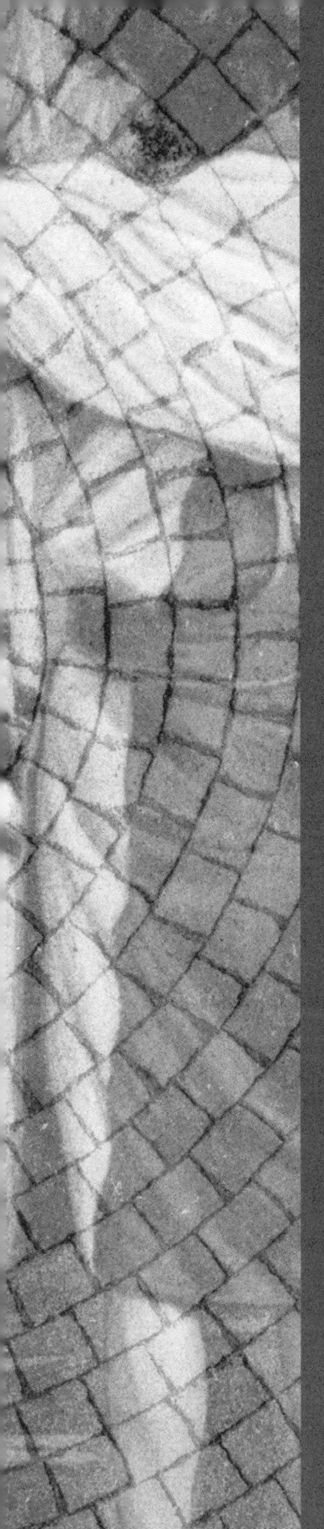

CHAPTER 4

THE MESSIANIC THREAD IN THE HISTORICAL BOOKS

The historical books of the Old Testament—Joshua through Esther—are a disparate collection. No two are alike in style. Judges is quite different from Kings. Joshua and Esther seem worlds apart both in style and in historical setting. So what holds these books together as a set? One might argue that they are all concerned with the history of the people of Israel. Yet that hardly seems enough to merit their being gathered into a collection. The Israel in Joshua is twelve tribes descended from Jacob taking possession of the land of Canaan (Jsh 3:12; 4:8), while the Israel in Ezra and Nehemiah is just two tribes—Judah and Benjamin, plus the Levites—who have recently returned to Jerusalem and its vicinity (Ezr 1:5; 4:1; 10:9; Ne 11:4). In Esther, the proper noun *Israel* is never even used—and the name of God is entirely absent! Instead, Mordecai is called *hayehudi,* "the Judean,"[67] a term deriving from the name of the tribe of Judah alone. Mordecai's people are *hayehudim*, "the Judeans."[68]

So what holds these books together? Like a string of separate pearls, they are united by one thread that runs through them—the message about the Messiah. We will look at a few of the many messianic pictures in these books.

PREDICTIONS: THE ANOINTED ONE

Although the high priest is called "the anointed priest" in Leviticus,[69] no one is called simply *meshiakh,* "anointed, messiah," until the Books of Samuel, where this title is used eleven times to refer to King Saul and three times to refer to King David,[70] both of

67 Est 5:13; 6:10; 8:7; 9:29, 31; 10:3; ESV translates as "the Jew."

68 E.g., Est 3:6; ESV translates as "the Jews."

69 Lv 4:3, 5, 16.

70 See, e.g., 2Sm 22:51; 23:1.

whom were anointed by Samuel to rule Israel (1Sm 10:1; 16:13). However, before there was a king of Israel, God's Anointed One, His Messiah, was mentioned twice.

THE HORN OF GOD'S ANOINTED ONE (1 SAMUEL 2:10)

The story of Hannah's desire for a child is filled with rivalry, pathos, angst, and ultimately joy at the birth of Samuel. When Hannah fulfilled her vow by dedicating the boy to God, she prayed the prayer recorded in 1 Samuel 2:1–10, often called the "Song of Hannah." She began her prayer by rejoicing in what God had done for her and speaking of His incomparable nature and His ability to judge those who are arrogant (1Sm 2:1–3). Next, she described the reversals of circumstance that God brings about: those who are mighty He can reduce to nothing, and those who have nothing He can supply with good things (1Sm 2:4–9). Hannah ended her prayer speaking of God's judgment:

> The Lord—his adversaries will be shattered; he will thunder in the heavens against them. The Lord will judge the ends of the earth. He will give strength to his king and lift the horn of his Anointed One. (1Sm 1:10, authors' translation)

Both Saul and David would fill the role of anointed one imperfectly, even though they would bear the title "messiah." In his psalm celebrating his victories through God's power, as recorded in both 2 Samuel 22 and Psalm 18, David would employ imagery from Hannah's song, especially God thundering from heaven (2Sm 22:14; Ps 18:13). Yet Hannah's words were not fulfilled by David or any of his successors in Jerusalem. For instance, none of them would "judge the ends of the earth." Instead, David recognized Hannah was speaking of the Great Messiah and built on her words to prophesy that God would show favor to "David and *his offspring* forever" (2Sm 22:51; Ps 18:50, emphasis added).

The last line of Hannah's prayer speaks of God lifting the horn of His Messiah, a poetic way of unfolding the meaning of the previous line, "He will give strength to His king." Here the Messiah is a king surpassing even the great David, who would call the Lord "the horn of my salvation," thereby identifying the Messiah with God (2Sm 22:3; Ps 18:2). In Psalm 132:17, David would use this same imagery to speak of the Messiah: "There I will make a horn to sprout for David; I have prepared a lamp for My anointed."

The New Testament confirms that Hannah's Messiah is Jesus. Mary, Jesus' mother, pointed to this after learning from the angel Gabriel that she would bear the Messiah. The words of her praise to God, the Magnificat, echo Hannah's prayer and its reversals of circumstance (Lk 1:46–55). Moreover, in the same chapter in Luke's Gospel, Zechariah, father of John the Baptist, recognized that Mary, a direct descendant of David, would bear the Messiah in the coming months. He began his prophesy by stating this: "Blessed be the Lord God of Israel, for He has visited and redeemed His people and has raised up a horn of salvation for us in the house of His servant David as He spoke by the mouth of His holy prophets from of old" (Lk 1:68–70). Hannah's song spoke of that horn: the Messiah.

GOD'S ANOINTED ONE AS THE FAITHFUL PRIEST (1 SAMUEL 2:35)

In contrast to the faithful Hannah and her son Samuel, the rest of 1 Samuel 2 presents the wickedness of the family of the high priest Eli. Eli's sons contemptuously misused the Lord's sacrifices (1Sm 2:12–17) and committed adultery with the women who served at the tabernacle (1Sm 2:22). While Eli warned his sons about their sins, he did nothing with his authority as high priest to stop them. Because of this situation, God sent a man of God, a prophet, to Eli with words of condemnation for him and his house. Eli's family would be removed from Israel's priesthood. This was fulfilled during the early reign of Solomon when the high priest Abiathar (a descendant of Eli) was banished (1Ki 2:26–27).

Yet God would not neglect His people and leave them without a high priest to intercede for them. The unnamed prophet promised: "I will raise for myself a faithful priest who will act in harmony with what is in my heart and my soul. I will build a secure house for him, and my Anointed One will serve in my presence forever" (1Sm 2:35, authors' translation). Just as the high priest is called "the anointed priest" in Leviticus, here God identifies this promised "faithful priest" as "my Anointed One," that is, "my Messiah." This priest will serve before God the Father forever. This cannot be a reference to Zadok, the high priest who replaced Eli's descendant Abiathar (1Ki 2:35). While the Zadokite line would supply Israel's high priests for many generations, they, too, would eventually yield the high priesthood to another family from Aaron's line. Instead, this prophecy is about the Messiah in His office as Priest. He would be the ultimate High Priest, serving forever before the heavenly Father on our behalf.

The New Testament recognizes Jesus as the faithful Priest prophesied to Eli. The writer to the Hebrews notes it was necessary for Jesus, to come from the human line of Abraham, stating, "Therefore He had to be made like His brothers in every respect, so that He might become a merciful and *faithful high priest in the service of God*, to make propitiation for the sins of the people" (Heb 2:17, emphasis added). Moreover, this priest was prophesied to have a "secure house" (1Sm 2:35), and Hebrews 10:21 says of Jesus, "We have a great *priest* over the *house of God*" (emphasis added). What can be more secure than God's house? Nothing. What faithful high priest can serve in it forever? Only the Messiah.

THE KING FROM DAVID'S LINE (2 SAMUEL 7:11–16; 1 CHRONICLES 17:10–14)

David's palace must have been the best that money could buy. He referred to it as "a house of cedar" (2Sm 7:2), built from the impressive cedars of Lebanon supplied by his friend King Hiram of Tyre (2Sm 5:11). Yet it brought David a feeling of impropriety: he had a magnificent cedar palace, but God's dwelling was a tent. When David proposed building a house for God, the prophet Nathan encourage him to do it—until God intervened. Nathan returned with a prophecy for David, perhaps the most influential prophecy for the rest of the Old Testament. The first part of the prophecy recalls what God did for David and then moves on to speak of what He would do for both David and Israel during the remainder of his life (2Sm 7:8–11). One important promise in this section occurs in verse 9: "And I will make for you a great name, like the name of the great ones of the earth." Next, the prophecy speaks of what God will do for David after his lifetime:

> Moreover, the Lord declares to you that the Lord will make you a house. When your days are fulfilled and you lie down with your fathers, I will raise up your offspring after you, who shall come from your body, and I will establish his kingdom. He shall build a house for My name, and I will establish the throne of his kingdom forever. I will be to him a father, and he shall be to Me a son. When he commits iniquity, I will discipline him with the rod of men, with the stripes of the sons of men, but My steadfast love will not depart from him, as I took it from Saul, whom I put away from before you. (2Sm 7:11–16; see 1Ch 17:10–14)

This prophecy speaks of one of David's offspring—one who would come from his own body. This phrase, literally "who will come from your internal organs," always refers to procreation of the next generation.[71] This part of the prophecy is speaking about Solomon, and gives details that apply especially to him:

1. He will be a product of David's body (2Sm 12:24).
2. God will establish his kingdom (1Ki 3:6).
3. He will build a house for God's name (1Ch 22:9–10).
4. God will be his father, and he will be God's son (1Ch 22:9–10).
5. When he sins, God will discipline him (1Ki 11:1–40).
6. Yet, God's love will not be removed from him (1Ki 11:11–12).

Yet this prophecy is not simply about Solomon. Embedded within it are these words: "I will establish the throne of his kingdom forever." This points beyond Solomon to a throne that is eternal, the throne of King Messiah.

Did David understand the messianic nature of this prophecy? He certain did, since God promised him that "the LORD will make you a house." This involves a play on words. David wished to make God a house—a building. But God was going to make David a house—a royal dynasty that would supply King Messiah to sit on the throne of the eternal kingdom. After Nathan finished his prophecy, David went and sat "before the LORD" (2Sm 7:18), before the ark of the covenant. There he gave thanks to God for these great promises. Contained within these words are David's statement "You have also

71 Gn 15:4; 25:23; Ru 1:11; 2Sm 16:11; 2Ch 32:21; Ps 71:6; Is 48:19; 49:1.

spoken about your servant's house for a long while to come: This is the teaching about *the man*" (2Sm 7:19, authors' translation). The writer of Chronicles reported David's words in a similar way, "You have viewed me according to the teaching about the *ascending man*" (1Ch 17:17, authors' translation). In both cases, David is stating that God is speaking about "*the* man," that is the Messiah, the perfect man. In 1 Chronicles, He is called "the ascending man," the man who will ascend into heaven.[72]

How did David come to this conclusion? Most obviously, the promise of an eternal kingdom entails an eternal king. But David also had been promised that God would give him a great name. In the Old Testament, only three have a great name: God, Abraham (Gn 12:2), and David (2Sm 7:9; 1Ch 17:8). The promise to David of an everlasting kingdom is like the promise to Abram that he would be a father of kings (Gn 17:6). This promise was associated with the changing of his name to Abraham (Gn 17:5), the name by which he would be more commonly known. The great patriarch of Israel was also promised a descendant who would do the royal work of conquering the gates of his enemies and through whom the nations would be blessed (Gn 22:17b–18). In addition, the promise to Abraham included the pledge of the land of Canaan for the people of Israel (Gn 12:7; 15:7, 18), a promise repeated to David (2Sm 7:10). It is impossible to escape the conclusion that David had been made Abraham's heir and received the promises first given to his ancestor Abraham—a father of kings, possessor of a great name, and one from whose line the Messiah would be born.

This prophecy about the Messiah coming from David's line is so important that it influenced the rest of the prophetic revelation in the Old Testament.[73] The identity of the Messiah is so strongly asso-

72 Pr 30:4; Lk 24:50–53; Jn 3:13; Ac 1:9–11; Eph 4:10.

73 E.g., Ps 18:50; 89:3–4, 20, 35–36, 49; 132:11–18; Is 9:6–7; 16:3–5; Jer 23:5; 33:15.

ciated with David that at times the prophets simply call the promised Savior "David."[74]

In the New Testament, Matthew's genealogy of Jesus calls Him "the Son of David" even before listing His ancestors (Mt 1:1). In the Gospels, those who acknowledge Jesus as the Messiah often proclaim Him "Son of David" (eleven times). Even Jesus' opponents admitted that the Messiah is "the son of David."[75] This great son of David is Jesus, the Christ, the fulfillment of Nathan's prophecy.[76]

PATTERN: BOAZ AND DAVID

The story of Naomi, Ruth, and Boaz is a poignant depiction of loyalty to God and family. More than that, however, it is an important link in the messianic line, with Boaz showing traits that parallel those of the Messiah. Boaz willingly took on the role of *go'el,* family redeemer.[77] As described in Leviticus 25, this is a close family member who is permitted to defend his family's interest against misfortune. He can buy back a close relative's land that has been sold to restore it to the family. The family redeemer may also redeem a brother from debt slavery. Numbers 35 grants the *go'el* the right to seek the punishment of someone who slays his relative.[78] In Ruth, Boaz redeemed the land of Elimelech to provide for Naomi (Ru 4:3). In fact, Boaz is the only person in the Old Testament who is portrayed as fulfilling the duties of a family redeemer. As such, his actions point forward to Jesus' role as redeemer of His own people, Israel (Lk 1:68; 24:21).

74 Jer 30:9; Ezk 34:23–24; 37:24–25; Hos 3:5.

75 Mt 22:42; see Mk 12:35; Lk 20:41.

76 Rm 1:3; Rv 3:7; 5:5; 22:16.

77 Ru 2:20; 3:9, 12; 4:1, 3, 6, 8, 14.

78 Nu 35:12, 19, 21, 24–25, 27; see also Dt 19:6, 12.

Yet there is more to Boaz as a foreshadowing of the Messiah: Boaz went beyond the simple requirements of the Law of Moses by agreeing to marry Ruth. In the Law, Moses commanded that when a man died without having a son, his widow was to marry one of her brothers-in-law to produce sons who would continue their father's name when they inherited the deceased brother's land (Dt 25:5–10). Ruth's husband, Mahlon, died before Ruth bore any children. Unfortunately for Ruth, she had no brother-in-law to marry her, since Chilion, Mahlon's only brother, had also died (Ru 1:5). Boaz, however, went beyond the letter of the law. Although he was not Ruth's brother-in-law, he agreed to marry her to perpetuate Mahlon's name on his property (Ru 4:10). This selfless act foreshadowed Jesus, whose supreme selflessness of making Himself cursed redeemed all humanity from the Law's curse (Gal 3:13).

In the five final verses in Ruth, we encounter a short ten-generation genealogy that connects Judah's son Perez to David through Boaz (Ru 4:18–22). This genealogy is not complete in that it does not list every generation during the span from Perez's day (the nineteenth century BC) to David's era (the eleventh century BC), a span of more than 800 years. In comparison, the complete Levite genealogy from Korah to Heman at 1 Chronicles 6:33–37 contains eighteen generations, and it covers only the period from the exodus (the fifteenth century BC) to David's day, a span of only 400 years. Clearly, the author of Ruth has strategically included only select ancestors of David in his genealogy. This selectivity in the genealogy allowed the author specifically to highlight two men: Boaz and David. Boaz occupies the privileged seventh position in the list; David, the honored tenth position.

What, then, is the point of this genealogy? Does it simply tell us of David's ancestry? No—the genealogy traces the Messiah's lineage, and it does this by reference to Genesis. That earlier book contains two genealogies that also trace the lineage of the bearers of the messianic promise from Adam to Abraham (Gn 5:3–32; Gn 11:10–26). These genealogies are also selective and make use of the numbers *7* and *10* to highlight prominent persons. Enoch, the man who "walked with God, and he was not, for God took him" is seventh (Gn 5:21–24). Noah, through whom humanity was saved from extinction, is tenth (Gn 5:32). Eber, the man whose name would become enshrined in the ethnic designation *Hebrew*, is fourteenth—double 7 in the combined lists (Gn 11:16–17). Abraham, the great patriarch of Israel, is twentieth—double 10 (Gn 11:26). By imitating the Genesis genealogies, the author of Ruth is sending his readers a message: This story in not simply about how a Moabite woman and an Israelite man came to marry. It is not just about how David came to be born in Bethlehem. This is the story of God's dedication to the messianic promise. The genealogy says, "Keep your eyes on the Messiah!"

Thus, Ruth ends with David (Ru 4:22). David's life also, then, foreshadows the Messiah, and there are distinct parallels to Jesus. Both were from Bethlehem (1Sm 17:12; Mt 2:1). Both were given a great name by God. David was promised this (2Sm 7:9). Jesus, however, received the greatest name of all: "Therefore God has highly exalted Him and bestowed on Him *the name that is above every name*, so that at the name of Jesus every knee should bow, in heaven and on earth and under the earth, and every tongue confess that Jesus Christ is Lord, to the glory of God the Father" (Php 2:9–11, emphasis added).

Moreover, both David and Jesus were triumphant over seemingly invincible enemies. In David's case, the enemies were the Philistines whom previous Israelites fought but could never subdue. Samson killed many Philistines, but he only began "to save Israel from the hand of the Philistines" (Jgs 13:5). The prophet Samuel called on God to defeat the Philistines, and there was a great victory of Israel (1Sm 7:2–13). Yet the Philistines remained a threat. Saul had battles against the Philistines, but when he died, they were still a menace to Israel.

Yet in David, the Philistines were subdued and confined to their narrow strip of land along the Mediterranean. David went forth from the Israelite battle lines to defeat the Philistine giant Goliath (1Sm 17). When he became king, he relied on God to defeat the Philistines twice and bring their threat to Israel to an end (2Sm 5:17–25).

Jesus defeated greater enemies. He conquered darkness, demons, and death itself: "Since therefore the children share in flesh and blood, He [Jesus] Himself likewise partook of the same things, that through death He might destroy the one who has the power of death, that is, the devil, and deliver all those who through fear of death were subject to lifelong slavery" (Heb 2:14–15).

In a foreshadowing of the Messiah's eternal kingdom, David founded a dynasty that lasted an extremely long time, from 1009 to 587 BC—422 years. Jesus inherited the throne of His ancestor David (Lk 1:32) and founded a kingdom that is eternal (2Pt 1:11).

It is not surprising, then, that David is compared to the Messiah not only by the prophets but also during his own lifetime, when he was favorably compared to the Messenger of God.[79] No other person in the entire Old Testament is so approvingly mentioned in connection to the preincarnate Savior.

79 1Sm 29:9; 2Sm 14:17, 20; 19:27 (a title given to the Messiah in, e.g., Gn 16:7; 22:11; Ex 3:2).

PRESENCE: COMMANDER AND MESSENGER

The Messiah's guidance for Israel throughout its forty years under Moses' leadership was seen in the fiery, cloudy pillar's manifestation of God's Messenger. After Moses' death, however, the pillar is never again mentioned as leading Israel. Yet the Savior continued to be present with Israel, not only as enthroned over the ark of the covenant (1Sm 4:4; 2Sm 6:2) but also as Commander and Messenger.

THE COMMANDER OF THE LORD'S ARMY (JOSHUA 5:13–15)

In the spring of 1404 BC, Joshua and the army of Israel crossed the Jordan River into the land of Israel, led by the ark of the covenant (Jsh 3). Shortly thereafter, Joshua approached Jericho, and he encountered a man with a drawn sword in His hand, ready for battle. Joshua's question to Him was a reasonable one: "Are You for us, or for our adversaries?" (Jsh 5:13). In which army did this man serve, Israel's or Jericho's? His answer was interesting: "Neither. I have now come as the Commander of Yahweh's army" (Jsh 5:14, authors' translation). From this reply, Joshua immediately knew this was God come to lead God's heavenly army into battle to support Israel as it went to conquer the land. Therefore, Joshua bowed face down on the ground and awaited instructions from the supreme Commander, asking "What does my Lord wish to say to his servant?" (Jsh 5:14, authors' translation). The next words of the Commander were momentous: "Take off your sandals from your feet, for the place where you are standing is holy." The echoes of the Messenger of the Lord's words to Moses at the burning bush (Ex 3:5) must have rung in Joshua's ears! He was in the presence of God the Messiah, who would continue to be with him to strengthen him as Israel's new leader (Jsh 1:9).

THE MESSENGER OF THE LORD IN THE HISTORICAL BOOKS

The Messenger of the Lord continued to be with Israel throughout its time in the Promised Land. He would come to Bochim to pronounce judgment on Israel because they had fallen into idolatry (Jgs 2:1–5). He would place a curse on Meroz when the men there failed to support Deborah and Barak's battle against Sisera (Jgs 5:23). He came to Gideon to call him to action as one of Israel's judges (Jgs 6:11–24). He also appeared to Samson's parents to announce the birth of their son, and Manoah recognized him as God (Jgs 13:1–23, especially 13:22).

When David conducted a census to discover how many Israelites were of fighting age to serve in his army, thereby trusting in human strength rather than God, the Messenger of the Lord would mete out punishment on David and his people (2Sm 24; 1Ch 21). In a later era, Elijah fled the wicked Queen Jezebel, and the Messenger of the Lord came to strengthen him with food. That miraculous food fortified Elijah to journey forty days on his way to Mount Horeb (1Ki 19:1–9). During Elijah's ministry, King Ahaziah faithlessly turned away from Israel's God to seek advice from the Philistine idol Baal-zebub. The Messenger of the Lord gave Elijah a prophecy condemning the king to die (2Ki 1, especially 1:3, 15). In 701 BC, the Assyrian army besieged Jerusalem, and the faithful King Hezekiah trusted God and refused to surrender. The Messenger of the Lord defended His city and His people by slaying Sennacherib's army, sending him packing all the way back to Nineveh (2Ki 18:13–19:36, especially 19:35).

In all these passages, we see glimpses of the Savior's work among Israel that would be characteristic of His ministry. For instance, He sharply condemned sin (e.g., Mt 23:13–39). He strengthened the weak, healing those who were blind, lame, and paralyzed.[80] The Messiah also defended His people from exploitation as He overturned the money changers' tables in the temple courtyard.[81]

THE HISTORICAL BOOKS—UNITED BY THEIR WITNESS TO THE MESSIAH

From Israel's entry into the land of Canaan in Joshua to the reign of Xerxes in Esther, the historical books are unified through the Messiah as the person who holds them together. The Books of Kings and Chronicles trace the Davidic kings as evidence that God would keep His promise to send a Savior, preserving the messianic line of rulers in Jerusalem as a "lamp for David."[82] After the exile, the Book of Ezra records the building of a new temple in Jerusalem that would await the arrival of the Messiah within its courtyard. Nehemiah chronicles the final stages of the rebuilding of Jerusalem's walls, a necessary step on the way to God's new covenant with His people (Jer 31:38–39; see 31:31–34). In 474 BC, God's people were threatened with genocidal extinction by Haman, thereby also endangering the messianic promise that all families on earth would be blessed by Abraham's descendant (Gn 12:3). But God delivered His people through the efforts of Esther and Mordecai.

Thus, the historical books are unanimous in their message: look for the Messiah. He was with Israel throughout its history so that He could bless people of all nations when He would come as the great Son of David in a lowly manger—in a little backwater town in Roman Judea, a place called Bethlehem.

80 Mt 11:5; 15:30–31; 21:14; Lk 7:22; Jn 5:3–9.

81 Mt 21:12–13; Mk 11:15; Jn 2:14–17.

82 See 1Ki 11:36; 15:4; 2Ki 8:19; 2Ch 21:7; Ps 132:17.

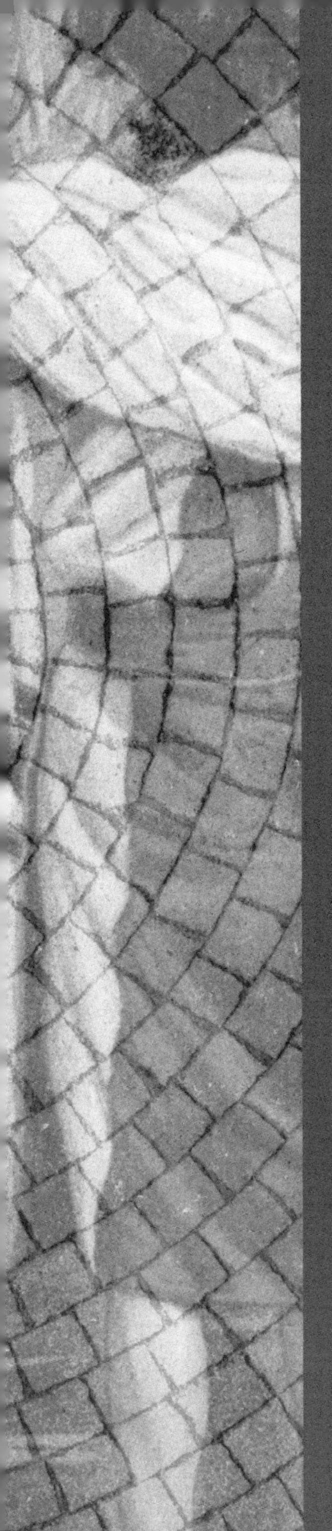

CHAPTER 5

THE MESSIANIC SIDE OF THE WISDOM BOOKS

The story about an afflicted man, the sayings of a wise king, the observations on the futilities that attend to earthly human existence, and a song of love between a woman and a man—could there be a more diverse collection in the Bible? Yet these are the wisdom books of the Old Testament: Job, Psalms, Proverbs, Ecclesiastes, and Song of Solomon.[83] Each in its own unique way gives us another view of the Messiah in the Old Testament as it also instructs readers in wise, godly living.

JOB: MESSIAH AS INTERCESSOR

There are times when we cannot represent ourselves before others. We may need a person to introduce us to someone of power and influence, a person to plead our cause in a certain matter, or even an attorney to represent us in a legal matter. Having someone to intercede for us can be extremely helpful. But suppose you are suffering from a terrible series of setbacks. In short order, you have lost most of your property, your family, and your health, and it appears as if your only appeal is to God. Who could intercede? That was Job's dilemma, and his words demonstrate that he believed he had an intercessor with God—the Messiah.

THE MEDIATOR (JOB 9:32–35)

According to Job, the problem he experienced was that God is not a man (Jb 9:32)—a problem that would ultimately be solved with the incarnation of the Messiah, who would then serve as a mediator between God and people to remove the fear of divine judgment

83 The Wisdom Literature Book of Psalms will be covered exclusively in the next chapter.

(Jb 9:33–35). Job 9:33 calls the Messiah an arbiter—someone who would function like a referee who "might lay his hand on us both." Job envisions the Messiah as a reconciler who would enable God and Job to settle their differences in a just and equitable manner, as Job confessed that he was completely unable to accomplish such reconciliation with God on his own (Jb 9:34).

It is noteworthy that this messianic mediator would remove from Job God's "rod" or "staff," which punishes sin (Jb 9:34). This is the same word used in 2 Samuel 7:14 to refer to God's chastening "rod" upon the Davidic kings. Finally—and most ironically—the rod of divine judgment would fall upon the sinless Son of David, who would serve the "mediator of a new covenant" and whose blood "speaks a better word than the blood of Abel" (Heb 12:24). Job's longings would one day be realized. The Messiah's blood would reconcile all people to God the Father (Eph 2:16).

THE ADVOCATE (JOB 16:18–21)

Having been relentlessly accused by his three friends of refusing to admit to some unstated sin, Job was not only afflicted physically with boils and pains but also tormented by knowing that he was being falsely accused. His only appeal was to God. Yet he was unsure why God was permitting him to suffer. So he placed his confidence in an advocate:

> O earth, cover not my blood, and let my cry find no resting place. Even now, behold, my witness is in heaven, and He who testifies for me is on high. My friends scorn me; my eye pours out tears to God, that He would argue the case of a man with God, as a son of man does with his neighbor. (Jb 16:18–21)

Despite all his troubles, Job was confident that he had an advocate before God whom he calls "my witness . . . He who testifies for me." Even as his "eye pours out tears to God," he knows that this advocate "would argue the case of a man with God." Job knew of the Messiah's role as an intercessor between God and humans and was confident that his case was being appealed in heaven even as he was beset with false friends on earth.

This same understanding of Jesus' role as messianic advocate is still a comfort to Christians today. Paul reminds us, "Who shall bring any charge against God's elect? It is God who justifies. Who is to condemn? Christ Jesus is the one who died—more than that, who was raised—who is at the right hand of God, who indeed is interceding for us" (Rm 8:33–34).

THE LIVING REDEEMER (JOB 19:23–27)

Job's suffering was so severe that at times he thought he might die. In Job 19, he noted his dire physical condition: "My bones stick to my skin and to my flesh, and I have escaped by the skin of my teeth" (Jb 19:20). Since he did not know how long he might live, the most famous passage in Job begins with his wish that his thoughts would be made permanent: "I wish that my words were written down! I wish they were inscribed on a scroll or engraved in stone forever with an iron stylus and lead!" (Jb 19:23–24, authors' translation). What he was about to say was so important that Job wanted it to be made long-lasting—eternal in the heavens.

In Job's day, few things were recorded in writing since writing materials were expensive and often had to be handmade. Scribes were trained to make their own ink and quills. Moreover, few people knew how to write. Most people never owned a written text of any kind. Those scrolls that were in existence were considered precious and carefully archived to preserve the words in them. Carved inscriptions were more durable than scrolls, and so Job mentions a stone engraving as an even more ideal medium to record what he was about to say.

"For I know that my Redeemer lives, and at the end he will stand upon the earth" (Jb 19:25, authors' translation). Job knows that he has a Redeemer, a *go'el*. (Recall the discussion of Boaz in chapter 4.) This person will act as his defender when Job is defenseless. He will be one to rescue Job. Later, the prophet Isaiah would use this term *go'el* to describe God as the defender of His people.[84] Job was confident that he had a divine Redeemer.

At the same time, Job said that this Redeemer would "stand upon the earth." He pictured his Redeemer not simply as God but also as a man—the Messiah who would be both human and divine. Moreover, He would do this "at the end," that is, at the end of time when God executes His final judgment. Job's confidence here is that even though he may die, his Redeemer will continue to live and will be at the judgment to defend him and rescue him.

Then Job added, "Even after my skin has been destroyed, yet in my flesh I shall see God, whom I shall see for myself, and my eyes shall behold, and not as a stranger. My heart faints within me!" (Jb 19:26–27, authors' translation). Not only did Job anticipate that he would die, but also that his corpse would decay. Nevertheless, he boldly proclaimed, "Yet in my flesh I shall see God." This is not the first time Job spoke of the resurrection. Earlier, he had said to God,

> I wish you would hide me in Sheol, that you would conceal me until your wrath is past, that you would appoint a set time for me, and remember me! If a man dies, will

84 Is 41:14; 43:14; 44:6, 24; 47:4; 48:17; 49:7, 26; 54:5, 8; 60:16; 63:16.

> he live again? All the days of my service I would wait, until my renewal would come. You would call, and I would answer you. You would long for the work of your hands. For then you would number my steps, but you would not keep a record of my sin. My transgression would be sealed up in a bag, and you would cover over my iniquity. (Jb 14:13–17, authors' translation)

Job answers his own question, "If a man dies, will he live again?" with a positive affirmation that he will—God will call, and Job will answer. Not only that, but Job knows that he will be forgiven by God.

In chapter 14, Job describes this landscape of his life. "Man who is born of a woman is few of days and full of trouble. He comes out like a flower and withers" (Jb 14:1–2). Like a flower, Job is withering away. "The mountain falls and crumbles away" (Jb 14:18). Like a mountain, Job's life is eroding and crumbling. "Water wears away the stones; the torrents wash away the soil" (Jb 14:19). Like stones and soil, Job's life is wearing and washing away.

Job's world is filled with pain and sorrow. But amid wilting flowers, eroding and crumbling mountains, worn stones, and washed-away soil, Job contemplates the tree, which has hope since, if cut down, it can sprout again (Jb 14:7–9). Though Job sees no visible evidence for the hope of an afterlife (Jb 14:10–12), his faith overcomes human reason: "If a man dies, will he live again? All the days of my service I would wait, until my renewal would come" (Jb 14:14). The term *renewal* in Job 14:14 comes from the same word Job uses to describe the tree sprouting in Job 14:7. With renewal, therefore, Job is thinking of an afterlife. He also speaks of God hiding him in Sheol (denoting the general realm of the dead) until divine wrath passes over and God remembers him (Jb 14:13). Reconciliation would be a real possibility if God were to overlook sin, seal up transgression in a pouch, and plaster over iniquity (Jb 14:16–17). Resurrection and redemption—these are the Messiah's gifts for Job and indeed for all who believe.

Now in Job 19, he once again affirms that even after death he will have life, and not simply as a disembodied soul but in his flesh (v. 26). He will see God *with his own eyes* in his resurrected body. God will be no stranger. The thought of the Redeemer raising Job on the Last Day was so overwhelming that he could only say, "My heart faints within me!" (Jb 19:27).

Job's statement is clear: the resurrection at the end of time is tied to the living Redeemer and clearly points to Christ. Paul elaborates on this resurrection in Christ for those who trust in Him as Job did:

> Behold! I tell you a mystery. We shall not all sleep, but we shall all be changed, in a moment, in the twinkling of an eye, at the last trumpet. For the trumpet will sound, and the dead will be raised imperishable, and we shall be changed. For this perishable body must put on the imperishable, and this mortal body must put on immortality. When the perishable puts on the imperishable, and the mortal puts on immortality, then shall come to pass the saying that is written: "Death is swallowed up in victory." "O death, where is your victory? O death, where is your sting?" The sting of death is sin, and the power of sin is the law. But thanks be to God, who gives us the victory through our Lord Jesus Christ. (1Co 15:51–57)

THE MEDIATING MESSENGER (JOB 33:23–28)

Job was not the only person who knew about the Messiah as a mediator between God and humans. The young man Elihu, who waited to speak until Job and his friends had grown silent, also spoke of Him. In Job 33, he mentioned that God often spares a person from death (Jb 33:18), even when it appears as if the body is wasting away (Jb 33:19–22). He then speaks about how this can happen: "If there is a Messenger on his side, one mediator out of a thousand, to declare to a person what is right for him, then he is merciful to him and says, 'Release him from going down to the Pit. I have found a ransom.' Then his flesh will be healthier than in his youth. He will return to the days of his youthful vigor" (Jb 33:23–25, authors' translation). Elihu seems to not only anticipate what will happen to Job—that God will rescue Job and restore his heath—but also sees this as the result of "a Messenger, . . . one mediator out of a thousand." The Messiah is the Messenger of the Lord (see the discussion of the Messenger of the Lord in chapter 2). Moreover, this Messenger is quoted as saying, "I have found a ransom." The tormented man was rescued because the Messenger had paid the price to ransom him.

Next, Elihu depicts the reaction of the man who is rescued: "Then man prays to God, and He accepts him; he sees His face with a shout of joy, and He restores to man His righteousness. He sings before men and says: 'I sinned and perverted what was right, and it was not repaid to me. He has redeemed my soul from going down into the pit, and my life shall look upon the light'" (Jb 33:26–28). The rescued man is not only forgiven but also recognizes that he did not receive what he deserved for his sins. He recognizes that the Messenger redeemed his soul—paid the price so that he would live forever.

Elihu's description of the Messenger is remarkably like the New Testament description of Jesus, who paid the price to ransom the world. "For there is one God, and there is one mediator between God and men, the man Christ Jesus, who gave Himself as a ransom for all, which is the testimony given at the proper time" (1Tm 2:5–6).

A major issue in the interpretation of the Book of Job is the identity of the mediator, witness, redeemer, and messenger. There is good reason to believe that Job is thinking of a single figure rather than of a separate figure in each of the passages we have discussed. In chapters 9, 16, 19, and 33, the redeemer figure has the same role. He has the legal function of ensuring Job's end-time acquittal or justification, and He appears before God when God is going to render judgment. The contexts of the four pericopes abound with legal terminology such as "justice," "litigate," "mediate," "witness," "intercede," and "redeem." Job is concerned with the problem of justification as well in chapters 14, 16, 19, and 33, with the existence of lasting, permanent evidence for his acquittal. In 13:15–16; 14:7–17; 16:18–22; 19:23–27; and 33:23–28, his hope extends beyond his own death and involves an afterlife—an afterlife secured by the Messiah's death on a cross and resurrection on the third day.

PROVERBS: THE MESSIAH AS WISDOM

The Book of Proverbs is often viewed simply as a book of sayings that offer advice for practical living. While one cannot deny that Proverbs has much to say about real-world situations and how to navigate a wise course in life, this is not all that Proverbs offers. In fact, Proverbs is a book of wisdom that derives from God, who grants His people the ability to live and know Him. Therefore, it is not surprising that we meet God in the pages of this book and learn of His Messiah, the embodiment of divine wisdom.

THE MESSIAH AT CREATION (PROVERBS 8)

In the opening chapters of Proverbs, we find several extended poems that teach about wisdom and wise behavior. Perhaps the most important of these is Proverbs 8, a speech by and about personified Wisdom. Here Wisdom is depicted as a woman, drawing on the grammatical gender of the Hebrew word for wisdom, *khokmah*. Some may find it troubling that the personified woman Wisdom is a picture of the Messiah, since Jesus was clearly a man. However, Jesus Himself was not hesitant to use female images to speak of His relationship to His people when it was appropriate. For instance, at Matthew 23:37 and Luke 13:34, Jesus says, "O Jerusalem, Jerusalem, the city that kills the prophets and stones those who are sent to it! How often would I have gathered your children together as a *hen* gathers *her* brood under *her* wings, and you were not willing!" (emphasis added).

Wisdom as a woman not only appears in the opening chapters of Proverbs but also is seen at the very end. The poem to the wife of noble character in chapter 31 is a parallel to Lady Wisdom herself. Consider that both poems assert these women's value as being above that of jewels (Pr 3:14–15 and 31:10). Both refer to the work and benefits of her hands (Pr 3:16 and 31:19–20). Those who know Lady Wisdom or the wife of noble character are happy, and their children call them happy (Pr 3:18 and 31:28). What are we to make of these connections? Wise women are praised in Proverbs, and ultimately, they paint a picture of the Messiah as God's gift of incarnate Wisdom.

Proverbs 8 begins with Wisdom calling out to people at the access to a city (Pr 8:1–3; cf. Pr 1:20–21). She invites people to hear her words to become prudent (Pr 8:4–5). Then Wisdom describes her speech as containing noble things that are true, righteous, and upright (Pr 8:6–9). Following this, the value of wisdom is said to surpass those things that humans esteem, including silver, gold, and jewels (Pr 8:10–11).

Next, Wisdom describes where she lives. It is not a common neighborhood but instead, "I, wisdom, dwell with prudence, and I find knowledge and discretion" (Pr 8:12). Then Wisdom says, "I have counsel and sound wisdom; I have insight; I have strength" (Pr 8:14). These attributes of Wisdom match closely the description of God at Job 12:13, hinting for the first time that this person Wisdom is God Himself. Moreover, six wisdom attributes of the Holy Spirit mentioned at Isaiah 11:2 are claimed here by Wisdom. This serves for the first time to help the reader see Wisdom as the Messiah on whom the Spirit of God rests (see Mt 3:16; Jn 1:32–33).

WISDOM ATTRIBUTES OF THE SPIRIT IN ISAIAH 11:2 AND PROVERBS 8

THE GIFT OF THE SPIRIT IN ISAIAH 11:2	USE IN PROVERBS 8
Wisdom	8:1, 11–12
Understanding	8:14
Counsel	8:14
Might/Strength	8:14
Knowledge	8:9–10, 12
The Fear of the Lord	8:13

The next verses in Wisdom's discourse claim that those who rule justly will rule by Wisdom's power. This once again identifies Wisdom as divine, since only God establishes rulers.[85]

85 E.g., Ne 9:37; Jn 19:10–11; Rm 13:1–4.

Then Wisdom speaks of her value once again as riches and treasure, but this time calls it "fruit" (Pr 8:18–19). By using this metaphor, Wisdom is offering perpetual riches of an everbearing tree's fruit. Once again, readers are pointed to the Messiah in the person of Jesus, who makes it possible for sinners to receive the greatest riches: God's grace, forgiveness, and eternal life. Paul often refers to these riches of Christ (emphasis added):

> In Him we have redemption through His blood, the forgiveness of our trespasses, according to the *riches* of His grace. (Eph 1:7)
>
> Having the eyes of your hearts enlightened, that you may know what is the hope to which He has called you, what are the *riches* of His glorious inheritance in the saints. (Eph 1:18)
>
> And my God will supply every need of yours according to His *riches* in glory in Christ Jesus. (Php 4:19)
>
> To them God chose to make known how great among the Gentiles are the *riches* of the glory of this mystery, which is Christ in you, the hope of glory. (Col 1:27)

However, the most important passage from Paul that relates to Proverbs 8 is Ephesians 3:8–10 (emphasis added):

> To me, though I am the very least of all the saints, this grace was given, to preach to the Gentiles the unsearchable riches of Christ, and to bring to light for everyone what is the plan of the mystery hidden for ages in God, who created all things, so that through the church the manifold *wisdom* of God might now be made known to the rulers and authorities in the heavenly places.

This description of Christ matches closely the description of Wisdom in Proverbs 8, including the next verses where we will see Wisdom at creation:

PARALLELS BETWEEN PROVERBS 8 AND EPHESIANS 3:8–10

PROVERBS 8	EPHESIANS 3:8–10
Wisdom gives riches (8:10–11; 18–19)	Christ gives riches (3:8)
Wisdom participated in creation (8:22–31)	Wisdom is linked to God, who created all things (3:9)
God's wisdom empowers rulers (8:15–16)	God's wisdom in Christ is made known to rulers in the heavenly places (3:10)

Clearly, the New Testament sees Proverbs 8 as a messianic passage, a description of the Messiah according to the gifts of divine wisdom and riches that He brings to humankind.

The climax of Proverbs 8 is Wisdom's presentation of herself as present with God before the creation of the world and then participating in God's creative acts. Wisdom begins by saying:

> The Lord possessed me at the beginning of His work, the first of His acts of old [*better translated as* "before His acts of old"]. Ages ago I was set up, at the first, before the beginning of the earth. When there were no depths I was brought forth, when there were no springs

> abounding with water. Before the mountains had been shaped, before the hills, I was brought forth, before He had made the earth with its fields, or the first of the dust of the world. (Pr 8:22–26)

Wisdom was with the Lord from eternity past. Here is a key passage in the Old Testament—depicting both God the Father ("the LORD") and God the Son (Wisdom). It has an unmistakable echo in John's description of Jesus as "the Word" who was with God in the beginning (Jn 1:1–2; see also 1 Jn 1:1; 2:13–14). Wisdom in Proverbs 8:22–26 matches other messianic passages in the Old Testament that speak of both the Father and the Son and the Son's eternal generation from the Father (Ps 2:7, 12; 89:27–28).

Finally, Wisdom speaks of participating in creation:

> When He established the heavens, I was there; when He drew a circle on the face of the deep, when He made firm the skies above, when He established the fountains of the deep, when He assigned to the sea its limit, so that the waters might not transgress His command, when He marked out the foundations of the earth, then I was beside Him, like a master workman, and I was daily His delight, rejoicing before Him always, rejoicing in His inhabited world and delighting in the children of man. (Pr 8:27–31)

Who alone was at creation when God established the heavens? It was the triune God—the Creator Father, Son, and Spirit (see Gn 1:2). Once again, in the New Testament, John noted that Jesus was at creation, just as Wisdom claims, "All things were made through Him, and without Him was not any thing made that was made" (Jn 1:3).

It is little wonder, then, that Paul boldly asserted, "But we preach Christ crucified, a stumbling block to Jews and folly to Gentiles, but to those who are called, both Jews and Greeks, Christ the power of God and *the wisdom of God*" (1Co 1:23–24, emphasis added).

In addition, Jesus identified Himself with Wisdom. Luke 11:49 quotes Jesus as saying, "Therefore also *the Wisdom of God said*, 'I will send them prophets and apostles, some of whom they will kill and persecute'" (emphasis added). In the parallel at Matthew 23:34, we read, "Therefore *I send* you prophets and wise men and scribes, some of whom you will kill and crucify, and some you will flog in your synagogues and persecute from town to town" (emphasis added). Clearly, Jesus is identifying Himself as the Wisdom of God.

WHAT IS THE NAME OF HIS SON? (PROVERBS 30:4)

Near the end of Proverbs, we encounter the sayings of a certain Agur, son of Jakeh. At Proverbs 30:4, he issues a challenge to his audience in a series of questions:

- Who has ascended to heaven and come down?
- Who has gathered the wind in His fists?
- Who has wrapped up the waters in a garment?
- Who has established all the ends of the earth?
- What is His name, and what is His son's name? Surely you know!

The first question is based on Deuteronomy 30:12, where Moses notes that Israel has no need to ascend to heaven to receive God's Word, since God has brought it down to them. The next three questions are drawn from God's questions to Job in Job 38–39. The answer to all these questions is obviously "God." But then Agur's final question has no complete answer for the Old Testament people to whom it was addressed. They could reply with God's name, Yahweh, the Lord. But they had no idea of the name of God's Son. That would remain a mystery, and Agur's final, biting words, "Surely you know!" are identical to God's challenging words to Job (Jb 38:5).

Agur, therefore, affirms the existence of the Son of God. He affirms, as in Proverbs 8, that the Son was with God the Father at creation, establishing "all the ends of the earth." But His name would not be revealed until many centuries later by the angel Gabriel to Jesus' mother, Mary: "And behold, you will conceive in your womb and bear a son, *and you shall call His name Jesus.* He will be great and will be called the *Son of the Most High*" (Lk 1:31–32, emphasis added).

ECCLESIASTES: ONE SHEPHERD

Near the end of Ecclesiastes, we find these words: "Man is going to his eternal home" (Ec 12:5). The author goes on to write, "And the dust returns to the earth as it was, and the spirit returns to God who gave it" (Ec 12:7). Because of the Messiah's death and resurrection, when we die, we go to our eternal home. We return to God. Our best years have not passed us by. Our biggest moments are not in the past. Death is the first chapter of a story that has no end. The Messiah's return will set in motion God's final plan to defeat death. Our spirits will reunite with our perfect, resurrected bodies. The spouse snatched by disease will run into our arms. The health that eluded us in the winter of our life will return a thousandfold. The friends and family members who died in the faith will sit next to us, singing in the heavenly choir.

Ecclesiastes, however, often discusses life and its futility "under the sun," and it is easy to miss the few—but important—notes of hope. Yet, in closing his book, the author summarizes the source of all wise sayings: "The words of the wise are like goads, and like nails firmly fixed are the collected sayings; they are given by one Shepherd" (Ec 12:11). The one that is called "Shepherd" is responsible for the wise words that act like goads—cattle prods—to move His people to do what they are sometimes reluctant to do. The Shepherd's words are also like firmly embedded nails that hold life together.

While elsewhere in Ecclesiastes the author frequently mentions God (thirty-six times), this is the only place in the book where God is called *Shepherd.* The change is significant and should alert us to the Messiah as the Shepherd of God's sheep. The prophets will use the shepherd imagery to prophesy of the Messiah (e.g., see the discussion of Ezk 34 in chapter 8). Of course, Jesus will speak of Himself as the Good Shepherd (Jn 10) and Peter will call Him "the Shepherd and Overseer" of the souls of God's people (1Pt 2:25). Here in Ecclesiastes, we glimpse the Messiah Shepherd, who uses the words of the wise to guide and sustain His people.

SONG OF SOLOMON: THE MESSIAH AS HIS PEOPLE'S BELOVED

In the Song of Solomon, we meet a man and a woman whose courtship and wedding will lead ultimately to the consummation of their relationship. The Song teaches us about God's good gift of marriage (see Gn 2:24) and the need to eschew promiscuity. But is that all there is to this short book? From antiquity, readers of the Song have recognized that it also looks beyond marriage to the bond between God and His people, a theme in the prophets who saw Israel as God's

Bride.[86] This, in turn, anticipates the New Testament's teaching that the Church, the New Jerusalem, is Christ's Bride, whom He purifies in Holy Baptism and among whom He lives now (Eph 5:22–33) and forever (Rv 21:1–4).

WISDOM'S MULTIFACETED MESSIAH

The Old Testament's wisdom books present several pictures of the Messiah. Among them are a renewing Redeemer, the Wisdom of God, the Son of God, the Shepherd, and the Bridegroom. Though in many ways the Wisdom Literature's portraits of the Messiah are much more subtle than the prophecies found in the Pentateuch or the Prophets, they are nevertheless important. Together they function as a gem with several facets, each of which reflects the light of the Messiah in unique ways to help us see His beauty from different perspectives. We can fully appreciate the many gifts that Jesus, the Christ, has bestowed upon His people.

86 E.g., Is 54:5; Jer 31:32; Hos 2:16.

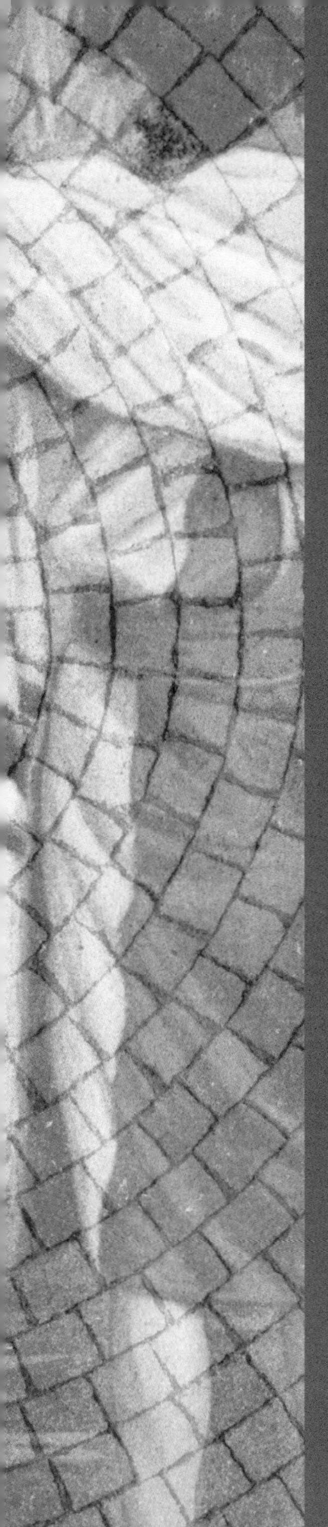

CHAPTER 6

THE MESSIANIC PSALMS OF ISRAEL

Have you ever looked at a 500-piece puzzle and asked, "How in the world do I put this together?" The key, as you probably know, is to keep looking at the picture on the front of the box. How do we make sense of 150 psalms that appear in all sorts of shapes and sizes? Keep looking for the predictions, patterns, and presence of the Messiah. He is the key to understanding this vast array of poetry and praise.

True, there are just a handful of messianic psalms.[87] Additionally, the term *messiah* appears only in Psalms 2:2; 18:50; 20:6; 28:8; 45:7; 84:9; 89:20, 28; and 132:10, 17. The messianic promise, however, dominates the Psalter in other ways.

First, consider this example from Hebrews 1. To support his claim that Jesus, the Messiah, is God's Son (Heb 1:2), the author cites six passages from the Psalter:

1. For to which of the angels did God ever say, "You are My Son, today I have begotten You?" (Heb 1:5, quoting Ps 2:7)

2. And again, when He brings the firstborn into the world, He says, "Let all God's angels worship Him." (Heb 1:6, quoting Ps 96:7)

3. Of the angels He says, "He makes His angels winds, and His ministers a flame of fire." (Heb 1:7, quoting Ps 104:4)

4. But of the Son He says, "Your throne, O God, is forever and ever, the scepter of uprightness is the scepter of Your kingdom. You have loved righteousness and hated wickedness; therefore God, Your God, has anointed You with the oil of gladness beyond Your companions." (Heb 1:8–9, quoting Ps 45:6–7)

87 E.g., Ps 2; 16; 18; 20; 21; 45; 72; 89; 101; 110; 118; 132; 144.

5. And, You, Lord, laid the foundation of the earth in the beginning, and the heavens are the work of Your hands; they will perish, but You remain; they will all wear out like a garment, like a robe you will roll them up, like a garment they will be changed. But You are the same, and Your years will have no end. (Heb 1:10–12, quoting Ps 102:25–27)

6. And to which of the angels has He ever said, "Sit at My right hand until I make Your enemies a footstool for Your feet"? (Heb 1:13; quoting Ps 110:1)

This is amazing, isn't it? In just one chapter of the New Testament ,the Book of Psalms is cited six times as proof that the Messiah is God's Son, whose name is Jesus.

Second, another feature in the Psalter that provides its messianic shape is that—while compiled after the Babylonian exile of 587 BC—it still gives prominence to David's dynasty. Given the absence of a Davidic ruler in post-exilic times, this emphasis is stunning. The book held on to its messianic priority even after Jerusalem's downfall and the exile of Judah's last king, Zedekiah, in August of 587 BC. Israel did not give up waiting for the Messiah. Every mention of a Davidic king in the Psalter is both a past reality and a future hope.

One simple example is from Psalm 2, which is an enthronement psalm. Why include this liturgy when there is no king to enthrone? The answer: Because one is on the way!

The Book of Psalms is a forward-looking collection of prayers and hymns that points to the final and perfect descendant of David—Jesus. Little wonder, then, that of the 283 direct quotes from the Old Testament in the New Testament, 116 are from the Book of Psalms. That is 41 percent. Jesus goes so far as to announce that the Book of Psalms is about Him (Lk 24:44).

The third point we want to make regarding the Psalter being a *messianic* Psalter is that the book's storyline centers upon Yahweh, the heavenly king, who appoints an earthly vice regent—or Messiah—to establish His kingdom by overthrowing unruly and ungodly rulers. This is the gist of Psalm 2. The Book of Psalms then divides into five sections, or books.

Book I of the Psalter (Ps 3–41) are Davidic (except for Ps 33). They mostly describe David's reign and his struggles with enemies like Absalom and Saul. For the most part, Book II (Ps 42–72) moves beyond David and concludes with a psalm by Solomon (Ps 72) which describes how the king is to reign as Yahweh's vice regent. This psalm also reflects the transition of the Davidic covenant to subsequent Judean kings. Book III (Ps 73–89) ends with the Babylonian destruction of Judah and Jerusalem in 587 BC and the last Davidic king's exile to the land of the two rivers. "Lord, where is Your steadfast love of old, which by Your faithfulness You swore to David?" (Ps 89:49). All hope seemed lost.

Enter Moses! The only Mosaic psalm is Psalm 90, which introduces Book IV (Ps 90–106). In his day, Moses commanded Yahweh to relent from destroying Israel when Aaron made a golden calf and people worshiped it (Ex 32:12). Yet, because of His steadfast love, God relented (Ex 32:14). Just so, the compilers of the Psalter place Moses' prayer for Yahweh to relent (Ps 90:13) in the context of the apparent end of David's dynasty. And wonder of wonders—God remembered His Davidic covenant promises and again relented (Ps 106:45). Book V (Ps 107–145) is full of thanksgiving and joy because divine promises to the house of David are back in play. The book fittingly ends with its "Hallelujah Chorus" (Ps 146–150) as each of these psalms begin and end with the word "Hallelujah."

Perhaps you already noticed that several messianic psalms are placed at important junctures in the Psalter. Psalm 2 is part of the collection's introduction; Psalm 72 comes at the end of Book III; Psalm 89 concludes Book IV; and Psalm 145, a Davidic prayer, concludes the Book of Psalms before its grand Hallelujah celebration. The Psalter, therefore, has a unified storyline with a beginning, middle, and end. It describes the death and resurrection of the Davidic monarchy.

INTRODUCING THE MESSIAH IN THE PSALTER (PSALMS 1 AND 2)

Psalms 1 and 2 introduce the Psalter with their twin themes of God's Word (or *Torah,* meaning *instruction*) and the Messiah. That these psalms should be interpreted together becomes clear through the words they have in common: "blessed" (Ps 1:1; 2:12); "way" (Ps 1:1; 2:12); "meditate/plot" (Ps 1:2; 2:1); and "perish" (Ps 1:6; 2:12). Also linking the psalms is that both lack titles, or superscriptions (unlike most of the psalms in Book I, Ps 3–41).

Psalm 1 lays out a key motif in the Psalter by contrasting the way of the righteous and the way of the wicked, along with emphasizing God's Torah. Psalm 2 moves the focus to the Davidic king—the Messiah (Ps 2:2). Yahweh says to Him, "You are My Son; today I have begotten You" (Ps 2:7). As God's Son, the Messiah is invested with divine authority and power.

The Torah and Davidic Messiah are not only connected vis-à-vis Psalms 1 and 2. The next messianic psalms—16, 18, 20, and 21—revolve around Psalm 19, also a Torah psalm. The third and last Torah psalm, Psalm 119, is preceded by Psalm 118 which depicts the Messiah who is rejected—only to become the cornerstone of God's new kingdom (Ps 118:22).

Moses brings Psalm 1 (God's Word) and Psalm 2 (the Messiah) together in these words: "When he [the king] sits on the throne of his kingdom, he shall write for himself in a book a copy of this Torah, approved by the Levitical priests. And it shall be with him, and he shall read in it all the days of his life" (Dt 17:18–19, authors' translation). The king's chief responsibility is to study God's Word until he dies. Imagine that! When we place Psalms 1 and 2 within the context of these words of Moses, the Psalter points us to the perfect king who not only loves God's Word but also embodies it. Little wonder that John calls Jesus, the Messiah, simply "the Word" (e.g., Jn 1:1, 14).

LITANY FOR THE MESSIANIC KING (PSALM 2)

The Psalter's second poem was deliberately placed at the front of the Psalter to give the book its messianic stamp. Originally, however, Psalm 2 served as a coronation liturgy for a Davidic king.

Psalm 2 begins with a strong sense of conflict and revolt against the Lord and His Messiah (Ps 2:1–3). Psalm 2:4 then moves from the battlefield and into the heavenly throne room, where Yahweh is not worried in the least about this well-orchestrated attack. Earthly powers present no threat to His governance of the world. In fact, God scoffs at His adversaries. Why? "I have set My King on Zion, My holy hill" (Ps 2:6). "My King" signals a binding relationship between Yahweh and the Messiah. He even calls Him "My Son." There is an inseparable bond between God and His Messiah. To resist one is to resist the other. "You are My Son; today I have begotten You" (Ps 2:7). *Today* specifies the day of the king's enthronement on Zion, which refers to God's temple in Jerusalem.

The coronation litany continues. The Messiah will shatter His enemies (Ps 2:9), just as Genesis 3:15 predicted. Then the leaders of the raging nations will fall before the Messiah's throne and kiss His feet (Ps 2:12)—a sign of humility and servitude.

Psalm 2 is connected to another pivotal messianic poem—Psalm 110. Both envision the Messiah in these ways:

1. Triumphant over His enemies (Ps 2:8; 110:2–3, 5–7)
2. Displaying divine anger (Ps 2:5; 110:5)
3. Using a scepter as a weapon (Ps 2:9; 110:2)
4. Reigning from Zion (Ps 2:6; 110:2)

How would all this have sounded to the average person in the Old Testament? Pretty far-fetched. Who was able to conquer the world? Who had the resources to subdue the kings of the earth? Except for Josiah, who was killed at the battle of Megiddo in 609 BC, most Davidic kings turned out to be disappointments. Even the godly Hezekiah failed miserably when he displayed the royal treasuries to Babylonian envoys—something tantamount to giving away the government's top secrets (Is 39).

Finally, only one Davidic king would fit the bill. New Testament writers quote from Psalm 2 and apply it to Jesus. For instance, when John the Baptist baptized the Messiah, God the Father employed words from Psalm 2:7 (which derive, in turn, from 2Sm 7:14, the Magna Carta of the Davidic dynasty), saying, "You are My Son."[88] The Father used the same words at the Messiah's transfiguration.[89]

Jesus is Israel's Messiah, despite His less-than-expected royal upbringing and His betrayal, torture, and horrific execution on a cross. On Good Friday Jesus is called a King at

- Pilate's interrogation,[90]

88 See Mt 3:17; Mk 1:11; Lk 3:22.

89 Mt 17:1–8; Mk 9:2–8; Lk 9:28–36.

90 Mt 27:11; Mk 15:2, 9, 12; Lk 23:3; Jn 18:33, 39.

- the soldiers' mocking,[91] and
- the Roman sign placed on the cross.[92]

For many, a crucified Messiah was an oxymoron—it made no sense. But for those who believed, the cross demonstrated the compassion and love of God.

In the New Testament, Psalm 2 also appears outside of the Gospels. For instance, Acts 13:33, along with Hebrews 1:5 and 5:5 cite Psalm 2:7. Additionally, when Jewish authorities release Peter and John from prison, Luke records their prayer in Acts 4:25–26, where believers call Jesus the Messiah, citing Psalm 2:1–2. Then, in Romans 1:3–5, Paul employs terms that resonate with Psalm 2—including "Son," "David," "Son of God," and "the nations."

The Book of Revelation announces the consummation of Psalm 2 in bold strokes. In painting the scene of the Messiah's second advent, John employs Psalm 2:9 when he writes, "From His mouth comes a sharp sword with which to strike down the nations, and He will rule them with a rod of iron" (Rv 19:15). The Messiah's victory over the enemies of sin, Satan, and death is the climax of the biblical message.

THE MESSIAH FROM DAVID'S DYNASTY (PSALM 16)

Psalm 16, our next messianic psalm, unfolds in a straightforward way. In the first eight verses, David expresses his trust in God for this life, while in verses 9–11, he switches gears and describes the joys that await him in the life to come. The psalm tenderly describes

91 Mt 27:29; Mk 15:17–19; Jn 19:19, 21.

92 Mt 27:37; Mk 15:26; Lk 23:38; Jn 19:19, 21.

what God did, is doing, and will do for David as well as for the Davidic Messiah: from David's dynasty will come death's defeater and conqueror. How so?

On Pentecost, as recorded in Acts 2:29–31, Peter quoted from Psalm 16:8–11. The apostle proclaimed that David, writing these words as a prophet, was not referring to himself but was predicting the Messiah's resurrection from the dead. Note especially this verse: "For You will not abandon my soul to Sheol, or let Your holy one see corruption" (Ps 16:10). While David's body decomposed and disintegrated, the Messiah's body was raised from the dead. Death has no dominion over Him. David, speaking by God's Spirit (2Sm 23:2), trusted God's resurrection promises that cannot be broken (2Sm 23:5).

Later in the Book of Acts, when Paul was preaching about the Messiah's victory over death in Pisidian Antioch (Ac 13:33), he cited Psalm 2:7; then, to cement his case, he quoted from Psalm 16:11: "He whom God raised up did not see corruption" (Ac 13:37). The Messiah is risen indeed!

THE SUFFERING MESSIAH (PSALM 22)

David is called the "sweet psalmist of Israel" (2Sm 23:1). God gave him the gift of poetry and music (1Sm 16:18) as well as prophecy (Ac 2:30). But David also knew the darker side of life. He was rejected by Saul (e.g., 1Sm 18–19), who, at one point, even hunted David like one would hunt a wild animal (1Sm 23:25–26). Later in his life, David was betrayed by his son Absalom (e.g., 2Sm 15:12, 31). In fact, in the twelve psalms that present details in David's life that led to this psalm's composition (Ps 3, 7, 18, 51, 52, 54, 56, 57, 59, 60, 62, 142), the most frequent theme is his lament that people are persecuting him. The Book of Psalms, then, describes David as an innocent sufferer whom evildoers mock and condemn. This torment and hatred reach their pinnacle in Psalm 22—a poem that describes David's suffering but even more graphically predicts the anguish of the Messiah.

Often titled "The Crucifixion Psalm," Psalm 22 has two parts. Verses 1–21 describe God's desertion, which leads to humiliation and death. Verses 22–31 contain praise and thanksgiving for Yahweh's royal reign. "Kingship belongs to the LORD, and He rules over the nations" (Ps 22:28).

The psalm begins with the cry "My God, My God"! The expression "My God" indicates the close relationship between David and God the Father—and subsequently between the Messiah (Mt 27:46; Mk 15:34) and God the Father. The lament continues, "Why have You forsaken Me?" (Ps 22:1). "God, in light of our deep, personal fellowship, how could You make this unbridgeable chasm between us now?"

In verses 6–8, David says that just as people held him in disdain, even more they will reproach, scorn, ridicule, and insult the Messiah. The Messiah's enemies mockingly wag their heads as He hangs on the cross (Ps 22:7; Mt 27:39, 44). And echoing Psalm 22:8, they say, "You who would destroy the temple and rebuild it in three days, save Yourself! If You are the Son of God, come down from the cross" (Mt 27:40).

Other psalms add facets to the Messiah's suffering and death. His bones will not be broken (Ps 34:20; Jn 19:36). A close friend will betray Him (Ps 41:9; Jn 13:18). Vinegar will be offered to quench His thirst (Ps 69:21; Jn 19:28–30). And He will commit His spirit to the Father (Ps 31:5; Lk 23:46).

Yet the lowest point comes in this statement: "I am a worm and not a man" (Ps 22:6). Worms are agents of divine judgment (Dt

28:39); Isaiah envisions hell as a place where "their worm shall not die, their fire shall not be quenched" (Is 66:24). What does this mean? The Messiah will take upon Himself our sin and be placed under God's judgment. The Father will turn away when the Messiah dies—not because of His sin—but because He carries the sin of the world. "Christ redeemed us from the curse of the law by becoming a curse for us" (Gal 3:13).

The lament concludes: "They have pierced My hands and feet . . . they divide My garments among them, and for My clothing they cast lots" (Ps 22:16, 18; cf. Mt 27:35). But all is not lost! The lament transitions into a celebration of praise: "I will tell of Your name to My brothers; in the midst of the congregation I will praise You" (Ps 22:22). Hebrews 2:12 cites this verse as words of the risen Messiah speaking to His Church. The movement in Psalm 22 is from humiliation to exaltation (cf. Is 52:13–53:12; Php 2:6–11).

The psalm ends with this great affirmation: "They shall come and proclaim His righteousness to a people yet unborn, that He has done it" (Ps 22:31). Indeed, the Messiah has done it. He has defeated death and the grave, all for us.

THE MESSIAH RESTORES ALL THINGS (PSALM 72)

Much like Psalm 2, Psalm 72 depicts "all kings" and "all nations" subject to the coming Messiah (Ps 72:11). And, while Psalm 2 announces that the Messiah will possess the nations as His heritage, Psalm 72 clarifies what this means for Israel and the world. The Messiah's reign will be marked by peace and prosperity for the needy and the oppressed (Ps 72:12–14).

Psalm 72 is one of two psalms composed by Solomon. (The other is Psalm 127.) The setting for Psalm 72 is probably when David was on his deathbed and he charged Solomon to walk in God's ways (1Ki 2:1–4). In response, we may imagine Solomon composing Psalm 72. After all, when the queen of Sheba visits Solomon and sees his wisdom and wealth, she echoes important motifs in the psalm: "He [God] has made you king, that you may execute justice and righteousness" (1Ki 10:9; cf. Ps 72:1–2). Also note this link between the queen's visit to Solomon and Psalm 72: "May gold of Sheba be given to Him!" (Ps 72:15).

Psalm 72 begins with a request that the Messiah exhibit the virtues of justice and righteousness, which, in turn will do these things:

1. Assist the poor and the needy (Ps 72:2–4, 12–14)
2. Make for peace and harmony in creation and among the nations (Ps 72:5–17)
3. Elicit praise to God and thanksgiving (Ps 72:18–19)

For this vision to be realized, the Messiah must execute divine judgment, thus implementing God's plan to defeat enemies so they "lick the dust" (Ps 72:9)—a phrase that recalls God's curse upon the serpent in Genesis 3:14.

Here is one of the psalm's key points: "May He [the Messiah] have dominion from sea to sea, and from the River to the ends of the earth!" (Ps 72:8). "Have dominion" may imply raping, pillaging, and abusing the earth, but nothing could be further from the truth here. God commissioned our first parents, Adam and Eve, to govern the world in the same way God would—with great care and conservation (Gn 1:26, 28). However, with the fall into sin (Gn 3), who is going to rule the world to bring it into harmony with the divine plan? *The Messiah.* He will bring prosperity to the mountains and hills (Ps

72:3). The messianic age will also be a time of productive land with an abundance of grain and fruit (Ps 72:16). Isaiah likewise envisions creation at peace and living in harmony with the Creator (e.g., Is 11:6–8; 65:25).

The expression "to the ends of the earth" (Ps 72:8) harmonizes with the messianic prediction in Genesis 49:10 where Moses describes the Messiah as receiving "the obedience of the peoples." Isaiah 11:10 likewise promises the messianic reign over all the nations. In like manner, so does Zechariah 9:10.

Psalm 72, then, describes God's plan to use His Messiah to restore all things. Just like Psalm 2, its accolades go beyond any Old Testament monarch. For instance, Psalm 72 says that all people will prosper through the king's administration of justice and righteousness (Ps 72:12–17). Indeed, the monarch's rule will be flawless (Ps 72:2, 6, 17), limitless (Ps 72:8, 11, 17), as well as endless (Ps 72:5–7, 17). These are grandiose descriptions for any Old Testament king. They are realized only in God's Messiah—Jesus.

GOD'S ENDURING MESSIANIC COVENANT TO DAVID (PSALM 89)

Psalm 2 describes the inauguration of the Davidic Messiah, while Psalms 16 and 22 predict His resurrection and crucifixion, respectively. Psalm 72 reflects the reign of the perfect king, the coming Messiah. Psalm 89 doubts that any of this will happen. Its author—a Levite named Ethan (cf. 1Ch 15:17, 19)—laments over the apparent cancellation of God's intention to send the Messiah. After the Babylonian dismantling and destruction of Jerusalem in 587 BC, it appeared that God decided to cancel His messianic plans.

The first section of Psalm 89, verses 1–4, introduces the key words of the psalm: "forever," "steadfast love," "faithfulness," "covenant," and "David." Yahweh made a covenant with David to be His "servant" and "chosen one" (Ps 89:3–4). David is God's "firstborn" and "the highest of the kings of the earth" (Ps 89:27). Reflecting Psalm 2:7, Ethan celebrates that God is even David's "Father" (Ps 89:26).

After extolling divine power and faithfulness to the house of David, in verse 38, Ethan adds a startling "but now." The poem's mood changes, taking a sudden turn toward blaming God for everything that has gone wrong. God has spurned His pledge to the house of David, renounced His covenant, and defiled the royal crown (Ps 89:38–39). Judean cities are in ruins, and David's throne and splendor have ended (Ps 89:40–45). Verses 46–51 conclude the poem by appealing to God, asking Him to reverse the curse and restore the Davidic dynasty.

Book IV of the Psalter then begins with Psalm 90. Moses asks God to relent (Ps 90:13) and, by the end of Book IV, God does just that (Ps 106:45). He remembers His covenant with David; it follows that the Psalter's fifth book accents this Gospel turn in several ways. Psalm 110 announces the coming of a Davidic king who will defeat His enemies, while Psalm 132:17 celebrates that God will "make a horn to sprout for David." Moreover, the pairing of Psalm 144, which is messianic, with Psalm 145, which maintains that Yahweh is King, suggests that human and divine rule will surely combine to achieve Israel's messianic hopes.

MESSIAH AS GOD, PRIEST, AND WARRIOR (PSALM 110)

Luther called the Psalter "a little Bible," for he saw the entire messianic message summarized in its chapters. The reformer reveled in the fact that the Psalms are the fullest expression of God's Messiah in the Old Testament. Nowhere does this happen more distinctly than in Psalm 110, where David makes the most stunning claim in the Psalter—the Messiah is both God and man. It should come as no surprise, therefore, that there are thirty-three quotations and allusions to Psalm 110 in the New Testament.

Three psalms petitioning Yahweh for deliverance (Ps 107–109) precede Psalm 110, and the three psalms praising Yahweh for deliverance (Ps 111–113) follow Psalm 110. Psalm 110, therefore, functions as a hinge, binding these seven psalms together. It reveals the Messiah as God, Priest, and triumphant warrior. When Psalm 110 is read within this context—the Messiah's betrayal in Psalm 109 and God's everlasting promises in Psalm 111—the messianic message of victory becomes even more pronounced.

Both Jesus[93] and Peter[94] endorse the idea that David composed Psalm 110. We point this out because Davidic authorship is crucial to the psalm's proper interpretation.

Psalm 110 is organized by means of two divine oracles in verses 1 and 4—giving equal status to the Messiah's divine and priestly roles. Here is an outline of the psalm:

- Verses 1–3, the Messiah is God

93 Mt 22:41–45; Mk 12:35–37; Lk 20:41–44.

94 Ac 2:34–35.

- Verse 4, the Messiah is a Priest
- Verses 5–7, the Messiah gains victory over His enemies

"Yahweh says to *Adonai*: Sit at my right hand, until I make your enemies your footstool" (Ps 110:1, authors' translation). David calls the Messiah *Adonai* or "my Lord." This confession is like these words, "Your throne, O God, is forever and ever. The scepter of Your kingdom is a scepter of uprightness; You have loved righteousness and hated wickedness. Therefore God, Your God, has anointed You with the oil of gladness beyond Your companions" (Ps 45:6–7). Verse 6 introduces God, while verse 7 announces that this God has a God who anointed the God in the previous verse. What?

Of course, there are not two gods. There is one God in three persons—Father, Son, and Holy Spirit. "Your throne, O God" (Ps 45:6) refers to God the Son. "God, Your God" (Ps 45:7) refers to God the Father. In like manner, in Psalm 110:1, *Yahweh* refers to God the Father, while *Adonai* refers to God the Son—the Messiah.

Psalm 110:1 continues with these words from Yahweh to David's *Adonai*, or Lord—the Messiah: "Sit at My right hand." The last verse from Psalm 109 tells us what this means: "For He stands at the right hand of the needy one, to save him from those who condemn his soul to death" (Ps 109:31). The Psalter frequently pairs "the needy" with "the poor."[95] The Messiah, then, advocates for those who have little or no social standing. Other words for this are "justice and righteousness"—an expression found frequently in messianic texts.[96]

Psalm 110:4 is the poem's literary and theological focal point. The Messiah is not only David's Lord. He is also a priest—not from

95 E.g., Ps 12:5; 40:17; 70:5; 109:16.

96 E.g., Jer 23:5; see also Ps 72:1–2; Is 9:7.

the order of Aaron but from the order of Melchizedek. Just as Moses describes Melchizedek as both priest and king (Gn 14:18), so the Anointed One of the Most High will combine these offices and do so forever.

Hebrews 7–10 is an extended commentary on Psalm 110:4. Undergirding this section of the epistle is the idea that in the Old Testament the high priest was himself a sinner and had to offer sacrifices for his own sins as well as the sins of the people. He would also die and be replaced. Israel's Aaronic priesthood—just like the nation's entire history—was imperfect, inadequate, and incomplete. The Old Testament, therefore, points forward to someone greater—the Messiah who is the ultimate and perfect High Priest.

The Book of Hebrews explains the Messiah's priestly work in two ways: His completed sacrifice and His ongoing intercession. Christ's sacrifice established the new covenant (Heb 8:6–13), for He mediates direct access to God through the perfect removal of sin (Heb 9:13–14; 26–27). These two points appear side by side in the central appeal of Hebrews 10:19–22.

Additionally, the Messiah's appointment as High Priest is by an oath (Heb 7:17–21, 28; reflecting Ps 110:4). He is not appointed by God's Law (like Aaron and his descendants) but by God's promise. And the Messiah's qualification for the priesthood comes through His resurrection from the dead rather than through genetic ancestry like Aaron (Heb 7:15–17). The Messiah is the High Priest forevermore.

Throughout the Book of Psalms, God repeatedly rescues David from his enemies.[97] In the last part of Psalm 110, God permanently exalts the Davidic Messiah over all His enemies and even invites Him to share the divine throne. "He will execute judgment among the nations, filling them with corpses" (Ps 110:6). This may sound crass,

97 E.g., Ps 18:4–6; 55:1–3; 59:1; 61:3; 138:7.

yet the Messiah's all-out victory hearkens back to God's promise that He will strike the serpent's head (Gn 3:15). It also connects to Balaam's prophecy about crushing foreheads and destroying survivors (Nu 24:15–19). Observe that the Hebrew verb "crush" (*makhats*) in Psalm 110:5–6 appears within Balaam's messianic prediction in Numbers 24:17, "I see Him, but not now; I behold Him, but not near: a star shall come out of Jacob, and a scepter shall rise out of Israel; it shall crush (*makhats*) the forehead of Moab and break down all the sons of Sheth." Isaiah says as much about the Messiah in Isaiah 11:4, while John concludes the biblical story by depicting the Messiah's victory over every enemy of the Gospel (Rv 19:11–21).

Daniel 7:9–14 reflects upon Psalm 110 as Daniel envisions the Ancient of Days (God the Father) as well as the Son of Man (God the Son). Jesus then combines Psalm 110:1 ("right hand") and Daniel 7:13 ("Son of Man" and "clouds") when He answers the Sanhedrin: "I tell you, from now on you will see the Son of Man seated at the right hand of Power and coming on the clouds of heaven" (Mt 26:64).

Zechariah 14 likewise shares motifs with Psalm 110. The Messiah will fight His enemies (Ps 110: 2, 5–6; Zec 14:3–5). He will be accompanied by a holy army (Ps 110:3; Zec 14:5). In addition, He will crush His foes (Ps 110:5–6; Zec 14:12–14).

Psalm 110 plays a pivotal role in the New Testament. In a debate with scribes and Pharisees, Jesus quotes from Psalm 110:1.[98] On Pentecost, Peter likewise cites Psalm 110:1 in Acts 2:34. Paul alludes to Psalm 110:1 to declare that when the Messiah returns, He will destroy all evil powers (1Co 15:25–26; Eph 1:20). The apostle also employs Psalm 110:1 to announce that the Messiah, who is seated at the Father's right hand, intercedes for us (Rm 8:34).

98 Mt 22:41–46; Mk 12:35–37; Lk 20:41–44.

THE STONE REJECTED BY THE BUILDERS (PSALM 118)

The author of Psalm 118 arranged his poem to begin and end with a call to give thanks (Ps 118:1, 29). Between these two thanksgivings is a procession leading to the temple's gates (Ps 118:19) with this messianic verse, "The stone that the builders rejected has become the cornerstone" (Ps 118:22).

Although David probably did not compose Psalm 118, he experienced the kind of rejection that it describes. Much like the stone rejected by builders, David had been dismissed by his father, Jesse, who did not consider him worthy of divine anointing (1Sm 16:11). Following their father, David's brothers considered it presumptuous that he would join them in battle against the Philistines (1Sm 17:28–29). Other rejections include Saul's frequent attempts to kill David (e.g., 1Sm 19–20; 23:15–29); David's first wife, Michal, holding him in disdain (2Sm 6:20–23); and initially, Israel's northern tribes keeping David at arm's length (2Sm 1–3). Despite it all, David remained God's chosen king.

In like manner, Jesus, the Messiah, came to His own people and they rejected Him (Jn 1:11). Religious authorities plotted His death (Mk 3:6) and one of His disciples—Judas Iscariot—handed him over to be arrested and crucified (Mt 26:14–16). No wonder the crowds sang out to Jesus on Palm Sunday, "Hosanna to the Son of David!" (Mt 21:9)—with "Hosanna" coming from Psalm 118:22. Here is *the* rejected stone. That is what Peter teaches us: the Messiah is "a living stone rejected by men but in the sight of God chosen and precious" (1Pt 2:4).

THE DAVIDIC MESSIAH ON MOUNT ZION (PSALM 132)

Psalm 132 refers to David four times (Ps 132:1, 10, 11, 17). These references provide bookends around the psalm's two parts (Ps 132:1–10; 11–17)—with verse 18 functioning as an epilogue. The first section is a prayer to God on behalf of David and his dynasty (Ps 132:1–10). The second section records God's response and affirmation of the Davidic covenant (Ps 132:11–18). Psalm 132, then, balances what David has done for God (bringing the ark to Jerusalem) with what God has done and will do for David (showing faithfulness to him and his descendants forever).

The poem was composed to commemorate David's relocation of the ark to Jerusalem. His oath to Yahweh (Ps 132:2) is matched by Yahweh's oath to him (Ps 132:11); thus, the psalm reflects the events in 2 Samuel 6–7 and 1 Chronicles 13–17. Note that the term "footstool" (Ps 132:7) is synonymous with the ark of the covenant (see 1Ch 28:2). Thus, the psalm's plea is for God to look with favor on the current Davidic king—the first being Solomon. "For the sake of Your servant David, do not turn away the face of Your anointed one" (Ps 132:10).

Verse 1 indicates that David has endured great hardships. There is only one instance where this word applies to David. First Chronicles 22:14 quotes David as saying, "With great pains I have provided for the house of the Lord 100,000 talents of gold, a million talents of silver, and bronze and iron beyond weighing, for there is so much of it; timber and stone, too, I have provided. To these you must add." Psalm 132:1, therefore, is referring to the high cost for the temple's construction. Amassing it all brought David all kinds of hardship.

With David making his oath and fulfilling it (Ps 132:2–10), the psalm turns to the second half—Yahweh's oath (Ps 132:11–18).

Divine constancy to David's house is the backbone of the biblical narrative. This faithfulness to David is announced in Psalm 89:3, 35, and 49, as well as in Psalm 110:4. Come what may, David's offspring will forever succeed him (cf. 2Sm 7:12).

The "if" in Psalm 132:12 does not impact this certainty. It does, however, indicate that individual Davidic kings may forfeit participation in the promise. Yet even then, the covenant will stand. It is irrevocable. When Saul, Israel's first king, committed sin, God rejected him. But now, when David's descendants commit evil, Yahweh will only correct and chasten them (2Sm 7:14–15). David says as much: "For does not my house stand so with God? For He has made with me an everlasting covenant, ordered in all things and secure" (2Sm 23:5).

Psalm 132 concludes by stating that David's horn (a metaphor meaning strength) will always grow and flourish (Ps 132:17). The promise is for "My anointed"—that is, whoever is currently sitting on the Davidic throne. God's flame in the second half of Psalm 132:17 employs the imagery of David serving as the lampstand, with his successors symbolized by individual lights deriving their sustenance from him—a pledge that 2 Kings 8:19 and 2 Chronicles 21:7 cling to in Israel's darker moments.

Because Psalm 132 focuses upon the motif of finding a place for the Lord (Ps 132:5), Solomon employs verses 8–11 in 2 Chronicles 6:41–42 at the end of his prayer celebrating the ark's presence in His temple. The place (Zion/Jerusalem/temple) goes with the person (the Messiah). This connection is first stated in the king's coronation liturgy: "I have set My king on Zion, My holy hill" (Ps 2:6). Psalm 78:67–72 is the only other section in the Psalter that brings God's choice of David and Zion together.

The New Testament likewise combines the Messiah with the temple, often called His Church (e.g., Eph 2:19–21; Heb 12:22–24). In perhaps the most famous example, the Messiah pledges that He, along with His Church, will endure forevermore (Mt 16:13–21). The gates of hell will not overcome the messianic movement, because Jesus has conquered death and the grave.

THE PSALMS: A MESSIANIC HYMNBOOK

Psalms 1, 2, 16, 22, 72, 89, 110, 118, and 132 are just a small sampling of the Psalter's portrait of the Messiah. Others include the Messiah's temptations in the wilderness (Ps 91:11–12; Mt 4:6; Lk 4:10), cleansing the temple (Ps 69:9; Jn 2:17), teaching parables (Ps 78:2; Mt 13:35), feeding the 5,000 (Ps 78:24; Jn 6:31), and Palm Sunday (Ps 8:2; Mt 21:16). Additionally, Jesus is the royal messianic Bridegroom, and the Church is His Bride (Ps 45; Eph 5:25–27). Put all these pieces together and it's no wonder the Psalter is one of the most loved and treasured books in the entire Bible.

In conclusion, the Book of Psalms makes clear that Jesus is not an enigmatic person who dropped down from heaven unannounced and unanticipated. Rather, He completes, fulfills, and is the final reinterpretation of Israel's hymnbook. The poems are organized to be a network of interconnected texts that find their ultimate expression in the Messiah, Jesus of Nazareth.

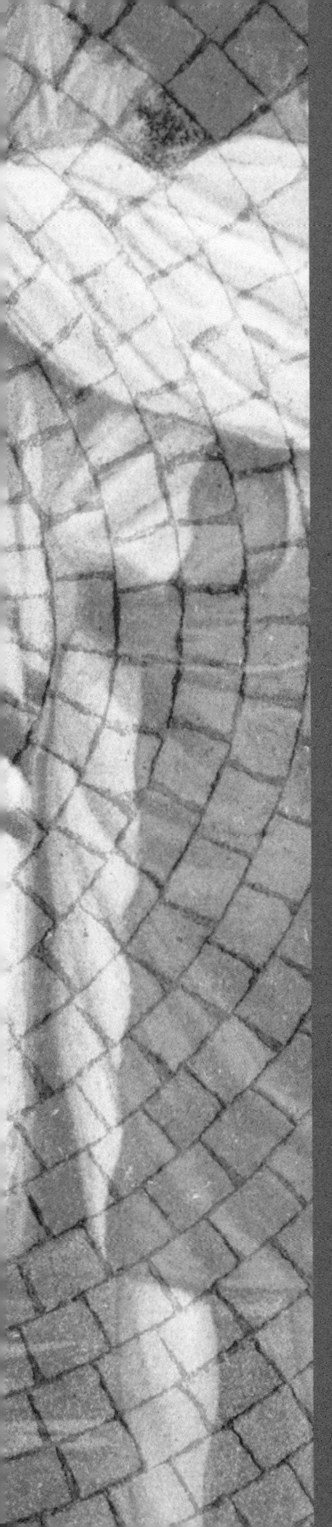

CHAPTER 7

ISAIAH, THE OLD TESTAMENT BIOGRAPHER OF THE MESSIAH

In some places, the Old Testament flows like a brook toward its fulfillment in the Messiah. Other places may be likened to a quiet backwater or small stream. In Isaiah, though, we come upon a rushing river that moves us mightily toward the New Testament's proclamation that Jesus of Nazareth is Israel's Messiah and the Savior of the world. Referring to the messianic age (Ac 3:18, 20), Peter states, "All the prophets who have spoken, from Samuel and those who came after him, also proclaimed these days" (Ac 3:24). Isaiah is the foremost of these prophets—he is the most frequently quoted prophet in the New Testament.

Isaiah, however, is also the most complex prophetic book in the Old Testament. This is because Isaiah encompasses a greater chronological sweep than the likes of Jeremiah and Ezekiel. Isaiah's vast historical scale may be symbolized by two names that appear in the book: Uzziah (Is 1:1) and Cyrus (Is 45:1). Uzziah was a king from Judah who reigned from 791 to 740 BC. Cyrus was a Persian emperor who reigned from 550 to 530 BC. Since Isaiah 6:1 refers to the death of Uzziah, there is a two-hundred-year period represented by these kings.

Digging through Isaiah to mine its messianic promises, though, is worth the effort. We begin with the prophet's most famous name for the Messiah—Immanuel.

MESSIANIC PREDICTIONS

IMMANUEL PREDICTIONS

CONTEXT

Isaiah 4:2 depicts a sprout that will be beautiful and glorious, granting forgiveness, cleansing, and shelter for God's people. Isaiah repeats this promise, depicting a scorched tree stump that has within it "a holy seed" (Is 6:13). Mention of the "seed" takes us back to Genesis 15:5 and 17:7, 19 and God's pledge to Abraham that he will have many seeds/offspring. The plural seeds/offspring will finally become one—the Messiah, the king of Israel (Gal 3:16; cf. Gn 3:15). He will be born of a virgin from the house of Ahaz, a descendant of David (Is 7:14; cf. Mt 1:23), and called *Immanuel*—or "God with us."

Isaiah's Immanuel prophecy appears within Isaiah 7–11—a section of the book that addresses Judah's terrifying dilemma of an imminent Assyrian attack in 735 BC. The prophet responds with divine promises that are embodied in children. Their names are Shear-jashub (Is 7:3), Maher-shalal-hash-baz (Is 8:1), and Immanuel (Is 7:14; 8:8, 10). Judah needs a warrior to take on and defeat Assyria. What can children do? Much, says Isaiah—very much.

A child is born, a son is given, whose name will be Wonderful Counselor, Mighty God, Everlasting Father, Prince of Peace (Is 9:6). He will be like a shoot coming up from a stump (Is 11:1) and will rule not with violence but through peaceful harmony (Is 11:4–9). All the nations will rally to the banner of this kingly child (Is 11:10–16) who wields God's Word and not a sword (Is 11:4). Power is not in the weapons of the world but in the truth of divine revelation. As we will see, this portrait of a humble Messiah in chapters 7–11 comports with the prophet's oracles about the Suffering Servant in chapters 42, 49, 50, 52, and 53.

GOD WITH US

Early in his reign, King Ahaz, Judah's reigning monarch (732–716 BC), became frightened because leaders in Syria and Israel (the Northern Kingdom) were pressuring him to join them in a war against the expanding Assyrian empire. To calm his fears, God sent His prophet Isaiah, who warned the king, "If you are not firm in your faith, you will not be firm at all" (Is 7:9). Ahaz refused to ask for a sign, so Isaiah continued, "Behold, the virgin shall conceive and bear a son, and shall call His name Immanuel" (Is 7:14).

The name *Immanuel* functions as a two-edged sword—Law and Gospel—as Isaiah turns an oracle of salvation into an oracle of judgment against Ahaz. Immanuel, and with Him the Lord's presence with the people, appears in the next chapter as well. On the one hand, "God is with us" (Is 8:10) promises the Lord's protection of Judah against foreign attack. On the other hand, Isaiah is told that Assyria "will sweep on into Judah, it will overflow and pass on, reaching even to the neck, and its outspread wings will fill the breadth of your land, O Immanuel" (Is 8:8).

The house of David (as represented by King Ahaz) did not accept God's offer of a sign. Hence the sign of Immanuel functioned as Law. By contrast, the future house of David—as embodied in the Davidic descendant Joseph—accepts the sign about Immanuel (Mt 1:20–25). Matthew goes on to repeat this promise in the middle of his Gospel (Mt 18:20) and again at the end (Mt 28:20). The promise of Immanuel thus provides the theme for the First Gospel and promises the Savior's abiding presence forever.

We can say more about Immanuel. As Matthew ends the first part of his Gospel (Mt 1:1–4:16), his fifth Old Testament citation comes from Isaiah 9:1–2—a section that includes these words about the Virgin Mary's child: "For to us a child is born, to us a son is given;

and the government shall be upon His shoulder, and His name will be called Wonderful Counselor, Mighty God, Everlasting Father, Prince of Peace" (Is 9:6). Matthew frames the first part of his Gospel with two of Isaiah's predictions about the Messiah—Immanuel and the Wonderful Counselor who will arrive as a little child.

PREDICTIONS IN FOUR DESCRIPTIVE NAMES FOR THE MESSIAH (ISAIAH 9)

While Isaiah 8 ends in darkness, chapter 9 begins with the promise of "no gloom" (v. 1) and continues in verse 2 with "great light" on the horizon. Not only does light dawn but in verse 3 there is also a reversal from depopulation (cf. Is 7:20–23) to the nation being multiplied (cf. Is 49:19–23), from lack of food (cf. Is 5:10) to plenty (cf. Is 35:1–2), and from being plundered (cf. Is 8:1) to dividing the spoil (cf. Is 33:23; 53:12).

Isaiah 9:4 then envisions the yoke upon the people being broken. This salvation is compared to the victory of Gideon, who freed the northern tribes of Asher, Zebulun, and Naphtali (Jgs 6:35) with a great light (Jgs 7:20). The next image is of war boots and cloaks being thrown into the fire and burned (Is 9:5). This cessation of war instruments is also pictured in Isaiah 2:4.

The reason for all this joy is spelled out in Isaiah 9:6. The names "Wonderful Counselor, Mighty God, Everlasting Father, Prince of Peace" are like the throne names used of David (2Sm 23:1). They describe the Messiah's power and authority. Furthermore, "to us a son is given" signifies the accession of a new king to the throne in Jerusalem (Ps 2:7). He makes peace—not through conquering rule but through upholding justice and righteousness (Is 9:7)

Isaiah calls the Messiah *Immanuel* ("God with us"; Is 7:14). In Isaiah 9:6, the prophet gives Him four more names. *Mighty God* employs the Hebrew term *'el* which is translated "God." *'El* recurs in Isaiah 10:21, where it refers to Yahweh. In fact, *'el* in the Old Testament exclusively means "divinity" or "the true God." Psalm 2:7 says of the Messiah, "You are *My* [*God's*] *Son*," while Psalms 45:6 and 110:1 call Him *God* and *Lord*.

Isaiah's throne name "Everlasting Father" adds to the Messiah's divine status. Israelite kings were never called *father*—making this title even more striking. In the Old Testament *father* is an established title for God.[99] Jesus helps us interpret what this means. He says, "Whoever has seen Me has seen the Father" (Jn 14:9).

Isaiah 9:6–7 unites several earlier messianic promises. The Messiah is the King promised to Abraham (Gn 17:6), from the tribe of Judah (Gn 49:10)—that is to say, from the house of David and a Judahite (2Sm 7)—who will execute justice and righteousness for all people (2Sm 8:15; Ps 72:1–2). Note that the motif of messianic justice and righteousness appears again in Isaiah 11:3–5. While Judah during Isaiah's day could neither "see" nor "hear" (Is 6:10), the Messiah will compassionately attend to people with no social capital—orphans, widows, and foreigners living in Israel. The prophet's vignettes in Isaiah 16:5 and 32:1 likewise reveal the same concern for justice and righteousness—an expression that denotes the ordering of society where everyone receives equal treatment, equal opportunity, and equal care.

While the tragic events of the Assyrian (723 BC) and Babylonian (587 BC) exiles led many to believe God had abandoned His commitment to David's house, Isaiah maintains that this promise still stood. Even though several of the Davidic kings who reigned in his day were corrupt, God would still send the Messiah who would reign as a King like no other. "Of the increase of His government and of peace there

99 E.g., Dt 32:6; Is 63:16; Mal 2:10.

will be no end, on the throne of David and over His kingdom, to establish it and to uphold it with justice and with righteousness from this time forth and forevermore" (Is 9:7).

Matthew announces that this Messiah and kingdom are present in Jesus (Mt 4:14–16). Citing Isaiah 9:1–2, the first evangelist then quotes Jesus as saying, "Repent, for the kingdom of heaven is at hand" (Mt 4:17).

A SHOOT FROM THE STUMP OF JESSE (ISAIAH 11)

In Isaiah's day, Davidic kings were a mixed bag. King Uzziah succeeded militarily but at one point insisted on offering incense, a duty reserved only for priests. He ended up dying under divine judgment (2Ch 26:16–23). King Ahaz did not respond in faith to enemy nations attacking him. When told to ask for a sign from God, he refused (Is 7:12). "In the time of his distress he [Ahaz] became yet more faithless to the LORD" (2Ch 28:22). Hezekiah stands out as the best of Judah's monarchs during Isaiah's ministry, yet even he showed Babylonian envoys the state treasures and then nonchalantly shrugged off divine retribution (Is 39). And Manasseh? He was too wicked to include in the list of kings in Isaiah 1:1. There is a better descendant of David on the horizon! This is what Isaiah 11 announces.

In Isaiah 11, we move from an emphasis on messianic titles (e.g., Is 7:14; 9:6) to messianic results. Out of the ashes of the Babylonian exile a new Davidic king will arise. Much like God's choice of Jesse's youngest son, David (1Sm 16:11–13), Jesse's stump will again bear fruit (Is 11:1). This Spirit-driven Messiah will bring justice and peace; indeed, "the earth shall be full of the knowledge of the LORD as the waters cover the sea" (Is 11:9).

In chapter 11, Isaiah calls the Messiah a small twig or sprout from a stump and root—images taken up from Isaiah 6, where the prophet speaks until "the land is utterly forsaken" (Is 6:12, authors' translation) and only a "holy seed" in the "stump" remains (Is 6:13). The axe that leveled Israel was the Lord's doing when He sent Assyria (Is 10:15) and later Babylon (Jer 25:9). But from "the stump of Jesse" (Is 11:1) will come a holy shoot—indeed, a Sprout (cf. Is 4:2). The use of "Jesse" rather than "David" in Isaiah 11:1 and 10 indicates that the Messiah is a new David—an idea also appearing in Hosea 3:5; Jeremiah 30:9; and Ezekiel 34:23–24.

"The Spirit of the LORD shall rest upon Him" (Is 11:2). To accent the role of the Spirit in the Messiah's ministry, Isaiah employs the term *Spirit* four times in this verse. The Spirit of the Lord also rested upon Saul and David when they were chosen by God to be Israelite kings (1Sm 10:10; 16:13).

The Holy Spirit is active in bringing about the Messiah's miraculous virgin birth (Mt 1:20). He is present to anoint Jesus at His Baptism (Mt 3:16; Ac 10:38) as well as to empower Him for ministry (Lk 4:14, 18). Indeed, Paul asserts that Jesus was declared God's Son when the Spirit raised Him from the dead (Rm 1:4).

The attributes of "the Spirit of wisdom and understanding" (Is 11:2) are called for in Israel's leaders (Dt 1:13). They also refer to the judicial capacity of a king to determine internal and foreign policy (e.g., 1Ki 3:16–28). Additionally, *counsel* and *might* (Is 11:2) describe two of the four names given of the Messianic king in Isaiah 9:6—thus connecting Isaiah 11 with this earlier prediction of the Messiah. All these attributes are rooted in the fear of the Lord, a phrase in both Isaiah 11:2 and 3. To fear God is to submit to the ways of the Holy One of Israel and work to bring about His righteous reign.

The fruits of the indwelling of the Spirit in the Messiah's ministry may be contrasted with the traits of corrupt leaders depicted in Isaiah 1:21–23 and 5:18–23. The Messiah will show righteousness by helping the poor and needy, the widows and orphans. And this Spirit-inspired Messiah will punish evildoers. His words are powerful; indeed, they are a sharp sword, just like those of the Suffering Servant (Is 49:2).

The Messiah's goal is to restore creation. This is, after all, what peace/*shalom* means—to put broken things back together again. The prey (lamb, young goat, fattened calf) allows predators (wolf, leopard, lion) to live with them; they no longer fear their enemies (Is 11:6). The bears and lions will graze as herbivores, recalling the time before the fall (Is 11:7; cf. Gn 1:29–30).

This change in relationships also includes reconciliation between dangerous creatures and people. The infant and the young child are left to play safely among venomous snakes (Is 11:8). Isaiah 35:9—another messianic prediction—likewise promises a life free from fearing ferocious wildlife. The Messiah who makes all things new does it on a holy mountain (Is 11:9). This is where the Lord dwells (Is 8:18), and this is where He delivers perfect peace.[100]

Matthew's genealogy (Mt 1:1, 6, 17), Luke's birth narrative (Lk 2:4), and Paul's sermon at Antioch in Pisidia (Ac 13:22–23) all confirm that Isaiah's promises of a Messiah are fulfilled in Jesus. There is, however, this enigmatic ending to Matthew 2: "And he [Joseph] went and lived in a city called Nazareth so that what was spoken by the prophets might be fulfilled, that He [Jesus] would be called a Nazarene" (Mt 2:23). Who are these prophets? And where does it say in the Old Testament that the Messiah will be a Nazarene?

Isaiah is one of the prophets Matthew is referring to. Isaiah 11:1 employs the Hebrew term *netser*, rendered by the ESV as the word *branch:* "There shall come forth a shoot from the stump of Jesse, and a branch [*netser*] from his *roots* shall bear fruit" (emphasis

100 Is 2:2–4; 25:7; 65:25.

added). *Netser* is a wordplay on *Nazareth*. Nathanael echoes the sentiments of many people of his day regarding this little out-of-the-way village: "Can anything good come out of Nazareth?" (Jn 1:46). Connect Nathanael's disdaindisdain together with these words: "For He grew up before Him like a young plant, and like a *root* out of dry ground; He had no form or majesty that we should look at Him, and no beauty that we should desire Him. He was despised and rejected by men, a man of sorrows and acquainted with grief; and as one from whom men hide their faces He was despised, and we esteemed Him not" (Is 53:2–3). How do these verses relate to Nazareth? Nazareth was despised and rejected by people. So was the Messiah—and then some, ultimately at the cross on Calvary. *He would be called a Nazarene.*

UNIVERSAL SALVATION IN THE MESSIAH (ISAIAH 35)

Much like Isaiah 24, with its worldwide judgment followed by universal salvation in Isaiah 25:6–9, so the cosmic judgment of chapter 34 is followed by universal salvation in Isaiah 35. This chapter begins after a rainfall with a flower suddenly springing up in a dry place, turning the desert floor into a carpet of golden colors. This transformation will remind people of Lebanon, Carmel, and Sharon—referring to areas in northern Israel known for their fertility. All of this is likened to the "glory of the LORD" (Is 35:2)—a common theme throughout the Book of Isaiah, mentioned thirty-seven times.[101] This glory foreshadows the Messiah. John writes: "We have seen His glory, glory as of the only Son from the Father, full of grace and truth" (Jn 1:14).

After seeing God's glory, people prepare to enter an abundant and fertile land. As they do so, the prophet commands them to be strong (Is 35:3). When Joshua was preparing to take the Promised

101 See, e.g., Is 6:3; 40:5; 60:1; 62:2.

Land, he was likewise commanded to "be strong and courageous."[102] Messianic days flowing with milk and honey are on the horizon!

Courage rises through these Gospel promises: "Then the eyes of the blind shall be opened, and the ears of the deaf unstopped; then shall the lame leap like a deer, and the tongue of the mute sing for joy. For waters break forth in the wilderness, and streams in the desert" (Is 35:5–6). Jesus paraphrased these two verses to summarize His Gospel gifts—announcing to John the Baptist that He is the promised Messiah (Mt 11:5; Lk 7:22). There is a road, a highway, that leads to paradise restored. "The redeemed shall walk there" (Is 35:9).

To be redeemed is to be restored by a relative who assists his family members when they have no other recourse.[103] The Messiah is the world's great Redeemer. He restores us through His blood (1Pt 1:18–19). This gift of liberating blood leads to some of the most significant messianic verses in the Old Testament—Isaiah's Servant Songs.

THE SERVANT SONGS PREDICTIONS

The prophet's four Servant Songs appear in Isaiah 42:1–4; 49:1–6; 50:4–9; and 52:13–53:12. The most important issue related to these passages is the Servant's identity. Who is He? After reading Isaiah 53:7–8, the Ethiopian eunuch asks Philip: "About whom, I ask you, does the prophet say this, about himself or about someone else?" (Ac 8:34).

Isaiah 42:1–4 is the first Servant Song, and the Servant is described in terms like Jacob/Israel in Isaiah 41:8–10. Both are upheld by Yahweh (Is 41:10; 42:1) and both are chosen (Is 41:8, 9; 42:1). These links suggest that the servant figure in Isaiah 42:1

102 Jsh 1:6, 9, 18; see also Jsh 1:7.

103 E.g., Ru 3:13; 4:4, 6.

and throughout chapters 40–48 is Jacob/Israel—exiles in Babylon in the mid-sixth century BC. These people are blind and deaf (Is 42:19–20), idolatrous (e.g., Is 44:9–20), and therefore unable to be a covenant people and light to the nations. Yahweh still loves Jacob/Israel, despite the nation's fatal flaws, and so He sends a replacement Servant to do what the exiles are unable to do.

The prophet introduces a new Servant in chapters 49–55, where he employs the term *servant* seven times.[104] In each case, the word denotes Yahweh's new Servant, who is righteous and just and perfect. He is the Messiah. The literary structures of Isaiah 42:1–4 and 49:1–6 correspond with each other, indicating that the substitute Servant and Messiah share a similar mission with the failed Babylonian exiles. Both songs are followed by Yahweh's speech (Is 42:5–9; 49:7–13), and within each is God's promise to make them a covenant for the people (Is 42:6; 49:8). The Servant in the second song is given the additional assignment of restoring Jacob/Israel (Is 49:5). Here is the prophet's point. *The servant nation needs the individual Suffering Servant—the Messiah—to reconcile them to Yahweh and accomplish what they were unable to do.* The new Servant will not only "raise up the tribes of Jacob and . . . bring back the preserved of Israel" (Is 49:6). Yahweh will also make Him "a light for the nations, that My salvation may reach to the ends of the earth" (Is 49:6).

TWO SERVANTS

It follows, then, that within Isaiah 40–55, there are two servants: servant Israel in Babylon and the Suffering Servant, who loves us with an everlasting love. Servant Israel is the nation introduced in Isaiah 41:8 and 42:1–4. After it fails (e.g., Is 42:19–20), Yahweh rejects the nation—but not forever.

---

104 Is 49:3, 5, 6, 7; 50:10; 52:13; 53:11.

Isaiah 48, accordingly, plays a pivotal role in Isaiah's presentation of these two servants. He dismisses servant Israel and introduces the Suffering Servant, who is also the Messiah. Yahweh says, "From this time forth I announce to you new things, hidden things that you have not known" (Is 48:6). The prophet, thus, closes out his emphasis on Cyrus, King of Persia (559–530 BC), who is at the heart of the message of chapters 41–47. Yahweh's attention becomes focused upon Israel's replacement, the Suffering Servant, who says, "But now the Lord God has sent me by his Spirit" (Is 48:16, authors' translation).

There are several connections between Isaiah 48:16 and 49:1-6—as well as with 50:4–9. The expression "but now" in Isaiah 48:16 anticipates a similar word usage in 49:4, while the title "Lord God" appears again in Isaiah 50:4, 5, 7, 9. Moreover, the word "Spirit" reaches back to the first song in Isaiah 42:1; both servant Israel and the Suffering Servant are directed by Yahweh's Holy Spirit. The first, however, is defeated by idolatry; the second is victorious, and this means reconciliation for the world.

Isaiah 48:17–22 follows the first-person revelation of the obedient Servant in 48:16. In these verses, this new Servant-Messiah issues Yahweh's call to leave Babylon and begin a new exodus. However, in Isaiah 49:4, He laments over the fact that the people are not yet free from captivity. Yahweh responds to the cry of despair by promising that His new Servant will not only restore Israel but will also bring salvation to the ends of the earth (Is 49:6). But His mission will be accomplished through acute rejection and suffering (Is 50:4–9; 52:13–53:12). Because of the Servant's submission, even to the point of death, Yahweh will declare many righteous (Is 53:11). Servant Israel, spurned in chapter 48, is recommissioned as the "servants of Yahweh," for their righteousness is from the victorious Servant-Messiah (Is 54:17, authors' translation).

Isaiah 40–55, then, presents two servants: one who is unfaithful and the other whose loyalty to Yahweh restores the faithless nation. The Messiah reconstitutes Israel (Is 49:5, 8; 53:8), yet He is far different from servant Israel. He listens to Yahweh (Is 50:4–5), while the nation does not.[105] In Isaiah 40:27, Israel laments that Yahweh disregards their cause. However, in Isaiah 49:4 the Servant knows that his cause will be vindicated by Yahweh. Israel is punished for her own sins,[106] whereas the Servant-Messiah suffers for the sins of others (Is 53:4–6).

While there are differences between servant Israel and the Suffering Servant, similarities also exist. The faithless nation is formed in the womb (Is 44:1), while the faithful Servant is called from the womb (Is 49:1). Yahweh seeks to beautify Himself through His servant Israel (Is 44:23) and in His Suffering Servant (Is 49:3). In Isaiah 49:2, Yahweh makes the mouth of His Suffering Servant to be like a sharp sword, whereas in Isaiah 51:16, He puts His words into the mouth of Israel. In a similar way, Yahweh preserves both His Suffering Servant (Is 49:2) and His people (Is 51:16) "in the shadow of His hand."

To summarize, Isaiah is telling a story about two servants. The first is the nation of Israel—captive in Babylon. The second is the Messiah. There is—to import Pauline terms (e.g., Rm 8:4–5)—a servant "according to the flesh" and a Servant "according to the Spirit." Just as the first Adam needed a Second Adam, so the first servant (Israel in exile) needs the Second Servant. The Messiah is this Second and Suffering Servant, who came not to be served but to serve and give His life as a ransom for many (Mt 20:28; Mk 10:45).

---

105 E.g., Is 42:19–20; 43:8; 48:8.

106 Is 40:2; 43:27–28; 50:1

THE FOURTH SERVANT SONG

The New Testament announces a change in how God delivers grace. It does not reveal a change in God or His grace. While God gives grace in the Old Testament through Israel's sacrificial system, in the new era divine forgiveness and grace will come through the Messiah. There is no better example of this good news than in Isaiah's fourth Servant Song.

This song is the epitome of the prophet's description of the Lord's Messiah—who is also the Second Servant. Here is how it begins: "Behold, My servant shall act wisely; He shall be high and lifted up, and shall be exalted" (Is 52:13). In the Book of Isaiah, only Yahweh is "high and lifted up,"[107] yet here the prophet describes the Servant with these same words. The Messiah clarifies this concept when He tells us that He and the Father are one (Jn 10:30). Paul, for his part, likewise maintains that the Messiah is God (Php 2:6) and, at His second coming, "every tongue [will] confess that Jesus Christ is Lord" (Php 2:11).

The fourth Servant Song begins with a cry of victory (Is 52:13). It ends with the spoils belonging to the victor (Is 53:12). We need to emphasize this point because nothing in between looks remotely triumphant.

Instead, there are comments like this: "As many were astonished at you—His appearance was so marred, beyond human semblance, and His form beyond that of the children of mankind" (Is 52:14). In the New Testament, the word "many" is connected to Jesus several times.[108] Paul interchanges "many" (Rm 5:15) with "all" (Rm 5:18). With this understanding, we interpret "many" in the fourth Servant

107 Cf. 6:1; 33:10; 57:15.

108 Mt 20:28 and similarly Mk 10:45; Mt 26:28 and similarly Mk 14:24; Rm 5:15; Heb 9:28.

Song—appearing again in Isaiah's 52:15; 53:11, 12—to be inclusive. It means all people. This is congruent with the Messiah's commission to be a light to all nations (Is 49:6).

The following passages (emphasis added) confirm our interpretation:

- The bread that I will give for the life of *the world* is My flesh. (Jn 6:51)
- Behold, the Lamb of God, who takes away the sin of *the world*! (Jn 1:29)
- Who gave Himself as a ransom *for all*. (1Tm 2:6)
- One has died *for all*. (2Co 5:14)
- By the grace of God He might taste death *for everyone*. (Heb 2:9)

The Messiah's suffering and death is for all sin, for all people, for all time.

Isaiah goes on to record the Servant's humble beginnings (Is 53:2); His rejection (Is 53:3); His atonement for sin (Is 53:5); His death, "like a lamb that is led to the slaughter" (Is 53:7); as well as the corruption of legal justice that marked the Messiah's trials (Is 53:8).

During Christ's trials, both the Jews and Romans failed to follow agreed-upon legal procedures. Pilate acquitted Jesus (Lk 23:4), as did Herod (Lk 23:15). As Christ stood before Pilate a second time, the governor announced His innocence three more times (Lk 23:14, 20, 22). But he finally caved in and gave Jesus over to be crucified (Mt 27:24). Little wonder that Jesus quotes from Isaiah 53:9 on the evening of His death: "For I tell you that this Scripture must be fulfilled in Me: 'And He was numbered with the transgressors'" (Lk 22:37).

A righteous Messiah from the house of David is promised many times in the Old Testament.[109] The fourth Servant Song is one such promise. God describes the Messiah this way: "By His knowledge, shall *the righteous one*, My servant, make many to be accounted righteous" (Is 53:11, emphasis added). By God's grace, and by faith alone, we are reckoned as righteous (Rm 3:28)—that is, completely accepted by the Father.

THE MESSIAH IS THE SUFFERING SERVANT

In Matthew 22:42, Jesus asks, "What do you think about the Christ?" In other words, can He be both a Davidic king and a Suffering Servant? Peter finally believed that. So did Paul. Matthew, Mark, Luke, and John organize their Gospels around this confession. Where does this connection between royalty and a servant come from? The book of the prophet Isaiah.

How do the messianic oracles—rooted in God's promises to David—in Isaiah 7, 9, and 11 connect with the prophet's portrayal of a Suffering Servant in chapters 49, 50, 52, and 53? While it is true that Isaiah does not explicitly link the title "Messiah" with "the Servant of the Lord," he does identify these figures as one and the same person. Both are empowered by the Holy Spirit (Is 11:2; 48:16), each brings light unto the Gentiles (Is 9:1–2; 49:6), neither is pretentious (Is 7:14–15; 11:1; 53:1), and lowly vegetation titles are employed for both (Is 11:1; 53:2).

There are additional connections. Within the Book of Isaiah, the title "servant" is used for royal figures. For example, the prophet quotes Yahweh as saying, "My servant David" (Is 37:35). It is noteworthy that dozens of verses outside of Isaiah identify David as Yahweh's servant.[110]

109 E.g., Is 32:1; Jer 23:5; Zec 9:9.

110 E.g., 1Sm 23:10; 2Sm 3:18; 1Ki 3:6; 2Ki 8:19; 1Ch 17:4; 2Ch 6:15; Jer 33:21; Ezk 34:23.

The Servant's royal/messianic links also appear right after the prophet's third Servant Song, where kings and princes bow before the Servant (Is 49:7). And, within the fourth Servant Song, kings are silent (Is 52:15) because the Servant, like royalty, is high and lifted up (Is 52:13). It is accurate to say, therefore, that David—who is a pattern of the coming Messiah—and the Suffering Servant do not represent two different figures. They are one and the same person. The prophet gives us two facets of the one Messiah.

These links are so clear that Jewish scholars of the early Christian era, in their Aramaic Targum on the prophets, begin the fourth Servant Song with these words: "Behold My Servant Messiah will prosper." This is important because we may have the impression that Judaism has always maintained that Israel—not the Messiah—is the servant in the fourth song. While Jewish teachers who debated with early Christian leaders did not believe Jesus was *the* Messiah, they did embrace the idea that Isaiah's words describe *a* messiah. Judaism and Christianity were united for a millennium in believing Isaiah 52:13–53:12 described a messiah. The difference of opinion was only with the Messiah's identity.

The stumbling block, not only for Jews but also for many unbelievers, is that the Messiah's kingdom comes through the most unlikely means—bloody suffering and death on a cross. Even there, though, His redemptive love topples the power structures of every other so-called king, prince, leader, and ruler.

MESSIANIC PATTERNS

THE SPIRIT OF THE LORD UPON THE MESSIAH (ISAIAH 61:1–2)

Isaiah is not done with his portrait of the Messiah. He continues with these words: "The Spirit of the Lord God is upon Me, because the Lord has anointed Me" (Is 61:1). There are several reasons to believe that Isaiah is referring to someone other than himself:

- In Israel—with one exception (1Ki 19:16)—only kings[111] and priests[112] were anointed.
- The messianic King in Isaiah 11:1–3 is also empowered with the Spirit.
- In his book, Isaiah himself does not speak at length in the first person.
- The Suffering Servant speaks in the first person also in Isaiah 49:1–6 and 50:4–9.

Put all this together and what do we have? The speaker in Isaiah 61 is the messianic Servant. Our Savior's appropriation of Isaiah 61:1–2 in Luke 4:18–19 confirms that He is the Messiah who is—at the same time—the Suffering Servant. The trinitarian connections in Isaiah 61:1 are also clear: the Father is *the Lord God*, Jesus is the anointed speaker, and the Holy Spirit is *the Spirit of the Lord God*.

The motif of God's Spirit further links the Davidic Messiah (Is 11:1–2) with the anointed Servant (Is 61:1). The same Holy Spirit descended upon Jesus at His Baptism, thus completing the

111 E.g., 1Sm 10:1; 16:13; 2Ki 9:3.

112 E.g., Ex 28:41; 40:13

connections between Isaiah 11, 61, and Jesus.[113] The Savior is the world's Spirit-empowered sin-bearer, who rules not with the bravado of this world's leaders but by depending on His Father and seeking His glory.

The Lord God sends the Servant "to proclaim the year of the Lord's favor" (Is 61:2). The expression "year of the Lord's favor" is synonymous with the Jubilee Year. According to Moses, every fifty years everyone under oppression and bondage was to be set free.[114] All slaves were released, and all debts were erased. Moreover, everyone who was bankrupt had their debts paid. *Jubilee* takes its name from the word for a ram's horn trumpet that was blown to signal the event's beginning.

The Jubilee was announced on the Day of Atonement (Lv 25:9; see chapter 3). This is a significant point. Canceling the debts of fellow Israelites flowed out of God's canceling their debts to Him. Social and economic justice issue forth from divine mercy. The Messiah's death is the final Day of Atonement and ushers in the eternal Jubilee.

The messianic Jubilee reverses the destiny of God's people. They had walked in the dark but now live in the light (e.g., Is 59:9; 60:1). They had been lost, but now are found (e.g., Is 60:15; 62:4, 12). Once they were blind, but now they see (Is 59:10; 61:1). Who wouldn't tenaciously cling to these Jubilee gifts?

People were puzzled when Jesus, a local person, claimed to initiate the Jubilee (Lk 4:22). Soon, however, they changed into a lynching mob when the Messiah defined the poor, captives, blind, and oppressed people—not as the Jews in Nazareth but as the dispersed Gentiles in the world. Recalling earlier Old Testament

113 Mt 3:13–17; Mk 1:9–11; Lk 3:21–22; Jn 1:32–34.

114 Lv 25:10; Jer 34:8–9; Ezk 46:17.

narratives about the prophets Elijah and Elisha, Jesus indicated that the Jubilee target was not only Israel but also Gentiles (Lk 4:25–27; cf. Is 56:1–8). How dare the Messiah announce God's love for the world! The Jews of the Messiah's day believed that Isaiah 61:1–2a was for them while the divine vengeance announced in Isaiah 61:2b was for the Gentiles.

John the Baptist was also confused. While sitting in prison and fearing for his life, he sent messengers to Jesus, asking, "Are You the one who is to come, or shall we look for another?" (Mt 11:3). Against this background of many confusing messianic expectations, Jesus undertook an enormous task—to reeducate people about the Messiah. In Matthew 11:4–5, Jesus helps John the Baptist (and us) by referring to the messianic message in Isaiah 35:5–6 and 61:1–2.

The message? Jesus is the Jubilee. The year of freedom, first articulated by Moses, announced by Isaiah, begun in Nazareth, ongoing throughout Luke's Gospel, marches on today. Wherever the Gospel is preached and the Sacraments administered, Jesus is there, releasing people from the burden of sin and setting them free to live in joy and gratitude.

AN EVANGELIST'S PORTRAIT OF THE MESSIAH: IMMANUEL, SPROUT, KING, SERVANT, AND JUBILEE

Located on the front of historic Trinity Church in Boston are the sculptures of six men. At the center are the four Gospel writers, who are flanked on the right by Paul and on the left by Isaiah. Isaiah's presence in this distinguished group speaks volumes about his importance for understanding the Messiah. Jerome (ca. 342–420) wrote of Isaiah, "He should be called an evangelist rather than a prophet because he describes all the mysteries of Christ and the Church so clearly that you think he is composing a history of what has already happened rather than prophesying about what is to come."[115] Likewise, when Augustine (345–430) asked Ambrose (ca. 327–400) for his advice on what he should read, the latter suggested Isaiah, saying, "I believe, because he above the rest is a more clear fore-shower of the Gospel and of the calling of the Gentiles."[116] The Book of Isaiah composes a beautiful portrait of Israel's messianic hope and the Savior of the world—Jesus.

---

115 Jerome, "Prefaces to the Books of the Vulgate Version of the Old Testament: Isaiah," in *The Principal Works of St. Jerome*, ed. Philip Schaff, trans. W. H. Freemantle (Grand Rapids, MI: Christian Classics Ethereal Library, 1892), 1055.

116 Augustine, *The Confessions of Saint Augustine*, trans. Edward B. Pusey (Grand Rapids, MI: Christian Classics Ethereal Library, 1909), Book 9, ch. 5.

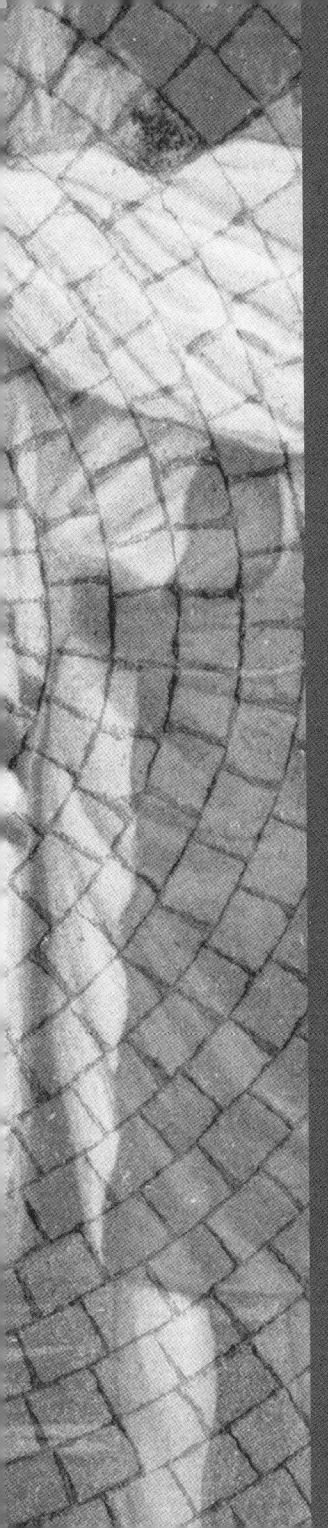

CHAPTER 8

JEREMIAH, EZEKIEL, AND DANIEL: VISIONS OF THE MESSIAH

Israel's prophets frequently announce God's coming judgment. Their oracles are filled with messages of divine anger and wrath. For example, Jeremiah predicts his nation's demise, foreseeing Babylon bulldozing Judah and Jerusalem (e.g., Jer 4:5–18; 5:14–17). He even goes so far as to bury his underwear to make it clear that Babylon will consign Judah's brightest and best to the grave (Jer 13:1–11). Ezekiel's first twenty-four chapters describe—in vivid detail—how God will punish His people through King Nebuchadnezzar and his Babylonian hordes. Then there is Daniel, with his vision of a ravenous bear, a flying leopard, and an iron-teethed monster—symbols of foreign nations that are God's agents of devastation and destruction (Dn 7:1–8).

However, while Jeremiah sharply criticizes the Davidic kings of his day (e.g., Jer 21:1–7; 22:10–30), he also expresses confidence that God will raise up a godly king from the house of David (e.g., Jer 23:5–6; 33:15). Ezekiel adds to the anticipation, envisioning a new David (Ezk 37:24–25), whom he frequently calls a prince.[117] And Daniel announces that the Messiah is coming—likening His kingdom to a rock that will crush the kingdoms of this world and endure forever (Dn 2:44–45).

Jeremiah, Ezekiel, and Daniel have much to say about the Messiah. The predictions, patterns, and presence of the Messiah in their prophecies have strengthened the faith of believers for millennia.

117 E.g., Ezk 34:23–24; 44:3; 46:2, 18; 48:21.

JEREMIAH: PROPHET TO THE LAST KINGS OF JUDAH

KING DAVID

The prophet Jeremiah begins his book by mentioning several of Judah's last kings—Josiah, Jehoiakim, and Zedekiah (Jer 1:2–3). We may not always be able to tell a book by its cover, but we know one of Jeremiah's main themes by means of these initial comments. The prophet will frequently shine the spotlight upon the Davidic house. Asaph helps us understand this longing for another King David. He writes of Jesse's famous son, "With upright heart he shepherded them and guided them with his skillful hands" (Ps 78:72).

King David was the yardstick by which Judah's kings/shepherds were critiqued. For instance, King Ahaz "did not do what was right in the eyes of the Lord his God, as his father David had done" (2Ki 16:2). Even the Joash-Amaziah-Azariah-Jotham succession—which gets a good report and whose kingships are generally likened to that of their father (e.g., 2Ki 14:3; 15:3)—are measured against David's rule. Their failure to remove high places (where idols were worshiped) makes them inferior to him.

It was no different in Jeremiah's day. He sees kings falling far short of the Davidic ideal. Several of these leaders—along with princes and other royal elite—worshiped Canaanite gods on high places. They also deprived God's people of justice and righteousness. Jeremiah offers this appraisal: "They judge not with justice the cause of the fatherless, to make it prosper, and they do not defend the rights of the needy" (Jer 5:28). Judah's kings failed to be shepherd-like—along the lines of David. Instead, they were more like wolves. But not all of them.

Josiah, who ruled from 641 to 609 BC, enacted justice and righteousness (Jer 22:15). "He judged the cause of the poor and needy; then it was well. Is not this to know Me? declares the LORD" (Jer 22:16). Tragically, Judean kings after Josiah ignored the cries of their people. Jehoahaz (609 BC), Jehoiakim (609–598 BC), Jehoiachin (598 BC), and Zedekiah (598–587 BC) failed miserably. These last four kings of the Judean state—often called shepherds—cared nothing for the sheep (Jer 23:2).

Enter the new David! "But they shall serve the LORD their God and David their king" (Jer 30:9). "David," in this verse, denotes the coming Davidic Messiah. David's dynasty will rise from the ashes. The Babylonian invasion in 587 BC brought death, but divine promises to the house of David guaranteed resurrection.

That is what God says through Jeremiah: "Look, the days are coming—this is the Lord's declaration—when I will raise up a Righteous Sprout for David. He will reign wisely as king and administer justice and righteousness in the land. In his days Judah will be saved and Israel will dwell securely. This is the name he will be called: Yahweh Is Our Righteousness" (Jer 23:5–6, authors' translation). These verses overflow with messianic hope.

Jeremiah calls the Messiah "a Righteous Sprout." In like manner, Isaiah 4:2 and Zechariah 3:8 and 6:12 employ the term "Sprout" (also translated "Branch") to speak of the coming Messiah. And, although Isaiah 11:1 and 53:2 do not employ this specific term, they use seedling imagery messianically. Just as a greenery grows from an unseen seed beneath the surface of the ground, so the Messiah will spring forth when all seems lost—both when He is born and, after His death, in His rising again on the third day.

The Messiah's lowly beginning, humble ministry, and frequent refusal to exercise divine power led the Jewish elites to conclude that Jesus could not be David's heir. They held that Jesus associated with the wrong kind of people, preached the wrong kind of sermons, gathered the wrong kind of followers, carried out the wrong kind of mission, and offered the wrong kind of redemption. It culminated on Good Friday. "And over His head they put the charge against Him, which read, 'This is Jesus, the King of the Jews'" (Mt 27:37).

It is on the cross, though, that Jeremiah's other messianic name finds its fulfillment. In a clear rebuff against Zedekiah—whose name means "Yahweh is righteous"—Jeremiah calls the Messiah "Yahweh Is Our Righteousness" (Jer 23:6, authors' translation). Zedekiah had the name. Jesus gives the gift—the gift of righteousness. It is ours because the Messiah laid aside His glory and became sin for us (2Co 5:21). Now we are free from striving to be self-righteous. Instead, we can rest in the Messiah's gift of declared righteousness. This is such a wonderful promise that the prophet says it again in Jeremiah 33:14–15. Good things are worth repeating!

Jeremiah goes on to declare that creation's permanence testifies to God's promises to the house of David: "Thus says the Lord: If you can break My covenant with the day and My covenant with the night, so that day and night will not come at their appointed time, then also My covenant with David My servant may be broken, so that he shall not have a son to reign on his throne, and My covenant with the Levitical priests My ministers" (Jer 33:20–21). The "if" in verse 20 may appear to sound a note of conditionality. Nothing could be further from the truth. The cessation of the heavens and the earth is impossible—it will never happen (cf. Gn 8:21–22; Rm 8:19–23). Just so, God's pledge to David will never cease. The covenant is completely reliable. It is fixed. It is irrevocable. It is forever.

In 597 BC, Nebuchadnezzar imprisoned the Davidic king Jehoiachin (2Ki 24:10–12). Zedekiah, Judah's last king, was captured in 587 BC. Then at Riblah, Nebuchadnezzar slaughtered Zedekiah's sons and then blinded him (2Ki 25:6–7; Jer 52:10–11). It appeared that God's promises to David's house were null and void. Jeremiah says, "Not so!"

A NEW COVENANT

Hebrews 8:8–12 contains the longest Old Testament quotation in the New Testament—Jeremiah 31:31–34. The author partially repeats it in Hebrews 10:16–17. Moreover, four times, New Testament writers link the "new covenant" with the Messiah's Holy Supper.[118] Although Jeremiah 31:31 is the only place in the Old Testament where the expression "new covenant" appears, synonymous terms include "new heart" and "new spirit,"[119] as well as the word "covenant" when it appears in a promise for the future.[120]

Most English translations include these words in Jeremiah 31:31: "make a new covenant." This is not completely accurate—for two reasons. First, the Hebrew adjective rendered "new" can mean something created new, from scratch. Or it may denote something refreshed and restored that is "as good as new." The context of Jeremiah 31 suggests that "new covenant" denotes "renewed covenant." The prophet tells a story of redemption, not replacement. God is working to fix what is broken, mend what is torn, heal what is sick, and make all things new, not to make all new things.

God does not send a wrecking ball. He sends the remodeling crew. He renews earlier promises. He also amplifies and intensifies them. The Messiah's renewed covenant is the old reborn, reaffirmed, and re-inaugurated—in a more profound and intimate way. It may be likened to a marriage gone bad but then reborn. That is what

---

118 Mt 26:28; Mk 14:24; Lk 22:20; 1Co 11:25.

119 Ezk 11:19; 18:31.

120 Is 42:6; 49:8; 59:21; Hos 2:18–20.

Jeremiah says. Within his renewed covenant oracle are the words "though I was their husband" (Jer 31:32).

One of the Jeremiah's primary metaphors to describe God's relationship with Israel is that of a relationship between a husband and wife. According to the prophet, the marriage began well (Jer 2:2–3), then deteriorated (Jer 2:5–13), leading God to judge His Bride (Jer 13:22–26). The marriage, however, did not end. There was no divorce. There was, however, a long separation. We call that the seventy-year Babylonian exile (cf. Jer 25:11–12; 29:10). In Jeremiah 31:31, however, the prophet announces that the relationship is now renewed, thus portending the Messiah's unwavering commitment to His Bride—the Holy Christian Church.[121]

The second word that needs comment within the expression "make a new covenant" is "make." More accurately, the word is "cut." In the Old Testament, covenants were not made. People did not sign their names to paper. There were no attorneys or notaries public with stamps and seals. There was, however, blood. In the Old Testament, people cut covenants. They killed animals, slit throats, and poured blood. It was a messy business. A more accurate way to render the Hebrew of Jeremiah 31:31, then, is "I will cut with them a renewed covenant."

The renewed covenant is central to the New Testament's understanding of the Messiah. Jesus came because God remembered "His holy covenant" (Lk 1:72)—that is, He acted upon His earlier promises to the house of David. The Savior then refers to Jeremiah's prophecy when He says that the Holy Supper is "the new covenant in My blood" (Lk 22:20). The Messiah poured out His blood "for the forgiveness of sins" (Mt 26:28). With these words, He further connects Himself with Jeremiah's renewed covenant. "For I will forgive their iniquity, and I will remember their sin no more" (Jer 31:34).

121 Cf. 2Co 11:2; Eph 5:27; Rv 21:1–9.

The messianic renewed covenant does not mean earlier covenants were failures. It is not as though God looked at His prior promise to the house of David, became fed up, cast it aside, and then made plans to start all over again. Instead, God said that His Davidic covenant promises were going to be delivered in greater, better, and fuller form—through the Messiah, Jesus of Nazareth.

KING JEHOIACHIN

In Jeremiah 52, the prophet reviews the tragedy of Jerusalem's destruction at the hands of the Babylonians in 587 BC. The description is devoid of the charged and powerful language that saturates Jeremiah's oracles about the nations in chapters 46–51. Instead, the prophet's last chapter has the sense of a news report told by a passionless observer. The account lacks emotion and comes across as grim and hopeless—but not for those who still believed in God's everlasting promises to the house of David.

Jehoiachin—Jehoiakim's son and Judah's second-to-last king—had been stuck in Babylon for decades. This Davidic heir was exiled, along with Ezekiel and others, in 597 BC. Night fell. Everything looked impossible. Then, daybreak! In 561 BC, the Babylonian king Evil-merodach (also known as Amel-marduk) ordered Jehoiachin to take off his prison clothes. The expression "put off his prison garments" (Jer 52:33 and 2Ki 25:29) elsewhere in the Old Testament indicates a change for the better (see Gn 45:22; Zec 3:4–5). How much better? Evil-merodach welcomed Jehoiachin at the royal table and even gave him daily financial assistance.

Though this short vignette at the end of Jeremiah's book might not seem much to hold on to, it is a prelude to the restoration of the Davidic monarchy. The Judean king is given "a seat above the seats" of other captive kings (Jer 52:32).

But what about Jeremiah's earlier reference to Jehoiachin? "Write this man down as childless, a man who shall not succeed in his days, for none of his offspring shall succeed in sitting on the throne of David and ruling again in Judah" (Jer 22:30). Jehoiachin not only spends most of his life in a Babylonian prison cell but is also "childless," says Jeremiah. The same word describes Abraham and Sarah in Genesis 15:2. We know that story! Abraham was an old man and Sarah was an infertile postmenopausal woman. When it came to the ability to procreate, Abraham was "as good as dead" (Heb 11:12).

Do you see the link between Jehoiachin and Abraham? Abraham's offspring were multiplied beyond imagination. David's house will also rise from the dead. God will reverse the curse of being childless. Jehoiachin finally had a family (1Ch 3:17–18). His grandson Zerubbabel became a Persian-appointed leader in Judah (Hg 1:1). Jehoiachin even became an ancestor of the Messiah (Mt 1:12). It is significant that Matthew features Jehoiachin twice in his genealogy (Mt 1:11–12). Jehoiachin straddles the end as well as the beginning—Judah's exile and restoration. Death gives way to resurrection, paving the way for the Messiah, who says, "I am the resurrection and the life" (Jn 11:25).

EZEKIEL: PROPHET TO THE JUDEANS IN EXILE

Like Jeremiah, Ezekiel envisions hope for the house of David through Jehoiachin, who is a new sprig, taken from a cedar, and raised into a great tree. All the birds of the forest find in it both shade and shelter (Ezk 17:22–24). Ezekiel has much more to say about Israel's messianic hope—especially through the gift of divine glory.

GOD'S GLORY

Ezekiel organizes his book in three parts, centering on the motif of God's glory. In his inaugural vision, the prophet sees the glory of God and describes it in stunning detail (Ezk 1:4–28). Then, in Ezekiel 8–11, he watches divine glory depart from Jerusalem's temple—it happens in stages.[122] Yahweh abandons the city and temple before He unleashes the Babylonian juggernaut whose army will destroy these sacred places. This, however, is not the last word.

At the end of his book, Ezekiel envisions God's glory returning to a new temple (Ezk 43:1–5). The book ends with this affirmation: "The name of the city from that time on shall be, The Lord Is There" (Ezk 48:35). Divine glory will permanently lodge in the new Jerusalem.

This is the bare outline of the book. Ezekiel's story about divine glory is worth considering in greater detail. The prophet sees God's glory, which he likens to a super-charged chariot. Four creatures are under the chariot, and each has four faces: a human, a lion, an eagle, and an ox. Next to each creature are four wheels. Each wheel is full of eyes.

Ezekiel includes this description: "On the throne, high above, was someone who looked like a man" (Ezk 1:26, authors' translation). This *man* is the Messiah. Earlier in the Old Testament, biblical authors also call Him a man.[123] Ezekiel goes on to describe Him as surrounded by brightness (Ezk 1:27–28), thus giving us a foretaste of the Messiah's transfiguration,[124] as well as His glorification after ascending to the Father's right hand (Rv 1:12–20). At the end of chapter 1, Ezekiel writes of the Messiah, "Such was the appearance of the likeness of the glory of the LORD" (Ezk 1:28). Like the prophet

---

122 Ezk 8:4; 9:3; 10:4, 18–19; 11:22–23.

123 See, e.g., Gn 18:2, 32:24–28; Jsh 5:13.

124 Mt 17:2; Mk 9:2–3; Lk 9:29.

Isaiah (Is 6:3; cf. Jn 12:41), Ezekiel sees the Messiah's glory. Both testify that He is "the radiance of the glory of God and the exact imprint of His nature" (Heb 1:3).

In Ezekiel 8–11, the prophet envisions Yahweh's withdrawal from the Jerusalem temple. It begins with people making an altar in the temple that exhibits an "image of jealousy" (Ezk 8:5). Leaders have their own idols (Ezk 8:12), women worship Tammuz (Ezk 8:14), and others are bowing down to the sun (Ezk 8:16). Bloodshed and violence fill the land (Ezk 9:9). These abominations drive divine glory from the temple (Ezk 8:6). Leaving in stages, as a jilted lover, God finds it heart-wrenching to leave the one He loves (e.g., Ezk 9:3; 10:4, 18–19). Finally, after the prophesied seventy years of exile (e.g., Jer 25:11), God's glory comes back: "The glory of the Lord filled the temple" (Ezk 43:5).

This is the message that reverberates throughout the New Testament. God's glory is back in the life and ministry of the Messiah. And John sees it: "The Word became flesh and dwelt among us, and we have seen His glory" (Jn 1:14). In the Book of Ezekiel, God's glory is connected to power—after all, in ancient warfare, there was nothing more powerful than a chariot. It is natural, then, to think that the Messiah's ultimate glory is connected to this kind of power: walking on water, raising Lazarus, healing the sick, and making people who are crippled whole. God's glory in His Messiah must mean the Savior was always walking an inch above the ground, right? It must mean Jesus was always emitting a glowing, heavenly light, right?

Wrong. Dead wrong. In John's Gospel, the Messiah's glory denotes His bitter suffering and death. How so? On Palm Sunday, Jesus says, "The hour has come for the Son of Man to *be glorified*" (Jn 12:23, emphasis added). In the Upper Room, right after Judas Iscariot leaves to betray Him for thirty pieces of silver, Jesus says, "Now is the Son of Man *glorified*" (Jn 13:31, emphasis added). Just before His arrest in the Garden of Gethsemane, Jesus says, "Father, the hour has come; *glorify* Your Son" (Jn 17:1, emphasis added). Do you see? The Messiah's supreme glory is His bloody death on a cross.

What does that look like? There is a legionnaire's whip of leather strips with lead balls on each end, beating His back into a bloody pulp. There is a crown of thorns caking His hair with blood. There are clenched fists deforming His face. And there are nails disfiguring His body as He twists and turns, writhing in pain. But that is not the end. How could it be? Recall that the Messiah said, "Destroy this temple, and in three days I will raise it up" (Jn 2:19).

THE NEW TEMPLE

John's Gospel picks up on Ezekiel's messianic motif of divine glory residing in the new temple. God's presence no longer lives in a building. Instead, it fills the Messiah—Jesus of Nazareth. And, by amplifying Ezekiel's vision of a river flowing out of the new temple (Ezk 47:1–12), John maintains that the Messiah is now this temple and the source of living water. It begins with just a trickle. Jesus tells Nicodemus, "Unless one is born of water and the Spirit, he cannot enter the kingdom of God" (Jn 3:5). It picks up momentum: "The water that I will give him will become in him a spring of water welling up to eternal life" (Jn 4:14). And then it becomes a surge: "Whoever believes in Me, as the Scripture has said, 'Out of his heart will flow rivers of living water'" (Jn 7:38).

But, in an ironic twist for the ages, this raging river completely dries up. The Messiah lamented on the cross, "I thirst" (Jn 19:28). Then the Roman spear thrust brought with it a sudden flow of blood and water (Jn 19:34). Here is *the* temple, crushed and cursed by the sin of the world. Could this be the end? Not at all! The Holy Spirit entered the dry bones in Ezekiel's most well-known vision, empowering them to stand on their feet—a vast army (Ezk 37:1–14). On the third day, this same Spirit vivified the Crucified One. The Messiah is now alive forevermore.

THE GOOD SHEPHERD

Another messianic reference appears in Ezekiel 34—an oracle that describes the failure of Judah's preexilic kings as well as God's plan to correct the disastrous situation. As Israel's benevolent shepherd, Yahweh appoints a human shepherd to restore peace and security. "I will set up over them one shepherd, my servant David, and . . . he shall feed them and be their shepherd" (Ezk 34:23). David—who is neither elected by the people nor self-appointed but divinely chosen—will shepherd the flock and inaugurate a covenant of peace.

Jeremiah 23:5; Hosea 3:5; and Amos 9:11 also explicitly name David as bringing about this new order. It is not as though these divine spokesmen envisioned a resurrected David. Instead, *David* functions as shorthand or an abbreviation for "the Davidic Messiah." The new David not only will serve as shepherd but also will be a servant (Ezk 34:23). Two times in 2 Samuel 7, God calls David "My servant" (2Sm 7:5, 8). In this same chapter, David acknowledges this role ten times. Paul reminds us that, in the fullness of time, Jesus, the Messiah, took the form of a servant and humbled Himself to become obedient—even to the point of death (Php 2:7–8).

Additionally, in his oracle on the shepherd and his sheep, Ezekiel calls the new David a "prince" (Ezk 34:24). True, in most contexts, a prince holds a lower rank than a king. In Ezekiel, however, this is not the case. The prophet hesitates to call the Messiah a king because so many preexilic kings abused their office, dishonored God, and ignored justice and righteousness. This is consistent with earlier passages in the book that also sought to downplay earlier kings.[125]

125 E.g., Ezk 7:27; 12:12; 19:1.

Ezekiel, therefore, employs the term *prince* to denote a leader who carries out a royal role—and this is not new. Although for the most part, Israelite monarchs were called kings, there are times when one would be called a "prince" or "ruler" (e.g., Solomon, 1Ki 11:34). As such, the Messiah is Yahweh's representative and deputy.

The Messiah/prince leads His people to find good pasture, which in the New Testament is equivalent to abundant life (Jn 10:1–10). He is not like the shepherds in Ezekiel's day. "Son of man, prophesy against the shepherds of Israel; prophesy, and say to them . . . the weak you have not strengthened, the sick you have not healed, the injured you have not bound up, the strayed you have not brought back, the lost you have not sought, and with force and harshness you have ruled them" (Ezk 34:2, 4). Ezekiel is referring to Judah's last four kings—Jehoahaz, Jehoiakim, Jehoiachin, and Zedekiah. They fleeced the flock, caring only for themselves.

What will the Lord do? He will take matters into His own hands. "Behold, I, I myself will seek. . . . I will search for my sheep. . . . I will search for my sheep. . . . I will rescue. I will bring them. . . . I will gather them. . . . I will bring them. . . . I will shepherd them. . . . I will shepherd them. I myself will shepherd. . . . I myself will cause them to lie down" (Ezk 34:11–15, authors' translation). In five verses, God refers to Himself seventeen times. Talk about taking matters into your own hands! Sheep are desperate for His new shepherd. It is the Messiah, Jesus (Jn 10:11, 14).

How good is this Shepherd? When we wander astray, He leaves the ninety-nine and comes searching for us. When we are confused by the voices of demons and devils, He calls us by name. When we get lost in the lunacy of life, He loves us and forgives us. The Messiah gathers us into His arms until we are better, holds us until we can live with the hurt, and carries us close to His loving heart forever.

The Good Shepherd says, "I lay down My life for the sheep."[126] The Messiah's death stands at the center of the Fourth Gospel. Let us run some numbers by you: John's Gospel has twenty-one chapters. Palm Sunday is in chapter 12 and Good Friday closes out chapter 19. Thirty-eight percent of the Gospel is focused on events surrounding the Messiah laying down His life for the sheep. How did He do it? Paradoxically, the Shepherd became a slaughtered Lamb. "Like a lamb that is led to the slaughter, and like a sheep that before its shearers is silent, so He opened not His mouth" (Is 53:7).

TWO STICKS

Ezekiel's second reference to the restoration of David's house appears within the context of an enacted prophecy that involves two sticks of wood. They are inscribed with the names "Judah" and "Joseph"—standing for the Southern and Northern kingdoms, respectively. The fragmented people of God are reunified (Ezk 37:16–28). God will re-create one nation and one kingdom under one king (Ezk 37:22). He says through the prophet, "My servant David shall be *king* over them" (Ezk 37:24, emphasis added); as well as "David My servant shall be their *prince* forever" (Ezk 37:25, emphasis added). The terms "king" and "prince" are again interchangeable.

The prophet's fivefold use of the word (or translated words related to) "forever" in Ezekiel 37:25–28 points to an unending messianic reign—an idea David reiterates to his subjects as well as to Solomon in 1 Chronicles 28:4, 7, 8, 9. Gabriel's announcement to the Virgin Mary about the Messiah echoes these promises: "He will be great and will be called the Son of the Most High. And the Lord God will give to Him the throne of His father David, and He will reign over the house of Jacob forever, and of His kingdom there will be no end" (Lk 1:32–33).

---

126 Jn 10:15; see also Jn 10:11, 17, 18.

THE NEW CITY

Ezekiel leaves one of his greatest messianic passages for the very end of his book. "The name of the city from that day on shall be, The LORD Is There" (Ezk 48:35). The city the prophet is referring to has measurements that are a perfect cube (Ezk 48:16).

In like manner, the Holy of Holies (or Most Holy Place) is a perfect cube. Ezekiel should know. Ezekiel was familiar with sections of the Pentateuch, especially the Book of Leviticus. Hence, he writes that a day is coming when the holy, powerful, merciful, gracious, blazing presence of God will no longer be confined to a small space. God's presence will fill a city. But that is not all. The prophecy finally points to the Messiah, who is the presence of God in bodily form (Col 2:9). His name is Immanuel, "God with us" (Is 7:14; Mt 1:23).

DANIEL: PROPHET TO BABYLONIAN AND PERSIAN KINGS

Daniel is familiar to many people because of the vivid stories of God's people in Babylon: three men in a fiery furnace, Daniel in the lions' den, and mysterious handwriting on a wall all make for lively reading and memorable characters. But there is more to the Book of Daniel than accounts of miraculous happenings. It is also permeated with prophecies about the Messiah.

DREAM PROPHECY: THE COMING OF GOD'S KINGDOM (DANIEL 2)

In Daniel 2, we read of King Nebuchadnezzar of Babylon's strange dream. He must have sensed that this was no ordinary vision in the night. He demanded that his courtiers whom he employed to interpret omens tell him what he had dreamed as well as its meaning. Nebuchadnezzar threatened them with death if they could not but offered great rewards if they could (Dn 2:5–6). Of course, no one could tell the king what he had dreamed—such a demand was clearly ridiculous, and the courtiers responded that they simply could not comply with the royal mandate (Dn 2:10–11).

Daniel and his three friends were caught up in the king's command to execute the Babylonian wise men, since they were in training to serve in the king's court (Dn 2:13). Yet, God rescued them by revealing the dream and its meaning to Daniel (Dn 2:14–23), who then explained it to Nebuchadnezzar (Dn 2:24–49). The vision involved a statue made of four metals, each of which represented a successive kingdom that would dominate the ancient Mediterranean world. However, the climax of the dream was a stone that struck the statue and crushed it. The dust of the statue was blown away, but the stone became a large mountain that filled the earth.

When explaining the dream, Daniel noted that the stone was quarried from a mountain, but not by human hands. Thus, the stone had a divine origin—it represented the coming of the Messiah, who would end the kingdoms symbolized by the four metals. God was revealing to Nebuchadnezzar the Messiah who was also depicted in the Prophets this way.[127] The stone growing into a great mountain symbolized the growth of the Messiah's kingdom until it would fill the entire earth.

This dream was a prediction of the coming Messiah. Four kingdoms would dominate the ancient world between Nebuchadnezzar's day and the Messiah's advent. It would begin with Nebuchadnezzar's own Babylonian empire, which would be replaced by the Persian Empire, and then the Greek kingdoms that followed in the wake of

127 Is 8:14–15; 28:16; Zec 3:9; see also Ps 118:22.

Alexander the Great's conquests. Finally, the Roman Empire would dominate the Mediterranean world. According to the dream, this would be when the Messiah would come.

The setting for the New Testament is the Roman Empire. It is no surprise, then, that we find expectations among the persons mentioned in the Gospels that the Messiah would come and establish His kingdom at that time—they could count to four! For instance, many wondered whether John the Baptist might be the Messiah: "As the people were in expectation, and all were questioning in their hearts concerning John, whether he might be the Christ" (Lk 3:15). The disciples on the road to Emmaus after Jesus' resurrection voiced the opinion that Jesus might have been the expected Messiah (Lk 24:19–21). And God had revealed to the aged Simeon that he would see the Messiah before he died (Lk 2:26). These expectations were all fueled by the dominance of the Roman Empire—the fourth kingdom predicted by Nebuchadnezzar's dream.

In the Gospels, Jesus identifies Himself as the rock in Daniel's dream as He linked together Daniel 2:34; Isaiah 8:14–15; 28:16; and Psalm 118:22: "But He [Jesus] looked directly at them and said, 'What then is this that is written: "The stone that the builders rejected has become the cornerstone"? *Everyone who falls on that stone will be broken to pieces, and when it falls on anyone, it will crush him*'" (Lk 20:17–18, emphasis added; see also Mt 21:42–44). Daniel's prophecy of the rock is so important that many of the Early Church Fathers cited it as a prophecy of the incarnation of the Messiah as fulfilled in Jesus. These include Justin Martyr (ca. AD 100–165), Irenaeus (died ca. AD 195), Jerome (ca. AD 345–420), and Theodoret of Cyrus (ca. AD 390–458).

With the incarnation of Jesus, the kingdom of God arrived (Mk 1:15), and this was acknowledged by John the Baptist's message and

Jesus' teachings about the kingdom of God throughout the Gospels. This kingdom was to be a worldwide kingdom, as already prophesied in the Old Testament.[128] Jesus commissioned His disciples to spread His kingdom to the ends of the earth (Ac 1:8), a process that continues to this day wherever the Gospel of Christ is proclaimed.

VISION PROPHECY: THE ARRIVAL OF THE SON OF MAN (DANIEL 7)

Nebuchadnezzar's dream was not the only prophecy of the coming of the Messiah during a fourth kingdom that would dominate the ancient world. Daniel had a vision of four beasts who would arise and rule the earth (Dn 7:1–8). Then, in his vision, Daniel saw a courtroom scene with "the Ancient of Days," God the Father, presiding (Dn 7:9–12). The beasts were judged, and their dominion was taken from them.

Next Daniel saw a new figure coming into this setting: "I saw in the night visions, and behold, with the clouds of heaven there came one like a son of man, and He came to the Ancient of Days and was presented before Him" (Dn 7:13). In place of the beasts whose dominions were removed, this Son of Man was to replace their authority with an even greater one: "And to Him was given dominion and glory and a kingdom, that all peoples, nations, and languages should serve Him; His dominion is an everlasting dominion, which shall not pass away, and His kingdom one that shall not be destroyed" (Dn 7:14). Thus, Daniel 7:13–14 describes the Son of Man's enthronement. Once again, Daniel presents a picture of the Messiah and His kingdom.

In the Gospels, Jesus frequently refers to Himself as "the Son of Man." While this phrase can be used in the Old Testament simply to

128 E.g., Ps 65:5; 72:8; Is 41:9; 49:6; Mi 5:4; Zec 9:10.

designate that someone is human,[129] Jesus clearly used it to mean more than that. For instance, He notes that "The Son of Man will send His angels, and they will gather out of His kingdom all causes of sin and all law-breakers" (Mt 13:41). Obviously, the Son of Man has angels and is more than a mere human. In fact, Jesus uses this title to refer to Himself eighty times.[130] However, no one else in the Gospel accounts ever refers to Jesus by this title.

While on trial, Jesus revealed why He frequently used this title for Himself. When the high priest placed Him under oath and demanded that He say whether He was "the Christ, the Son of God," Jesus replied, "You have said so. But I tell you, from now on you will see the Son of Man seated at the right hand of Power and coming on the clouds of heaven."[131] The only passage in the Old Testament picturing one like a son of man coming on the clouds of heaven is Daniel 7:13. Jesus unmistakably told the high priest that He was the Messiah, the Son of Man, to whom would be given an eternal kingdom by God the Father.

Later in Daniel's vision, the prophet asked to have an explanation of what he had seen. Part of the interpretation involved the Son of Man's kingdom: "And the kingdom and the dominion and the greatness of the kingdoms under the whole heaven shall be given to the people of the saints of the Most High; His kingdom shall be an everlasting kingdom, and all dominions shall serve and obey Him" (Dn 7:27). Here the kingdom is given to the "people of the saints of the Most High" instead of "one like a son of man," as earlier in the vision (Dn 7:13–14). Thus, Daniel is shown the consequences of

---

129 E.g., Nu 23:19; Jb 25:6; God calls Ezekiel "son of man," that is, a mortal human, ninety-three times.

130 Thirty-two times in Matthew; fourteen times in Mark; twenty-six times in Luke; ten times in John.

131 Mt 26:63–64; see also Mt 24:30; Mk 14:62.

the Messiah's receiving His kingdom—the people of God will reign with the messianic king. Therefore, Paul could tell Timothy, "The saying is trustworthy, for: If we have died with Him, we will also live with Him; if we endure, *we will also reign with Him*" (2 Tm 2:11–12, emphasis added).

ANGELIC PROPHECY: MESSIAH AND PRINCE (DANIEL 9)

Daniel 9 opens during the first year after the fall of Babylon with the prophet praying about Jerusalem, based on the prophecies of Jeremiah.[132] Jeremiah had prophesied that Jerusalem would be restored after Babylon had dominated the ancient Near East for seventy years. Because the Babylonian Empire had fallen to the Persians, Daniel was now anxious to know about the Holy City's rebuilding. In response to his prayer, God sent the angel Gabriel to tell Daniel about the future of Jerusalem, symbolized by seventy weeks:

> Seventy weeks are decreed about your people and your holy city, to finish transgression, to put an end to sin, and to atone for iniquity, to bring everlasting righteousness, to seal both vision and prophet, and to anoint a Most Holy One. Know therefore and have insight that from the going out of the word to restore and rebuild Jerusalem until Messiah, a Leader, there will be seven weeks and sixty-two weeks when it will have been built with plaza and moat, but during troubled times. Then after the sixty-two weeks, Messiah will be cut off and have nothing. Both the city and the holy place will be destroyed with a Leader who is coming. Its end will come

132 Dn 9:1–2; see Jer 25:11–12; 29:10.

> with a flood. Until the end there will be war, and desolations are decreed. (Dn 9:24–26, authors' translation)

In this message from Gabriel, Jerusalem's history is seventy symbolic weeks to accomplish several goals (Dn 9:24): ending, finishing, and atoning for sin; bringing everlasting righteousness; sealing vision and prophets; and anointing a Most Holy One—the Messiah (which means "Anointed One"). All of these are messianic in nature, and the Messiah is mentioned as the last, climactic goal. He will bring an end to the curse of sin and usher in everlasting righteousness for His people. The Messiah will be the greatest Prophet, eliminating a need for ongoing prophetic revelation as in the Old Testament.

Next, the period required for Jerusalem's restoration is symbolized by seven weeks and its subsequent history until the coming of the Messiah by an additional sixty-two weeks. Here the Messiah is called a "Leader" (in some English versions, "prince"). The Messiah is to be "cut off and have nothing." However, with the coming of this messianic Leader, the City and the Holy Place (i.e., Jerusalem and its temple) would be destroyed during the final week of the seventy weeks predicted for Jerusalem as outlined by Gabriel.

That the 490 weeks are symbolic can be seen by other uses of related numbers in the Scriptures. For instance, "Jesus said to him, 'I do not say to you seven times, but seventy times seven'" (Mt 18:22, authors' translation). "Seventy times seven" equals 490. What is that about? Jesus does not mean that we should be counting to 490, through clenched teeth, so that when they finally offend us 491 times, we let our enemies have it. If that is how we are thinking, it shows we have never really forgiven once, let alone 490 times. What does Jesus mean? Seven is the perfect number in the Bible, so seventy times seven means perfect forgiveness—490. There are two important truths connected to 490.

When the Messiah commands us to forgive "seventy times seven" (Mt 18:22, authors' translation). He references Daniel's seventy sevens—490 (Dn 9:24). Daniel's 490 refers to Moses' 49 (seven times seven) in Leviticus 25:8. Here Moses writes that at the end of every 49 years, all debts are forgiven, the land is returned to its original owners, and all prisoners go free. That is why the fiftieth year is called the Jubilee. Leviticus 25:10 states, "Proclaim liberty throughout the land."

Daniel's 490 (49 x 10), therefore, envisions a universal and permanent Jubilee. There will come a time when God will perfectly forgive the world. The movement is from Moses to Daniel to the Messiah, who claims that He came to inaugurate an endless Jubilee (Lk 4:16–21). The New Testament identifies the Messiah of Daniel 9 as Jesus, who atoned for sin and was the Prophet extraordinaire.[133] He was the Anointed One of God (Lk 4:17–21). He was "cut off and had nothing" at His crucifixion, as God predicted through Gabriel; this was also later proclaimed by Peter and John (Ac 4:27–28). Finally, Jesus connected His ministry with the destruction of Jerusalem and its temple, expanding on Daniel 9:27 and its mention of desolations.[134]

THE MESSIAH'S PROPHECY (DANIEL 10)

The last of Daniel's visions occupies three chapters: Daniel 10–12. The revealer of this final vision to Daniel is described in Daniel 10:4–21. We will not review every detail of these verses since our focus is on identifying who this revealer of Daniel's ultimate vision was. The following table outlines the parallels between the revealer of the vision and both Ezekiel's inaugural vision of God and John's vision of the glorified Messiah:

133 Mt 21:11, 46; Lk 7:16; 24:19; Jn 6:14; 7:40.

134 Mt 24:1–2, 15–22; Mk 13:1–2, 14–20; Lk 21:5–6, 20–24; see also Dn 11:31; 12:11.

COMPARISON OF DANIEL 10, EZEKIEL 1, AND REVELATION 1

THE REVEALER (DN 10:5–21)	*GOD AND HIS CHERUBIM (EZK 1:4–48)*	*THE GLORIFIED CHRIST (RV 1:13–16)*
Appearance like a man, a Son of Man (10:5, 16, 18; see 7:13)	God's appearance is like a man (1:26–27)	Like a Son of Man (1:13)
Clothed in linen garments (10:5)		Clothed in a long robe (1:13)
A gold belt around His waist (10:5)	Appearance of gleaming metal above God's waist and fire below His waist (1:27)	A gold belt around His chest (1:13)
Face like lightning (10:6)	Flashes of lightning from the cherubim (1:13)	Face shining like the sun (1:16)
Eyes like burning torches (10:6)	God's presence like fire (1:4); torches flash between the cherubim (1:13); from the waist down, God appeared like fire (1:27)	Eyes like flames of fire (1:14)
Arms and feet like polished bronze (10:6)	God's presence like glowing metal (1:4); the cherubim had feet like polished bronze (10:7); from the waist up, God appeared like glowing metal (1:27)	Feet like polished bronze refined in a furnace (1:15)
Voice like an army (10:6); compare 12:6–7, where He is "above the waters of the stream"	The wings of the cherubim made the sound of many waters, like the voice of the Almighty, like battle tumult and an army camp (1:24)	Voice like many waters (1:15)

While the parallels in these three visions are not exact, it is quite clear that all three passages are speaking of the same person. Thus, the revealer of Daniel's final vision is the Messiah, the God whom Ezekiel saw on His throne surrounded by cherubim and the glorified Savior who appeared to John on the island of Patmos.

The identity of the revealer of Daniel's vision as the Messiah, Jesus before His incarnation, is central to this final vision. It is about both Christ's first and second advents. Daniel 11:30 is a prophecy that ships will come from Kittim. The combination of the words "ships" and "Kittim" occurs elsewhere in the Bible only at Numbers 24:24, part of Balaam's messianic prophecy of the Messiah's first advent that a star will arise from Jacob (Nu 24:17; see chapter 3).

Daniel 12:2–3 has what can be considered the clearest description of the resurrection of the dead at the final judgment when Jesus will come again. The statement that "many of those who sleep in the dust of the earth shall awake, some to everlasting life, and some to shame and everlasting contempt" is part of the Savior's final verdict on all humankind (Dn 12:2; see Mt 25:31–46). The promise that God's people, "those who are wise," will "shine like the brightness of the sky above" (Dn 12:3) suggests that believers in Christ will be conformed to the likeness of His glorified body (Php 3:21).

THE MESSIAH WITH HIS PERSECUTED PEOPLE (DANIEL 3)

Finally, we also encounter the Messiah's presence with His people at Daniel 3:24–25. In the familiar story of Shadrach, Meshach, and Abednego in the fiery furnace, King Nebuchadnezzar observed men in the furnace and said, "Did we not cast three men bound into the fire?" When he was assured that there were only three that had been thrown into the furnace he exclaimed, "But I see four men unbound, walking in the midst of the fire, and they are not hurt; and the appearance of the fourth is *like a son of the gods*" (emphasis added). From his pagan Babylonian point of view that believed in many gods, Nebuchadnezzar identified a fourth man in the furnace as a son of one of those gods. However, his words reveal more than he knew: he saw the Son of God walking in the furnace with Shadrach, Meshach, and Abednego, who were not burned by the fire (Dn 3:27). The fourth man in the furnace was the Messenger who appeared to Moses in the burning bush, yet the bush was not consumed (Ex 3:2; see also Is 43:2)

ENVISIONING THE MESSIAH: JEREMIAH, EZEKIEL, AND DANIEL

Jeremiah, Ezekiel, and Daniel saw King Nebuchadnezzar's onslaught, which would result in the Babylonian captivity of the Judean people. These three men all had marvelous visions of the Messiah, visions that were intended to give courage to God's faithful people and increase their trust in the Almighty even as Judah and Jerusalem fell to Nebuchadnezzar's armies. Their prophecies of the coming Savior pointed the true believers in Israel beyond their current sufferings to the glory of the Messiah to come and His work for them. So also, as we look at these three prophets, we see Jesus and envision the splendor of Christ, who will resurrect His people on the Last Day to live with Him in His eternal kingdom.

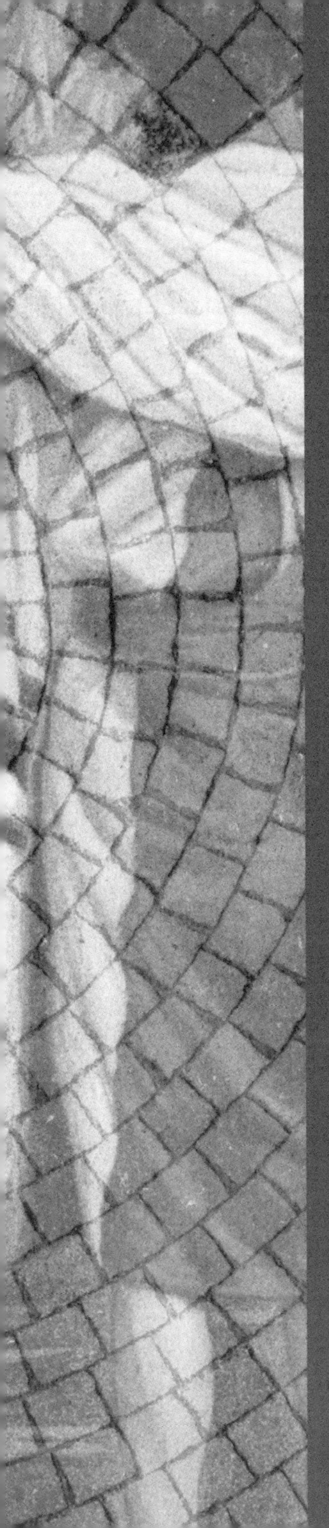

CHAPTER 9

THE MAJOR THEME OF THE MINOR PROPHETS: THE PROMISE OF MESSIANIC GRACE

In 1 Peter 1:10–12, the apostle tells us what Old Testament prophets believed about the Messiah:

1. He will come.
2. He will suffer.
3. He will be glorified.

Peter also maintains that this messianic message was for both the divine spokesmen's audience and the New Testament believers. Put another way, prophets wrote about the Messiah. The apostles identified Him to be Jesus. John makes it clear: "The testimony of Jesus is the spirit of prophecy" (Rv 19:10).

The Messiah appears regularly in the Minor Prophets. To employ a football analogy, He does not sit on the bench waiting for His fourth-quarter winning touchdown in the New Testament. No, in the Minor Prophets, the Messiah is the coach, manager, owner, and star player. He is marching purposefully toward His incarnation so that He can save the world.

THE MESSIAH AS ISRAEL'S BRIDEGROOM (HOSEA)

While the prophet Hosea is extremely critical of Israel's kings (e.g., Hos 8:4; 13:11), he has hope because of God's unconditional pledge to the house of David. After judgment falls upon Israel in 723 BC, God will reconstitute His people. "They shall appoint for themselves one head [*rosh*]" (Hos 1:11). The Hebrew word *rosh* in some contexts denotes "king."[135] In the Book of Judges, the term coin-

135 E.g., 2Sm 22:44; Is 11:16; Hos 2:15.

cides with "leader,"[136] while in 1 Samuel 15:17 and Job 29:25, *rosh* and "king" appear interchangeably. The Messiah will be a king—no doubt about it! Paul (1Tm 6:15) as well as John (Rv 17:14; 19:16) call him "the King of kings." This means God has made the Messiah the sovereign ruler in heaven and on earth.

Hosea clarifies this messianic hope: "Afterward the children of Israel shall return and seek the Lord their God, and David their king" (Hos 3:5). The prophet is referring to the final Davidic heir, who will reign on Israel's throne forever (2Sm 7:14–16). Hosea envisions the messianic era (e.g., Hos 6:1–3; 12:6, 9–10), which includes victory over the grave, death, plagues, and destruction (Hos 13:14). Jesus fulfills Hosea's hopes of a new David,[137] and His death is the death of death—along with pain, crying, mourning, and tears (Rv 21:4).

The New Testament likewise expands upon Hosea's understanding of Yahweh's marriage to Israel (Hos 1–2). The Messiah's relationship with His Church as that of a bridegroom and his bride (e.g., Eph 5:22–33). John the Baptist's role, therefore, was to lead the bride to her groom and rejoice in their successful union. "The bridegroom's voice"[138] is His triumphant shout indicating that He is united with His bride. The Baptist calls this his great joy (Jn 3:29b). In the Bible's final vision, John beholds the eschatological marriage between Christ and His Church (Rv 19:7–8; 21:2). "Blessed are those who are invited to the marriage supper of the Lamb" (Rv 19:9).

In Hosea 11:1, the prophet replaces the bridegroom/bride motif with that of father/son—appealing to Exodus 4:22, where God calls Israel His firstborn son. The Messiah is also firstborn— the firstborn of creation and the firstborn from among the dead (Col 1:15, 18).

136 E.g., Jgs 10:18; 11:8, 9, 11.

137 E.g., Mt 9:27; Mk 11:10; Lk 2:4; Rm 1:3.

138 Jn 3:29[a]: cf. Jer 7:34; 16:9; 25:10; Rv 18:23.

Little wonder, then, that His departure from Egypt as a child fulfills Hosea 11:1. Matthew writes, "[Joseph] remained there until the death of Herod. This was to fulfill what the Lord had spoken by the prophet, 'Out of Egypt I called My son'" (Mt 2:15).

RAISING UP DAVID'S BOOTH (AMOS)

It is significant that God's promise to Abraham and Sarah includes a line of kings (Gn 17:6, 16). By the end of Genesis, Moses clarifies that God chose the tribe of Judah to bear the coming royal Messiah, who will be like a conquering lion (Gn 49:8–12). Amos employs this messianic motif: "The LORD roars from Zion and utters His voice from Jerusalem" (Am 1:2). The prophet then lists six foreign nations that fall under divine judgment (Am 1:3–2:3)—all of which at one time had been a part of David's empire. This prepares us for Amos's last oracle; the rebirth of the Davidic dynasty that, once again, incorporates the nations (Am 9:11–12). The Lion will roar once again.

In the New Testament, the Jewish ruling council, along with Pharisees and scribes, did everything they could to cage the Lion—Jesus, the Messiah—but since they could not cage Him, they killed Him. And for three days, all the demons of hell thought they had won. But coming forth from the tomb, the Lion's fierce love roars on. "Behold, the Lion from the tribe of Judah, the Root of David, has conquered" (Rv 5:5).

Amos 1:2–9:10 burns and buries the world of power politics and phony religion as these were known in the prophet's day. Only after the killing message of the Law is the Gospel announced in Amos 9:11–15. Demolition is penultimate; salvation is ultimate. New life will burst forth, throbbing with hope. Yahweh has a plan for the entire created order, not just for Israel. The "remnant of Edom" will be restored (Am 9:12) and the mountains and hills will drip with new wine (Am 9:13). Much like the messianic promises in Isaiah 11:6–8 and Psalm 72:3, 16, 19, Amos links the golden age with creation's restoration. And, like several other Old Testament prophets, Amos peers into the future based upon messianic promises to the house of David. He quotes God as saying, "In that day I will raise up the booth of David that is fallen and repair its breaches, and raise up its ruins and rebuild it as in the days of old" (Am 9:11). Amos's use of the term "booth" implies David's house or dynasty (cf. 2Sm 7:12; Is 16:5).

The prophet Amos is pivotal to the convening of the Jerusalem Council in Acts 15. The council assembled to decide if Gentiles could be saved if they continued living as Gentiles. The issue at hand was articulated as follows: "Unless you are circumcised according to the custom of Moses, you cannot be saved" (Ac 15:1). Peter, Paul, and Barnabas testified that God confirmed the conversions of noncircumcised Gentiles by giving them the Holy Spirit—just as He had given this gift to the Jews. Salvation comes not by the "yoke" of intertestamental Jewish traditions but by the "grace of the Lord Jesus" (Ac 15:10–11).

James—the half-brother of Jesus—addressed the issue by invoking Amos 9:11–12. By means of these verses, James convinced the various sides of the debate that the Gentiles were included in the Davidic promise of an eternal kingdom, apart from circumcision. When God raised up the booth of David—that is, brought the Messiah back from the dead—the gift of salvation become available to "all the nations who are called by My name" (Am 9:12).

THE SIGN OF JONAH

Jonah is the only Old Testament prophet with whom the Messiah directly compares Himself. One "greater than Jonah is here" (Mt 12:41). This is a striking connection when we recall Jonah's flight to Tarshish (Jnh 1:3), his five-word (in Hebrew) sermon (Jnh 3:4), and his pity party at the end of the book (Jnh 4:1–11). Jonah pales in comparison to towering prophets like Elijah, Elisha, Isaiah, and Jeremiah. That both Jonah and Jesus were prophets from Galilee is suggestive, but this does not explain the significance of Jonah for Jesus. No, the real connection comes with the words "the sign of the prophet Jonah" (Mt 12:39).

The Messiah employs the word *sign* three times in Matthew 12:39. Here, it does not refer exclusively to Jonah's deliverance from the fish. When Jonah was swallowed, he—at the same time—received both God's judgment and salvation. When the Messiah referred to the sign of Jonah, He stated that He will likewise undergo judgment and salvation. The primary meaning of the "sign of the prophet Jonah," then, is the correspondence between Jonah's descent into Sheol and the Messiah's experience of death, especially when He—like Jonah—is "driven away from Yahweh's presence" (Jnh 2:4, authors' translation; cf. Mt 27:46).

The context of the Messiah's "sign of the prophet Jonah" saying raises a question over its common interpretation—that it refers only to Christ's resurrection. However, since Jesus is refusing to give a sign to this "evil and adulterous generation" (Mt 12:39), how likely is it that "the sign of the prophet Jonah" refers to His resurrection? Are we to understand that Jesus simply says, "No sign will be given to this generation, except a resurrection from the dead like Jonah's"? That would accede to His enemies' demands.

Three references confirm that the primary emphasis of "the sign of the prophet Jonah" is not the Messiah's resurrection. All three occur in contexts where Jesus is responding to opponents who ask Him for a "sign." In Matthew 12:38 and 16:1, the designations of the enquirers are "scribes and Pharisees" and "Pharisees and Sadducees," respectively. In Luke 11:16, the opposition of the questioners is indicated by a participle that could be rendered as the word "challenging."

To be sure, Matthew 12:40 implies the resurrection—not, however, simply as a miraculous wonder (as a "sign" in the Pharisee's sense of the word) but as deliverance from the experience of divine judgment. Jesus will be the one—so much more so than Jonah—whose cry to the Father from the depths of Sheol will be heard and answered. Like Jonah, the Messiah will be brought up from the pit (Jnh 2:3, 6).

In Luke 11:29–32, the "sign of Jonah" is different from Matthew's. In Luke, the expression denotes that Jonah himself is a sign to the Ninevites who repented at his preaching. Applied to the Messiah, the "sign of Jonah" here is that His preaching will bring many to repentance and faith—especially Gentiles. The Messiah's first sermon in Nazareth confirms this mission to Gentiles as He mentions Elijah's mission to Sidon as well as Elisha's mission to Naaman the Syrian (Lk 4:25–27). The "sign of Jonah" in Luke 11 is the power of the preached Word to move people—especially outsiders and the lost (see Lk 19:10)—to repentance and faith.

A RULER FROM BETHLEHEM (MICAH)

The Christmas carol "O Little Town of Bethlehem" comes from the prophet Micah. "But you, O Bethlehem Ephrathah, who are too little to be among the clans of Judah, one from you shall come forth for Me one who is to be ruler in Israel, whose coming forth is from of old, from ancient days" (Mi 5:2).

By Micah's time—the late eighth century BC—Bethlehem had long been associated with David. Boaz, who took Ruth for his wife, was from Bethlehem (Ru 2:4), and together, Boaz and Ruth made it their home (Ru 4:11–13). David—Ruth and Boaz's great-grandson—was born and raised in Bethlehem (1Sm 16:1; 17:12). When God sends the Messiah, He will choose David's birthplace, the little town of Bethlehem.

Micah was also from a small, out-of-the-way village—Moresheth (Mi 1:1). The prophet champions little places like Bethlehem ("too little to be among the clans of Judah"; Mi 5:2). Moresheth and Bethlehem, unlike the bustling capital city of Jerusalem, are places of divine favor. Because of its corruption, Jerusalem will become a heap of ruins (Mi 3:12).

Micah predicts that a ruler (*moshel*) will come forth from Bethlehem. First Kings 4:21 describes Solomon as a *moshel*—or ruler. Micah's messianic link with Solomon becomes stronger when we consider his oracle about the renewed Zion. There he says in part, "They shall sit every man under his vine and under his fig tree" (Mi 4:4). Compare these words with this description about Solomon's kingdom: "And Judah and Israel lived in safety, from Dan even to Beersheba, every man under his vine and his fig tree" (1Ki 4:25). It comes as no surprise, then, that the Messiah compares Himself with Solomon (Mt 12:42).

Micah's predicted "ruler in Israel"—the Messiah from the house and lineage of David—will come "from of old, from ancient days." The Messiah had a history before He arrived in history? His existence stretches back into eternity? He was planned before the creation of the world? Yes, yes, and yes!

This ruler—the Messiah—is one with the eternal God. The Nicene Creed puts it this way: Jesus is "God of God, Light of Light, very God of very God, begotten, not made, being of one substance with the Father." The Messiah is 100 percent, fully, actually, really *God.*

A new person did not come into existence when the Messiah was conceived and born. Instead, the Second Person of the Trinity took on flesh. He became incarnate. God took upon Himself a body. God slept and cried. God became hungry, thirsty, and tired. God felt disappointment, sorrow, hurt, and loneliness. We have seen that in the Old Testament, the Messiah occasionally took the *form* of a man. Conceived by the Holy Spirit and born of the Virgin Mary, He finally took the *flesh* of a man.

The Messiah did not change into flesh, morph into flesh, or transition into flesh. If He changed, morphed, or transitioned into flesh, He would no longer be God. But remaining what He was—God—the Messiah became what we are—flesh. Mary touched the hands that created the universe. Mary heard the voice that thundered, "Let there be light!" (Gn 1:3). Mary looked at the eyes that are all-seeing and all-knowing.

Micah has more to say about the Messiah. "He shall stand and shepherd His flock in the strength of the Lord, in the majesty of the name of the Lord His God" (Mi 5:4). In Micah 2:12–13, 4:6–8, and 7:14—much like the texts we looked at in Jeremiah and Ezekiel—the prophet employs shepherd/sheep imagery. These prophets drink deeply from 2 Samuel 7:7 and Psalm 78:70–72, passages describing David as a shepherd.

Micah, for his part, juxtaposes the Messiah's compassion as a shepherd with His strength as a mighty king. In the wilderness Yahweh attended to Israel's needs with this same mercy and might (cf. Dt 1:30–31), while the synthesis of tender and tough, personal and powerful occurs in other texts (e.g., Is 40:10–11). The Messiah is saving and sovereign. As true man, He demonstrates solidarity with the weak when He weeps, bleeds, and dies. As true God, He has authority over every evil that threatens His Church—including finally His defeat of death.

Matthew 2:5–6 announces that Micah's messianic prophecies point to Jesus. In doing so, the first evangelist adds a section from 2 Samuel 5:2 that refers to David: "You shall be shepherd of My people Israel." This cements the connection between Jesus and Israel's second and most famous king.

Yet Solomon is still in the picture. Matthew employs Micah's messianic prediction within the context of Magi bearing gifts for the newborn king (Mt 2:11). This reprises Solomon's international fame when the queen of Sheba brought Israel's monarch her costly treasures (1Ki 10:2, 10). The Solomonic psalm—Psalm 72—also envisions gifts for the Messiah coming from international locals (Ps 72:10–11, 15).

THE DIVINE WARRIOR (NAHUM)

The prophet Nahum foresees the downfall of Nineveh in 612 BC. He states his theme with these words: "The Lord is good, a stronghold in the day of trouble; He knows those who take refuge in Him. But with an overwhelming flood He will make a complete end of the adversaries, and will pursue His enemies into darkness" (Na 1:7–8). God does not step back from anyone who inflicts harm upon His people. He will fight for His own, in this case, by sending a massive flood of water.

The Book of Revelation announces that the Messiah also functions as the divine warrior. John writes, "I saw heaven opened, and behold, a white horse! The one sitting on it is called Faithful and True, and in righteousness He judges and makes war. . . . He is clothed in a robe dipped in blood, and the name by which He is called is The Word of God. . . . He will tread the winepress of the fury of the wrath of God the Almighty" (Rv 19:11, 13, 15). No stone in front of the tomb could hold back the Messiah's resurrection. And nothing is going to hold back His second coming to defeat evil and vindicate His elect. On the day when clouds no longer carry nourishing rains but rather bear the divine warrior and the thunder of His judgment, Satan and his minions will be thrown into the lake of fire (Rv 20:10).

No wonder Nahum launches his vision with a threefold emphasis on divine vengeance: "The Lord is a jealous and avenging God; the Lord is avenging and wrathful; the Lord takes vengeance on His adversaries" (Na 1:2). "Vengeance" does not denote a hostile spirit of revenge. Rather, it is action to thwart evil and restore creation to its original design. God has authorized the Messiah to rule the nations with an iron rod (Rv 19:15; cf. Ps 2:9), and at His second coming He will make all things new (Rv 21:5).

THE NEW TEMPLE (HAGGAI)

The people in Haggai's day were discouraged. When they began rebuilding the temple that the Babylonians had destroyed in 587 BC, it appeared to be a poor replacement for what had once been the nation's pride—Solomon's temple with all its glory (cf. 1Ki 6–8). The prophet asks, "Who is left among you who saw this house in its former glory? How do you see it now?" (Hg 2:3). Since Solomon's temple had been destroyed seventy years earlier (2Ki 24:8–9), few of the Judeans would have seen it. However, its reputation surely survived. The ruins had even become a site for pilgrimages (Jer 41:5). Haggai acknowledges the poor condition of the temple and then uses it as a stepping stone to promise its future glory. "The latter glory of this house shall be greater than the former" (Hg 2:9).

The Messiah is this new temple (Mt 12:5–6), for from Him radiates divine glory (Jn 1:14; Heb 1:3). Just as Israel's temple was resurrected in the days of Haggai, so Christ rose from the dead. Death has no more dominion over Him (cf. Jn 2:19–22; Rm 6:9).

At the end of his short, two-chapter book, Haggai addresses Zerubbabel, the governor of Judah who directed the temple's construction. God says through the prophet, "I am about to destroy the strength of the kingdoms of the nations, and overthrow the chariots and their riders" (Hg 2:22). The verb "overthrow" is employed in Genesis 19 to describe God's judgment of Sodom and Gomorrah (19:25, 29). When the Messiah comes, enemy thrones, kingdoms, chariots, and their riders will be dismantled and destroyed.

The prophet continues, "On that day, declares the LORD of hosts, I will take you, O Zerubbabel My servant, the son of Shealtiel, declares the LORD, and make you like a signet ring, for I have chosen you, declares the LORD of hosts" (Hg 2:23). God gave Zerubbabel a messianic title, "My servant." He is, therefore, a pattern of the coming Messiah, whom Isaiah frequently calls God's servant (e.g., 50:10; 52:13). A signet ring represented a king's throne or crown. When issuing decrees, commandments, and resolutions, the king would seal the scroll with clay or wax with the royal signet authenticating the message. How does this relate to the Messiah? The Father authenticates His presence through Jesus. When we see the Messiah, we see the Father (Jn 14:9). Small wonder, then, that Jesus says, "Do not work for the food that perishes, but for the food that endures to eternal life, which the Son of Man will give to you. For on Him God the Father has set His seal" (Jn 6:27).

THE PRIESTLY KING (ZECHARIAH)

The Book of Zechariah begins with eight visions that are intended to encourage God's people to complete the construction of the second temple. In the center of Zechariah's first vision (Zec 1:8–13) is a man riding on a red horse (Zec 1:8); he is the Lord's Messenger (Zec 1:11). He is Zec's constant companion throughout his eight visions.[139] The Man/Messenger is not a mere angel or divine apparition. His task throughout the visions is to explain and interpret God's actions and plans. This is how John explains the role of the Messiah—He interprets or explains the Father (Jn 1:18).

The Messenger/Messiah also intercedes for Israel: "O Lord of hosts, how long will You have no mercy on Jerusalem and the cities of Judah, against which You have been angry these seventy years?" (Zec 1:12). He likewise intercedes, shockingly, for the Roman soldiers crucifying Him: "Father, forgive them, for they know not what they do" (Lk 23:34). The Messiah's Spirit also intercedes for the baptized (Rm 8:26–27).

In Zechariah 3, the prophet envisions Satan accusing Judah's high priest, named Joshua. The Lord's Messenger—the preincarnate Messiah—advocates for the high priest to absolve him. "Behold, I have taken your iniquity away from you, and I will clothe you with pure vestments" (Zec 3:4). In this same chapter Zechariah calls the Messiah God's Servant and His Sprout/Branch (Zec 3:8). The term "Servant" derives from Isaiah's Servant Songs, in Isaiah 42, 49, 50, and 52–53, while "Sprout" is one of Jeremiah's names for the Messiah (Jer 23:5; 33:15). Additionally, Zechariah gives the coming Messiah the name "Stone." Messianic predictions employing the stone motif appear in Psalm 118:22; Isaiah 28:16; and Daniel 2:34. Peter picks up this motif, announcing that Jesus—the rejected Stone—has become the cornerstone through His resurrection from the dead (1Pt 2:4–8).

139 Zec 1:19; 2:3; 3:1, 5–6; 4:1, 4, 11; 5:2–3, 10; 6:4.

A PRIEST AND KING

Zechariah predicts that the Messiah will not only be the cornerstone for His Church; He will also be its builder. In Zechariah 6:9–15, the prophet employs the image of Solomon as a constructor and harbinger of peace. The "counsel of peace" (Zec 6:13) reflects this earlier promise: "In that day, declares the LORD of Hosts, every one of you will invite his neighbor to come under his vine and under his fig tree" (Zec 3:10). This verse, just like Micah 5:2, is a Solomonic link vis-à-vis the same description of his reign in 1 Kings 4:25. When the Messiah arrived, it is no coincidence that, within a heightened discussion on the Old Testament's messianic message (Jn 1:40–50), Jesus sees Nathanael sitting under a fig tree (Jn 1:48).

Within his vision of a messianically built new temple, Zechariah envisions two crowns—one for the high priest, Joshua, and one that foreshadows the coming messianic Sprout/Branch (Zec 6:11, 14). It is understandable, therefore, that the ancient Qumran community (connected with the Dead Sea Scrolls) expected two messiahs—one from the priestly line of Aaron and the other from David's royal line. The former would be sacred and the latter secular. The New Testament, however, announces that Jesus fulfills both the priestly and royal offices. The Magi worshiped the Messiah as King (Mt 2:1–12), and the writer of Hebrews understands Jesus as a priest according to the order of Melchizedek.[140] The fusion of these roles becomes most clear when the Messiah ascended into heaven to rule over all creation.[141]

---

140 Heb 7; cf. Gn 14:18–20; Ps 110:4.

141 Ac 2:23–36; Eph 4:8; 1Pt 3:22.

BEHOLD, YOUR KING COMES TO YOU

Zechariah's prediction of the Messiah's entry into Jerusalem on Palm Sunday is the prophet's best-known verse: "Rejoice greatly, O daughter of Zion! Shout aloud, O daughter of Jerusalem! Behold, your king is coming to you; righteous and having salvation is He, humble and mounted on a donkey, on a colt, the foal of a donkey" (Zec 9:9). When the term "righteous" appears in the context of "salvation," the latter gives the former a military meaning—conveying the ideas of "success" or "triumph." The Messiah is victorious over His enemies.

Zechariah also calls Him "humble." God called Israelite kings to be meek and lowly. "The king is not saved by his great army; a warrior will not be delivered by his great strength" (Ps 33:16). The Messiah's unpretentious demeanor comports with Isaiah's fourth Servant Song, as fifteen passive verbs describe the Messiah in Isaiah 52:13–53:13.

Note these additional similarities between Zechariah's messianic passages in chapters 9–14 and Isaiah's Servant Songs.

The Messiah

- blesses the nations (Zec 9:10; Is 42:6);
- releases captives (Zec 9:11–12; Is 42:7; 61:1);
- gathers exiles (Zec 9:11–12; Is 49:5–6);
- is struck (Zec 13:7; Is 53:4);
- is pierced (Zec 12:10; Is 53:5);
- is described using shepherd imagery (Zec 13:7–9; Is 53:6–7);
- is rejected (Zec 12:10; Is 53:3);

- suffers under Yahweh's direction (Zec 13:7; Is 53:6, 10);
- forgives (Zec 13:1; Is 53:5–6); and
- is mourned over (Zec 12:10–14; Is 53:4–12).

Zechariah 9:9 further describes the Messiah as "mounted on a donkey." Kings could ride on horses and use chariots in times of war (e.g., Jer 17:19–25) but they customarily rode male asses/donkeys in less combative situations (e.g., 2Sm 16:2). The Messiah places no confidence in military might. His hope is in Yahweh, who says, "I will cut off the chariot from Ephraim and the war horse from Jerusalem; and the battle bow shall be cut off" (Zec 9:10).

Matthew 21:5 and John 12:15 cite Zechariah 9:9 in their Palm Sunday narratives. It is surprising, however, that Matthew omits the phrase "righteous and having salvation." Both words appear frequently in the first Gospel, seventeen and fifteen times, respectively. By leaving them out here, Matthew places the emphasis on the Messiah's humility—a concept that elsewhere appears in the New Testament only in Matthew 5:5, 11:29, and 1 Peter 3:4.

Like Matthew in his Palm Sunday narrative, John does not mention Zechariah by name. He introduces his quote with "just as it is written" (Jn 12:14). Also like Matthew, John excludes the phrase, "Rejoice greatly, O daughter of Zion! Shout aloud, O daughter of Jerusalem!" (Zec 9:9). The fourth evangelist writes, "Fear not, daughter of Zion; behold, your king is coming, sitting on a donkey's colt!" (Jn 12:15). In all likelihood, John is alluding to Zephaniah 3:15–17. These verses announce, "The King of Israel, Yahweh, is among you" (Zep 3:15, authors' translation), "fear not, O Zion" (Zep 3:16), and "Yahweh your God is among you, mighty to save" (Zep 3:17, authors' translation). Notice that John's Palm Sunday crowd acclaimed Christ with the title "the King of Israel/the Jews" (Jn 12:13)—a title for the Messiah that appears frequently in the fourth Gospel.[142] John's emphasis on the Messiah's reign as well as His deity (e.g., Jn 1:1, 14; 8:58) suggests he wants us to recognize that, as the Messiah rides into Jerusalem on a donkey, He is both the Davidic king and God present to save His people.

Zechariah 9:9–10 shares these words with Psalm 72—a major messianic psalm: "king" (Ps 72:1, 10–11); "righteous" (Ps 72:7); "save/deliver" (Ps 72:4, 13); "poor/humble" (Ps 72:2, 4, 12); "peace/prosperity" (Ps 72:3, 7); and "nations" (Ps 72:11, 17).

THIRTY PIECES OF SILVER

Zechariah 11 is a retrospective view of Israel and Judah's monarchial history and provides the rationale for the judgment and salvation oracles delivered in chapters 9–14. Zechariah 11 not only looks back upon the demise of Israel and Judah but even more so points forward to the Messiah's ministry.

Matthew, therefore, interprets Zechariah 11:4–17 as predictive prophecy pointing to Jesus. Zechariah's clash between God and false shepherds gets transposed into a higher key, lived out through the Messiah. The disciples rejected Jesus when He was arrested (Mt 26:56), and Peter disowned Him (Mt 26:69–75). However, the most significant betrayal came when Judas handed Jesus over to the Jewish authorities for thirty pieces of silver. Matthew concludes his description of Judas's remorse and subsequent suicide (Mt 27:9–10) by citing Zechariah 11:12–13—albeit with several modifications, since the prophet does not mention a potter's field, an idea that derives from Jeremiah 19:1–13 and 32:6–9.

By quoting from Zechariah 11:13 to describe the Messiah's

142 Jn 1:49; 6:15; 18:33, 37, 39; 19:3, 12, 14, 15, 19, 21.

betrayal by Judas (Mt 27:9), the first evangelist invites us to interpret Zechariah 11 not only as God's judgment against Northern and Southern kings but also as divine condemnation of the Jewish leaders who arrested, tried, and pressured Pilate to have the Messiah crucified. The Sanhedrin (Jewish Council) are the fallen trees and evil shepherds whom the prophet targets with a sarcastic taunt (Zec 11:1–3). They are the blind guides (e.g., Mt 23:16, 24) who slaughter the flock (Zec 11:4–5). "If the blind lead the blind, both will fall into a pit" (Mt 15:14). God's judgment against the flock (Zec 11:6) portends the events in Jerusalem in AD 70 (e.g., Mt 24:2). Some, however, believed. Zechariah calls them the faithful remnant who became the church (Zec 11:7, 11). The Messiah did all He could to save the flock (Zec 11:7)—but most rejected Him (Mt 23:37). They detested the shepherd (Zec 11:8) and so the covenant was broken (Zec 11:10–11, 14). "The kingdom of God will be taken away from you and given to a people producing its fruit" (Mt 21:43). Zechariah 11, therefore, recapitulates monarchial Israel as well as the Messiah's ministry.

PIERCED

The amazing messianic predictions throughout Zechariah come to fruition with the vision of the Messiah's death—making Zechariah 12:10 one of the most profound passages in the book. We need to set this text in its messianic context. "David" is mentioned fifteen times in Jeremiah, ten times in Isaiah, four times in Ezekiel, twice in Amos, once in Hosea, but six times in Zechariah 12:7–13:1, where the Messiah—who is also God—is pierced and killed.

Should we be surprised that Zechariah says that God suffers and dies? When God saw evil and misery multiply, He grieved with heart-piercing sorrow (Gn 6:6). When He saw Israel's suffering in Egypt, He came down into the burning bush, saying, "I know their sufferings" (Ex 3:7). Yahweh is the only one in Isaiah's book who is "high and lifted up."[143] What a mystery it is, therefore, that Isaiah describes the Servant-Messiah with the same words, "high and lifted up" (Is 52:13). That is because Yahweh and the Servant-Messiah are one (cf. Jn 10:30).

The implications are overwhelming. The Messiah, as God, made the tree from which His cross was carved. The Messiah, as God, made the minerals from which His nails were forged. The Messiah, as God, made the woman whose son was Judas Iscariot. The Messiah, as God, set in motion the political events that sent Pontius Pilate to Judea, Herod to Jerusalem, and Caiaphas to serve as high priest.

God hung on a cross and was pierced with a spear? A split-lipped, puffy-eyed, blood-caked God on a cross? A sponge was thrust into God's face? Dice tossed at God's feet? God bled? God took nails? Yes. Yes. A thousand times, and forever, yes.

God even empowers us to look upon the Pierced One. "I will pour out my Spirit of grace and prayer" (Zec 12:10, authors' translation). In the Old Testament, Yahweh normally pours out His Spirit upon one person at a time—for instance, Balaam (Nu 24:2), Saul (1Sm 10:10), Asa (2Ch 15:1), Jahaziel (2Ch 20:14), Micah (Mi 3:8), and Ezekiel (Ezk 11:5). Yet in Zechariah 12:10, Yahweh pours out His Holy Spirit upon the entire community (cf. Jl 2:28).

John 19:37 quotes Zechariah 12:10, making it clear that the faithful will continue to "look on Him whom they have pierced." John also quotes from Zechariah 12:10 in Revelation 1:7: "Every eye will see Him, even those who pierced Him." At that time, "all the tribes of the earth will wail on account of Him" (Rv 1:7). Note the massive amount of mourning and lamenting for the Messiah in Zechariah 12:11–14.

143 Is 6:1; 33:10; 57:15.

Zechariah 12:10 concludes with these words: "They shall mourn for Him, as one mourns for an only child, and weep bitterly over Him, as one weeps over a firstborn." The Messiah is not only the firstborn of creation (Col 1:15) but also "the firstborn from the dead" (Col 1:18). But what about the child Elisha raised from the dead? Or Jairus's daughter? Or the widow of Nain's son? Or Lazarus? Weren't there several people who were raised from the dead before Jesus? Yes. Their bodies were temporarily resuscitated, but each eventually died. Jesus, on the other hand, rose from the dead in an immortal body never to die again. "Death no longer has dominion over Him" (Rm 6:9).

STRIKE THE SHEPHERD

Zechariah 13:7 begins with these words: "Awake, O sword, against My shepherd." Which shepherd does the sword strike? One of the false shepherds in Zechariah 11:4–15? Or the foolish shepherd of Zechariah 11:17? Neither. Instead, Yahweh commands the sword to strike the shepherd who is also His close associate. "Awake, O sword, against my shepherd, against the man who is my close associate" (Zec 13:7, authors' translation). The term "close associate" appears again only in the Book of Leviticus,[144] where it is frequently translated "neighbor" or "one another" (e.g., CSB, ESV, NIV, and NASB). Yahweh and His Shepherd/Close Associate—who is also the Messiah—stand side by side. They are equals. It is remarkable that such an exalted a figure should be struck down, and indeed, by the sword of God Himself!

If the thought of parents piercing their own son shocks us (Zec 13:3), the bombshell becomes a massive earthquake when we consider that, unlike the son who became a false prophet in Zechariah 13:3, this Shepherd/Close Associate had done nothing wrong. The

144 Lv 6:2; 18:20; 19:11, 15, 16; 24:19; 25:14, 15, 17.

great irony is that Yahweh commanded the sword to strike a person who is not only completely innocent and holy but also stands closest to Him. The Messiah will be killed in accordance with the will of God declared in the Scriptures. Isaiah concurs. "It was Yahweh's will to crush him" (Is 53:10, authors' translation).

THE SUN OF RIGHTEOUSNESS (MALACHI)

In about 450 BC, believers living in the Persian province of Yehud were losing hope. They asked, "Where is the God of justice?" (Mal 2:17). Malachi responded with an oracle that predicted the Messiah's advent: "Behold, I send My messenger, and e will prepare the way before Me. And the Lord whom you seek will suddenly come to His temple; and the messenger of the covenant in whom you delight, behold, He is coming, says the LORD of hosts" (Mal 3:1). This verse begs for some clarifying comments. John the Baptist is "My messenger," while the Messiah is "the Lord whom you seek" as well as "the messenger of the covenant."

Jesus refers to John the Baptist as Malachi's first messenger and therefore Elijah (Mt 11:10, 14; cf. Mal 4:5). Furthermore, the Messiah's role as initiator of the new covenant (cf. Jer 31:31–34) becomes clear on the night He was betrayed and gave His Church the gift of Holy Communion (e.g., Lk 22:20; 1Co 11:25).

Malachi ends his book with a vision of the Messiah's grand finale—His second coming: "The sun of righteousness shall rise with healing in its wings. You shall go out leaping like calves from the stall" (Mal 4:2). The Sun of Righteousness will bring with Him the eternal day, when every hint of darkness will be scattered, all gloom will be gone, and the night of terror and dread will be forever banished. On that day, our righteous standing, by faith, will become clear—just like the shining sun in all its brightness and beauty. The Messiah will also bring healing in His wings. He will restore everything we have lost. All the years of pain will be erased, every tear of disappointment will be wiped away, and the symphonies we missed and sunsets we did not see will be beautifully played over again and again. We will playfully jump like calves released from the stall. What joy! What exuberance! What freedom! We will no longer be confined by age, decay, or even death. It is fitting that Malachi, in the last book in the Old Testament, ends his prophecy with such a compelling vision of the Last Day—the Messiah's triumphant return.

THE MINOR PROPHETS' MESSIAH: HIS ORIGIN, IDENTITY, AND WORK

Although the Minor Prophets are books full of plots and subplots, twists and turns, and highs and lows; although their books consist of a marriage gone sour (Hosea) and a man swallowed by a fish (Jonah), this section of the Old Testament contains one unified story line—the Messiah is coming to restore all things.

The prophets Hosea through Malachi tell us where the Messiah will come from, what He will be like, and how He will suffer, die, and rise again. If we read these books carefully—along with the rest of the Old Testament—when we get to the New Testament, we will know what to expect.

In a whole new light, *we will see Jesus.*

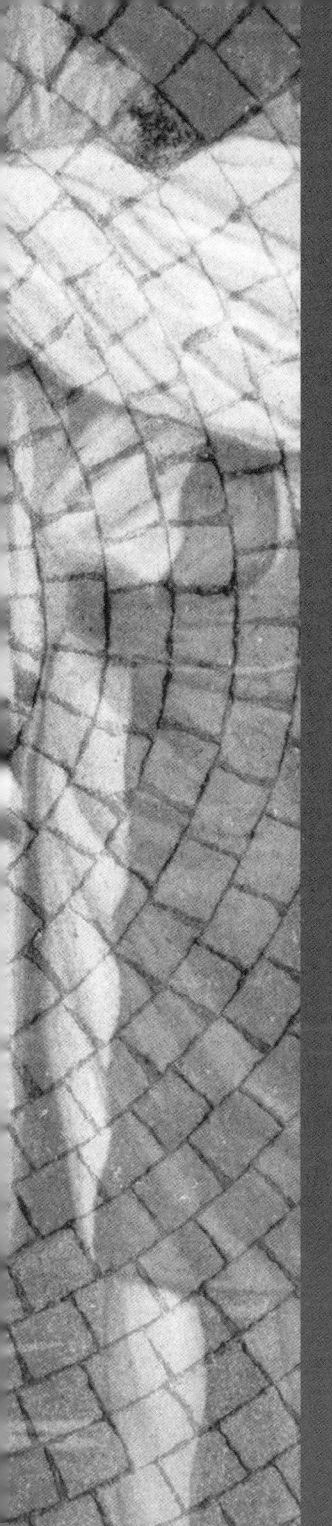

CHAPTER 10

THE BIBLE'S MESSIANIC MESSAGE

When you peruse the books in a library or a bookstore, you expect that they are shelved in sections by types of literature. All of the self-help books are in one place and all of the mysteries in another. Travel books are not mixed in with the biographies, nor are histories scattered among the computer and technology books. This arrangement is useful for library users or bookstore patrons, but it also has a downside: one does not often look for connections and commonalities among the various types of literature.

It is perhaps too easy also to view the collection of books in the Bible this way. It consists of two Testaments. The Old Testament is grouped in four divisions: Pentateuch, Books of History, Wisdom and Poetry, and Prophetic Books. They look like books on the shelves of the library—all arranged in categories. Yet there are some things that tie these books together for even the most casual reader: God and His people Israel are important characters in nearly every book. Israel's sin and God's grace are constant themes virtually everywhere we look. However, we have presented you with what we believe is an even more important thread that binds these biblical books together: the message about the Messiah. Let's review what the Old Testament tells us about Israel's messianic hope.

THE PENTATEUCH: MOSES LAYS THE MESSIANIC FOUNDATION

Genesis leads off the Pentateuch perhaps as the most intensely messianic book of the Old Testament. Here we see not only God's words directly referencing the promised Messiah not only as He speaks to Eve, Abraham, Isaac, and Jacob but also in prophecies uttered by Noah and Jacob. We meet the mysterious figure of the Messenger of the Lord who will appear not only in Moses' first book but subsequently in later books of the Pentateuch, the Books of History, and even the Prophets. A careful reading of these passages reveals that this is no ordinary messenger but a manifestation of God Himself—the Messiah appearing to humans before He later assumed human flesh and was born of the virgin mother, Mary. We also saw that Moses presents to us people whose lives, though imperfect and sinful, have aspects that parallel the work of the coming Savior. These include Noah, Melchizedek, and Joseph.

In the rest of the books of Moses, the messianic theme of Genesis is developed further. Balaam recycles some of the prophetic language from Genesis as he points to the Messiah as a star from Jacob whom he sees "but not near," whom he beholds "but not now." Moses speaks of a great prophet—one like himself—to whom Israel is to listen when God sends Him. The entire worship system of Israel, including the tabernacle, the various sacrifices, and the yearly festivals continually taught Israel about aspects of the coming Messiah's character, life, and ministry. Once again, the Savior appeared to His people before His incarnation not only as the Messenger of the Lord but also as the cloudy pillar and the rock that followed them in the wilderness.

Reading the Pentateuch correctly is not simply about learning Sunday School stories concerning Israel and its great ancestors. It is also an exercise in learning that God was working through Israel for a greater purpose than simply favoring one ethnic group over all others. He was working through them to bring blessings to all the families of the earth. The heavenly Father was patiently enduring their rebellion so that through them He could bring into the world the great deliverer from sin, death, and Satan. This means that wherever we choose to read in the Pentateuch, whether it be the narratives, the genealogies, or the laws delivered to Moses, we ought to be looking for messianic predictions, patterns, and presence as well as for the ways that these elements serve to connect God to Israel's great Son, the Son of God who would come in the flesh.

HISTORY FOR MORE THAN HISTORY'S SAKE: A CHRONICLE THAT CLIMAXES IN JESUS

The Old Testament's Books of History continue the messianic trajectory of the Pentateuch. Here, further prophecies build on previous ones: Hannah's Song of a messianic king, an anonymous prophet who speaks of a faithful priest to come, and Nathan's dramatic words to David, promising to establish an eternal kingdom ruled by David's descendant. Like the Pentateuch, the Books of History contain genealogies, and one of them—the line of David as outlined at the end of Ruth—continues the Messiah's genealogy that will eventually be embedded in the Gospels of Matthew and Luke. Once again, the Messiah makes appearances to Israelites. He is seen by Joshua as the Commander of the Lord's Army and by Gideon, David, and Elijah as the Messenger of the Lord.

When we read the Old Testament's historical books, we read them properly only when we read them as a record of God's determination to break into history in the person of Jesus Christ. The sins of Israel cannot derail God's work to love the world through His Son. The historical books teach us that all that happened in ancient Israel among its judges, kings, priests, prophets, and leaders was for the sake of the promised salvation through the Messiah, whose day was nearing as the story progressed through time.

POETRY AND WISDOM: SINGING THE MESSIANIC SONG

In the Wisdom Literature of the Old Testament, we see pictures of the Messiah that are familiar to us from the New Testament: an intercessor, God's Wisdom, a shepherd, and the Church's beloved. All of these anticipated aspects of Jesus and His ministry. In fact, whenever we read the Books of Wisdom and Poetry, we find the wisdom of Jesus and much of His teaching as related in the Gospels is reflected there.

In Psalms, we find a special emphasis on Jesus as the fulfillment of God's promise to David of an eternal kingdom. Several psalms speak of various facets of the Messiah as the great king from David's line. However, the psalms also speak of the Savior as one who suffers and as the Priest who offers the ultimate sacrifice. The psalms teach us that God's ancient people Israel not only praised God for what He had done for them in the past but also worshiped and adored Him for what He would accomplish through the Messiah as they looked forward in time.

THE PROPHETS: SPEAKING ABOUT THE SAVIOR TO COME

When we read the prophets, we not only are confronted with stern warnings to an errant Israel. We also read of God reaching out to His people in order to call them back to Him for forgiveness and life. An important aspect of that prophetic message was prophecy about the Messiah. Isaiah is saturated with passages that paint a virtual biography of Jesus centuries before His birth. Jeremiah, Ezekiel, and Daniel relate their visions of the Savior and His kingdom of grace. The Minor Prophets are peppered with images that cover His entire life and ministry, from His birth in Bethlehem to His suffering and resurrection. The prophets even point us beyond our time to Jesus' final return in glory.

While not every passage in the Prophets is directly about the Messiah, the prophets invite us to read their messages to Israel as calls for our repentance in light of God's promises of grace, forgiveness, and life in Christ Jesus. The messianic prophecies are not sidelights or foreign intrusions into the prophets' preaching. Instead, their pictures of the Redeemer are at the center of their communication to Israel and to us.

VIEWING THE OLD TESTAMENT AS THE NEW TESTAMENT DOES: SEEING THE HOPE OF ISRAEL FULFILLED IN JESUS

Perhaps the words of Balaam the Moabite prophet best summarizes the gist of our book: "I see Him, but not now; I behold Him, but not near: a star shall come out of Jacob, and a scepter shall rise out of Israel" (Nu 24:17). Balaam sees the Messiah—Israel's scepter-wielding king—but only from a distance. Yes, the Messiah will be like a bright shining star. Yes, He will come from Israel, the nation God promised to Abraham. And yes, the Messiah will defeat and thoroughly rout His enemies. That much we know. Yet even by the time we get to the end of the Old Testament, the details still are not crystal clear.

We might liken the Old Testament, then, to a sonogram. Sonograms give us a general idea of what a child looks like, but there are still so many unknowns. What's the color of her hair? Her eyes? What shape is his nose? Does he look more like his mother or his father?

God's Word from Moses to Malachi is a sonogram of sorts. We see general shapes and sizes. But we're still looking at shadows: black and white, without any color—yet. Then, at just the right time, it happened! You remember. On an ordinary night there were some ordinary shepherds with some ordinary sheep. But God loves to place an "extra" in front of ordinary, and that night He painted an extraordinary masterpiece.

The black sky exploded with brightness. Trees lurking in the dark jumped into clarity. Silent sheep became a chorus of curiosity. Angel choirs belted out their good news of great joy. And Mary and Joseph wondered in absolute amazement.

A baby was born. Yet He was no ordinary child. He was, and still is, the Messiah—Israel's long-awaited Davidic king who would crush the serpent's head. Little wonder that Balaam's hesitant "I see Him, but not now" in Numbers 24:17 transitions to the full-throated cry in Hebrews 2:9, "But we see Him [Jesus]!"

Seeing Jesus. That's our greatest joy, and that's why we wrote this book. In our first chapter, we presented the New Testament's view of the Old Testament as a thoroughly messianic collection of God-inspired words from His sages and prophets. We cataloged how the Gospels, Acts, Paul's Letters, and Revelation all make use of the Old Testament to demonstrate that Jesus is the Messiah, the Christ, of whom Moses and the prophets speak. We made the case that the New Testament invites us to read the Old Testament with eyes ready to see Jesus.

Subsequent chapters in our book pointed out messianic patterns, predictions, and His presence in Israel's sacred history. And what a history it is! Leah and Rachel. Joshua and Caleb. David and Goliath. Ezra and Nehemiah. There are so many stories, so many poems, so very many words!

God's Word called Abraham from Ur in the land of the Chaldeans, spoke to Moses from a burning bush, gave manna and quail in the wilderness, thundered from Sinai, and spoke to Elijah in a still, small voice. God's Word even made dry bones come to life—standing on their feet, a vast army! Just ask Ezekiel! God said it. That settles it. Faith believes it! We have His Word! And what an awesome Word it is.

It all points to John 1:14: "The Word became flesh and dwelt among us, and we have seen His glory, glory as of the only Son from the Father, full of grace and truth."

John doesn't say, "We glanced. We glimpsed." John doesn't say, "We previewed. We peeked." John doesn't stand at the back of the room or listen to someone describe Jesus. John pulls out his bifocals and his binoculars. John gets out his telescope and his microscope. John focuses and fixes his eyes. John *sees* Jesus.

Jesus. The Prophet from Galilee who spoke with such thunderous authority and who loved with such childlike humility. Jesus. The one who claimed to be older than time and greater than death. Jesus. The Alpha and the Omega. The King of kings and the Lord of lords. The Lion of the tribe of Judah. All the splendor of God revealed in a human body. The doors to the throne room were open and God came near. *Jesus!*

Changing weather patterns don't faze Him. Contested elections don't rattle Him. Pandemics don't worry Him. Problems don't shock Him. And death will never defeat Him. *Death will never defeat Jesus.*

Because we have no power to face the problems, we are told to look to Him (Heb 12). Because shame and sadness can overwhelm us, we want to see Jesus. When you're overwhelmed with shame and sadness, it's time to take a look. When you need a Savior from sin, a Friend who loves at all times, and a Redeemer who restores and renews, it's time to open your Old Testament again and join the faithful in saying . . . in saying what? "We have *seen* His glory!" (Jn 1:14).

HOW TO READ THE OLD TESTAMENT FOR ITS MESSIANIC MESSAGE

We believe that reading the Old Testament messianically is not something that is foreign to the pages of Moses and the Prophets, but how those ancient documents were intended to be understood. To read the Old Testament properly, we must see the Messiah at the heart of those divinely inspired books.

We offer these principles to guide you in your study of the Old Testament:

When the New Testament uses words, phrases, or images from the Old Testament to demonstrate that Jesus is the promised Savior, look closely at those Old Testament passages and their context to learn how God was teaching the Israelites about the Savior.

When reading the Old Testament, even in passages that are not speaking directly about the Messiah, always look for how the message relates to God's work of salvation through the Savior and how God wished to use that message to bring Israel closer to Him.

Understand that the Old Testament is looking at the Messiah from a different perspective than the New Testament. The Old

Testament is looking *forward in time* to the Messiah, who will come in the future—a future that is centuries away from even the latest of the Old Testament books. In contrast, the New Testament is looking *backward in time* to the work of Jesus in His life, death, and ministry. Simultaneously, it is urging readers to live in faith that trusts what Jesus not only did for our salvation but also will do for us when He comes again with the resurrection of all humans to establish His eternal kingdom.

With these three simple principles in mind, you will be able to better understand the love of God the Father, who sent His Son, Jesus, the Messiah. You, too, will see how the Old Testament points to Jesus every time you study the words of Israel's inspired prophets and sages.

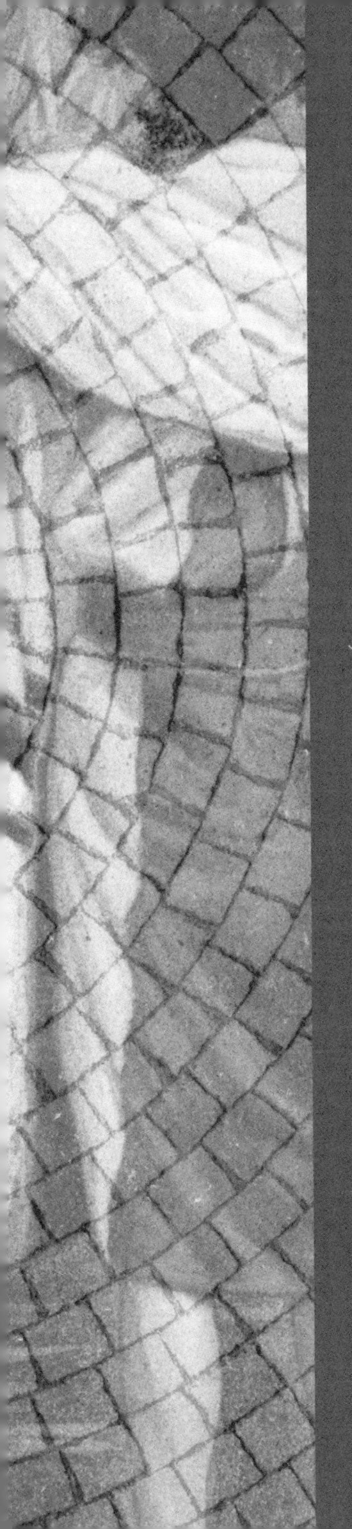

FOR FURTHER READING

GENERAL WORKS

Alexander, T. Desmond. *The Servant King: The Bible's Portrait of the Messiah*. Vancouver: Regent College Publishing, 2003.

Bateman, Herbert W. IV, Darrell L. Bock, and Gordon H. Johnston. *Jesus the Messiah: Tracing the Promises, Expectations, and Coming of Israel's King*. Grand Rapids, MI: Kregel, 2012.

Kaiser, Walter C. *The Messiah in the Old Testament*. Studies in Old Testament Biblical Theology. Grand Rapids, MI: Kregel, 1995.

Lessing, R. Reed, and Andrew E. Steinmann, *Prepare the Way of the Lord: An Introduction to the Old Testament*. St. Louis: Concordia Publishing House, 2013.

Murray, David. *Jesus on Every Page: Ten Simple Ways to Seek and Find Christ in the Old Testament*. Nashville: Thomas Nelson, 2013.

Nauman, Martin. *Messianic Mountaintops*. Concordia Seminary Monograph Series 2. Springfield, IL: Concordia Theological Seminary, 1975.

Rydelnik, Michael. *The Messianic Hope: Is the Hebrew Bible Really Messianic?* NAC Studies in Bible and Theology. Nashville: B&H Publishing Group, 2010.

Rydelnik, Michael, and Edwin Blum, eds. *The Moody Handbook of Messianic Prophecy: Studies and Expositions of the Messiah in the Old Testament*. Chicago: Moody Publishers, 2019.

Van Groningen, Gerard. *Messianic Revelation in the Old Testament*. Grand Rapids, MI: Baker, 1990.

Williamson, Paul R., and Rita F. Cefalu, eds. *The Seed of the Promise: The Sufferings and Glory of the Messiah: Essays in Honor of T. Desmond Alexander*. GlossaHouse Festschrift Series 3. Wilmore, KY: GlossaHouse, 2020.

CHAPTER 1: THE MESSIANIC EMPHASIS OF THE NEW TESTAMENT

Abernethy, Andrew T., and Gregory Goswell. *God's Messiah in the Old Testament: Expectations of a Coming King*. Grand Rapids, MI: Baker, 2020.

Bird, Michael F. *Jesus Is the Christ: The Messianic Testimony of the Gospels*. Milton Keynes, England: Paternoster, 2012.

France, R. T. *Jesus and the Old Testament: His Application of Old Testament Passages to Himself and His Mission*. London: Tyndale Press, 1971.

Jipp, Joshua W. *Christ Is King: Paul's Royal Ideology*. Minneapolis: Fortress Press, 2015.

Murray, David. *Jesus on Every Page: Ten Simple Ways to Seek and Find Christ in the Old Testament*. Nashville: Thomas Nelson, 2013.

Wright, Christopher. *Knowing Jesus through the Old Testament*. 2nd ed. Downers Grove, IL: InterVarsity Press, 2014.

CHAPTER 2: THE MESSIANIC FOCUS IN GENESIS

Alexander, T. Desmond. "Further Observations on the Term 'Seed' in Genesis." *Tyndale Bulletin* 48 (1997): 364–65.

———. "Genesis 12:1–3; 22:16–18: The Covenant with Abraham." In *The Moody Handbook of Messianic Prophecy*, edited by Michael Rydelnik and Edwin Blum, 259–70. Chicago: Moody Publishers, 2019.

Collins, C. John. "Galatians 3:16: What Kind of Exegete Was Paul?" *Tyndale Bulletin* 54 (2003): 80–86.

Hamilton, James M., Jr. "The Skull Crushing Seed of the Woman: Inner-Biblical Interpretation of Genesis 3:15." In *The Seed of Promise: The Sufferings and Glory of the Messiah*, edited by Paul R. Williamson and Rita F. Cefalu, 3–34. Wilmore, KY: GlossaHouse, 2020. First published in *The Southern Baptist Journal of Theology* 10.2 (2006): 30–54.

Köstenberger, Andreas J. "The Cosmic Drama and the Seed of the Serpent: An Exploration of the Connection between Genesis 3:15 and Johannine Theology." In *The Seed of Promise: The Sufferings and Glory of the Messiah*, edited by Paul R. Williamson and Rita F. Cefalu, 264–84. Wilmore, KY: GlossaHouse, 2020.

Lee, Chee-Chiew. "Once Again: The Niphal and the Hithpael of *brk* in the Abrahamic Blessing for the Nations." *Journal for the Study of the Old Testament* 36 (2012): 279–96.

Merrill, Eugene H. "Genesis 49:8–12: The Lion of Judah." In *The Moody Handbook of Messianic Prophecy*, edited by Michael Rydelnik and Edwin Blum, 271–84. Chicago: Moody Publishers, 2019.

Postell, Seth D. "Genesis 3:15: The Promised Seed." In *The Moody Handbook of Messianic Prophecy*, edited by Michael Rydelnik and Edwin Blum, 239–50. Chicago: Moody Publishers, 2019.

Steinmann, Andrew E. *Genesis: An Introduction and Commentary.* Tyndale Old Testament Commentary. London: InterVarsity; Downers Grove, IL: InterVarsity, 2019.

———. "Jesus and Possessing the Enemies' Gate (Genesis 22:17–18; 24:60)." *Bibliotheca Sacra* 174 (2017): 13–21.

Varner, William C. "Genesis 9:25–27: The Promise through Noah." In *The Moody Handbook of Messianic Prophecy*, edited by Michael Rydelnik and Edwin Blum, 251–58. Chicago: Moody Publishers, 2019.

CHAPTER 3: THE MESSIANIC THRUST OF EXODUS

Gordley, Matthew E. "Seeing Stars at Qumran: The Interpretation of Balaam and His Oracle in the Damascus Document and Other Qumran Texts." *Proceedings of the Eastern Great Lakes and Midwest Bible Societies* 25 (2005): 107–19.

Guyot, Gilmore Henry. "The Prophecy of Balaam." *The Catholic Biblical Quarterly* 2 (1940): 330–40.

Montgomery, John Warwick. "Old Testament Sacrifice." In *Chytraeus on Sacrifice: A Reformation Treatise in Biblical Theology*, 43–75. St. Louis: Concordia Publishing House, 1962.

Postell, Seth D. "Numbers 24:5–9, 15–19: The Distant Star." In *The Moody Handbook of Messianic Prophecy*, edited by Michael Rydelnik and Edwin Blum, 285–308. Chicago: Moody Publishers, 2019.

CHAPTER 4: THE MESSIANIC THREAD IN THE HISTORICAL BOOKS

Coakley, James F. "1 Samuel 2:1–10, 35: Hannah's Song of the Messianic King." In *The Moody Handbook of Messianic Prophecy*, edited by Michael Rydelnik and Edwin Blum, 361–71. Chicago: Moody Publishers, 2019.

McKeown, James. "Messianic Trajectories in Ruth: A Redeemer and a Great Name." In *The Seed of Promise: The Sufferings and Glory of the Messiah*, edited by Paul R. Williamson and Rita F. Cefalu, 74–89. Wilmore, KY: GlossaHouse, 2020.

Steinmann, Andrew E. *1 Samuel.* Concordia Commentary. St. Louis: Concordia Publishing House, 2016.

———. *2 Samuel.* Concordia Commentary. St. Louis: Concordia Publishing House, 2016.

———. "Genesis Genealogies and the Messianic Promise." *Bibliotheca Sacra* 176 (2019): 343–59.

———. "The Role of the Philistines in the Establishment of the Israelite Monarchy." *Journal of Biblical and Theological Studies* 4 (2019): 42–54.

———. "What Did David Understand about the Promises in the Davidic Covenant?" *Bibliotheca Sacra* 171 (2014): 19–29.

CHAPTER 5: THE MESSIANIC SIDE OF THE WISDOM BOOKS

Steinmann, Andrew E. *Proverbs.* Concordia Commentary. St. Louis: Concordia Publishing House, 2009.

Waters, Larry J. "Job 19:23–27: A Living Redeemer." In *The Moody Handbook of Messianic Prophecy*, edited by Michael Rydelnik and Edwin Blum, 437–49. Chicago: Moody Publishers, 2019.

CHAPTER 6: THE MESSIANIC PSALMS OF ISRAEL

Bullock, C. Hassel. *Encountering the Book of Psalms.* Grand Rapids, MI: Baker, 2001.

Cole, Robert L. "Psalms 1–2: The Divine Son of God." In *The Moody Handbook of Messianic Prophecy*, edited by Michael Rydelnik and Edwin Blum, 477–90. Chicago: Moody Publishers, 2019.

———. "Psalm 22: The Suffering of the Messianic King." In *The Moody Handbook of Messianic Prophecy*, edited by Michael Rydelnik and Edwin Blum, 529–42. Chicago: Moody Publishers, 2019.

Creach, Jerome F. D. *The Destiny of the Righteous in the Psalms.* St. Louis: Chalice, 2008.

Firth, David, and Philip S. Johnston, eds. *Interpreting the Psalms: Issues and Approaches.* Downers Grove, IL: InterVarsity, 2005.

LaRondelle, Hans K. *Deliverance in the Psalms: Messages of Hope for Today.* Berrien Springs, MI: First Impressions, 1983.

McKinnon, Randall L. "Psalm 69: The Lament of the Messiah." In *The Moody Handbook of Messianic Prophecy*, edited by Michael Rydelnik and Edwin Blum, 591–603. Chicago: Moody Publishers, 2019.

Merrill, Eugene H. "Psalm 89: God's Faithful Promise of Messiah." In *The Moody Handbook of Messianic Prophecy*, edited by Michael Rydelnik and Edwin Blum, 631–43. Chicago: Moody Publishers, 2019.

Postell, Seth D. "Psalm 16: The Resurrected Messiah." In *The Moody Handbook of Messianic Prophecy*, edited by Michael Rydelnik and Edwin Blum, 513–27. Chicago: Moody Publishers, 2019.

———. "Psalm 45: The Messiah as Bridegroom." In *The Moody Handbook of Messianic Prophecy*, edited by Michael Rydelnik and Edwin Blum, 573–89. Chicago: Moody Publishers, 2019.

Rydelnik, Michael A. "Psalm 110: The Messiah as Eternal King Priest." In *The Moody Handbook of Messianic Prophecy*, edited by Michael Rydelnik and Edwin Blum, 673–91. Chicago: Moody Publishers, 2019.

Snearly, Michael K. "Psalm 118: The Rejected Stone." In *The Moody Handbook of Messianic Prophecy*, edited by Michael Rydelnik and Edwin Blum, 693–700. Chicago: Moody Publishers, 2019.

Spencer, James. "Psalm 72: The Messiah as Ideal King." In *The Moody Handbook of Messianic Prophecy*, edited by Michael Rydelnik and Edwin Blum, 605–16. Chicago: Moody Publishers, 2019.

Vowell, Michael. "Psalm 132: The Messianic Restoration of the Davidic Throne." In *The Moody Handbook of Messianic Prophecy*, edited by Michael Rydelnik and Edwin Blum, 701–9. Chicago: Moody Publishers, 2019.

CHAPTER 7: ISAIAH, THE OLD TESTAMENT BIOGRAPHER OF THE MESSIAH

Brown, Michael L. "Isaiah 52:13–53:12: The Substitution of the Servant of the Lord." In *The Moody Handbook of Messianic Prophecy*, edited by Michael Rydelnik and Edwin Blum, 961–74. Chicago: Moody Publishers, 2019.

Coakley, James F. "Isaiah 35:1–10: The Messianic Era." In *The Moody Handbook of Messianic Prophecy*, edited by Michael Rydelnik and Edwin Blum, 907–19. Chicago: Moody Publishers, 2019.

Firth, David G. and H. G. M. Williamson. *Interpreting Isaiah: Issues and Approaches.* Downers Grove, IL: InterVarsity Press, 2009.

Hindson, Edward E. "Isaiah 9:1–7: The Deity of Messiah." In *The Moody Handbook of Messianic Prophecy*, edited by Michael Rydelnik and Edwin Blum, 831–43. Chicago: Moody Publishers, 2019.

———. "Isaiah 11:1–16: The Reign of the Righteous Messianic King." In *The Moody Handbook of Messianic Prophecy*, edited by Michael Rydelnik and Edwin Blum, 845–58. Chicago: Moody Publishers, 2019.

———. "Isaiah 61:1–6: The Spirit-Anointed Messiah and His Promise of Restoration." In *The Moody Handbook of Messianic Prophecy*, edited by Michael Rydelnik and Edwin Blum, 983–96. Chicago: Moody Publishers, 2019.

Johnson, Elliott E. "The Message of the Servant Songs." In *The Moody Handbook of Messianic Prophecy*, edited by Michael Rydelnik and Edwin Blum, 921–29. Chicago: Moody Publishers, 2019.

Lessing, R. Reed. *Isaiah 40–55*. Concordia Commentary. St. Louis: Concordia Publishing House, 2011.

———. *Isaiah 56–66*. Concordia Commentary. St. Louis: Concordia Publishing House, 2014.

McConville, J. Gordon. "Rhetoric and Truth in Isaiah: An Approach to Messianic Interpretation in the Old Testament." In *The Moody Handbook of Messianic Prophecy*, edited by Michael Rydelnik and Edwin Blum, 181–99. Chicago: Moody Publishers, 2019.

Oswalt, John N. "Kings and Kingdoms in the Book of Isaiah." In *The Seed of Promise: The Sufferings and Glory of the Messiah*, edited by Paul R. Williamson and Rita F. Cefalu, 200–218. Wilmore, KY: GlossaHouse, 2020.

Sawyer, John F. A. *The Fifth Gospel: Isaiah in the History of Christianity.* Cambridge University Press, 2000.

CHAPTER 8: JEREMIAH, EZEKIEL, AND DANIEL: VISIONS OF THE MESSIAH

Block, Daniel I. "Ezekiel 34:20–31: The Shepherd of Israel." In *The Moody Handbook of Messianic Prophecy*, edited by Michael Rydelnik and Edwin Blum, 1083–95. Chicago: Moody Publishers, 2019.

Brown, Michael L. "Jeremiah 23:5–6: The Divine Branch of the Lord." In *The Moody Handbook of Messianic Prophecy*, edited by Michael Rydelnik and Edwin Blum, 1011–19. Chicago: Moody Publishers, 2019.

Hummel, Horace D. *Ezekiel 1–20*. Concordia Commentary. St. Louis: Concordia Publishing House, 2004.

———. *Ezekiel 21–48*. Concordia Commentary. St. Louis: Concordia Publishing House, 2007.

Lessing, R. Reed. *Overcoming Life's Sorrows: Learning from Jeremiah*. St. Louis: Concordia Publishing House, 2021.

Mathews, Josh. "Jeremiah 31:31–34: The New Covenant." In *The Moody Handbook of Messianic Prophecy*, edited by Michael Rydelnik and Edwin Blum, 1035–47. Chicago: Moody Publishers, 2019.

McKinion, Randall L. "Jeremiah 33:14–26: The Branch and the Abrahamic Promises." In *The Moody Handbook of Messianic Prophecy*, edited by Michael Rydelnik and Edwin Blum, 1049–62. Chicago: Moody Publishers, 2019.

Price, J. Randall. "Ezekiel 37:15–28: The Restoration of Israel under the One Shepherd." In *The Moody Handbook of Messianic Prophecy*, edited by Michael Rydelnik and Edwin Blum, 1097–113. Chicago: Moody Publishers, 2019.

Steinmann, Andrew E. *Daniel*. Concordia Commentary. St. Louis: Concordia Publishing House, 2008.

Tanner, J. Paul. "Daniel 7:13–27: The Glorious Son of Man." In *The Moody Handbook of Messianic Prophecy*, edited by Michael Rydelnik and Edwin Blum, 1127–38. Chicago: Moody Publishers, 2019.

Woods, Andrew M. "Jeremiah 30:1–24: The Messiah: Israel's Deliverer and King." In *The Moody Handbook of Messianic Prophecy*, edited by Michael Rydelnik and Edwin Blum, 1021–33. Chicago: Moody Publishers, 2019.

CHAPTER 9: THE MAJOR THEME OF THE MINOR PROPHETS: THE PROMISE OF MESSIANIC GRACE

Blum, Edwin A. "Joel 2:28–32: The Messianic Outpouring of the Spirit." In *The Moody Handbook of Messianic Prophecy*, edited by Michael Rydelnik and Edwin Blum, 1177–85. Chicago: Moody Publishers, 2019.

Brown, Michael L. "Zechariah 6:9–15: The Royal Priesthood of Messiah." In *The Moody Handbook of Messianic Prophecy*, edited by Michael Rydelnik and Edwin Blum, 1247–59. Chicago: Moody Publishers, 2019.

Chou, Abner. "Zechariah 11:4–14: The Rejected Shepherd." In *The Moody Handbook of Messianic Prophecy*, edited by Michael Rydelnik and Edwin Blum, 1271–83. Chicago: Moody Publishers, 2019.

Clendenen, E. Ray. "Malachi 3:1; 4:1–5: The Messiah as Messenger of the Lord." In *The Moody Handbook of Messianic Prophecy*, edited by Michael Rydelnik and Edwin Blum, 1327–38. Chicago: Moody Publishers, 2019.

Engman, Leon. "Micah 5:2–5[a]: Bethlehem: Birthplace of the Messianic King." In *The Moody Handbook of Messianic Prophecy*, edited by Michael Rydelnik and Edwin Blum, 1207–17. Chicago: Moody Publishers, 2019.

Finkbeiner, David. "Haggai 2:6–9, 21–23: The Messiah: The Chosen Signet Ring of God." In *The Moody Handbook of Messianic Prophecy*, edited by Michael Rydelnik and Edwin Blum, 1219–34. Chicago: Moody Publishers, 2019.

———. "Hosea 3:4–5: Israel's Present Estrangement and Future Restoration." In *The Moody Handbook of Messianic Prophecy*, edited by Michael Rydelnik and Edwin Blum, 1153–66. Chicago: Moody Publishers, 2019.

Lessing, R. Reed. *Amos*. Concordia Commentary. St. Louis: Concordia Publishing House, 2009.

———. *Jonah*. Concordia Commentary. St. Louis: Concordia Publishing House, 2011.

———. *Zechariah*. Concordia Commentary. St. Louis: Concordia Publishing House, 2021.

Price, J. Randall. "Zechariah 13:7–9: The Striking of the Shepherd King." In *The Moody Handbook of Messianic Prophecy*, edited by Michael Rydelnik and Edwin Blum, 1301–13. Chicago: Moody Publishers, 2019.

Stallard, Mike. "Zechariah 3:1–10: The Messiah and His Restoration of Israel." In *The Moody Handbook of Messianic Prophecy*, edited by Michael Rydelnik and Edwin Blum, 1235–46. Chicago: Moody Publishers, 2019.

Stuart, Daniel E. "Zechariah 12:10–13:1: The Pierced Messiah." In *The Moody Handbook of Messianic Prophecy*, edited by Michael Rydelnik and Edwin Blum, 1285–1300. Chicago: Moody Publishers, 2019.

Zuber, Kevin D. "Zechariah 9:9–10: Rejoice Your King Is Coming." In *The Moody Handbook of Messianic Prophecy*, edited by Michael Rydelnik and Edwin Blum, 1261–70. Chicago: Moody Publishers, 2019.

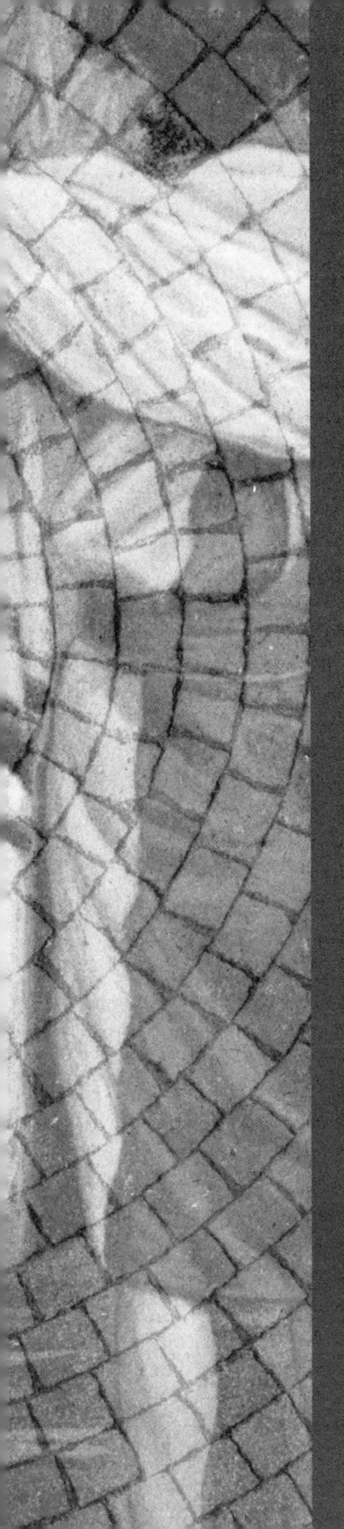

MESSIANIC PROPHECIES IN THE OLD TESTAMENT

This list is not intended to be exhaustive. Instead, it catalogs the most important messianic prophecies in the Old Testament.

Gn 3:14–15—Crushing the Serpent's Head

Gn 9:25–27—The God of Shem

Gn 12:2–3—The Call of Abram

Gn 22:15–18—Overcoming the Enemies' Gate

Gn 26:2–5— All Nations Blessed

Gn 27:27–29—Jacob Blessed

Gn 28:12–15—Jacob's Staircase Dream

Gn 49:8–12—The Lion of Judah

Nu 23:7–10, 18–24—Balaam's First Oracles

Nu 24:3–9; 15–24—Balaam Sees Him

Dt 18:15–19—Prophet like Moses

1Sm 2:1–10 (esp. v. 10)—King Messiah

1Sm 2:30–36—The Faithful Priest

2Sm 7:4–16; 1Ch 17:4–14—The Davidic Covenant

2Sm 7:18–29; 1Ch 17:16–27— David Acknowledges God's Promise

2Sm 23:1–7—David's Last Words

Jb 9:25–35 (esp. v. 33)—Job Longs for Mediator

Jb 16:18–22— The Advocate

Jb 19:23–27—Job's Living Redeemer

Jb 33:23–28—The Mediating Messenger

Ps 2—The Son of God

Ps 8—The Son of Man

Ps 16—God Will Not Abandon His Servant

Ps 22—The Suffering Messiah

Ps 40—Written about in the Scroll

Ps 45—The Messiah's Wedding

Ps 68—The Messiah's Ascent

Ps 69—Gall and Vinegar to Drink

Ps 72—Ruling to the Ends of the Earth

Ps 89—"David, My Servant"

Ps 110—A Scepter from Zion

Ps 118—The Rejected Stone

Ps 132—A Horn for David

Pr 3:13–20—Wisdom as Tree of Life

Pr 8:12–36—Wisdom as Creator

Pr 30:2–4—God's Son and His Name

Is 2:2–5; Mi 4:1–5—The Mountain of the Lord's House

Is 4:2–6—The Branch of the Lord

Is 7:13–16—Immanuel

Is 9:2–7—Wonderful Counselor

Is 11:1–16—A Shoot from Jesse's Stump

Is 24:21–23—Reign from Zion

Is 28:16—A Cornerstone in Zion

Is 35:5–6—The Eyes of the Blind Opened

Is 42:1–9—The Servant's Mission

Is 49:1–13—A Light to the Nations

Is 50:4–11—The Lord Helps His Servant

Is 52:13–53:12—The Suffering Servant

Is 55—A Witness to the Peoples

Is 61—Anointed to Bring Good News

Is 63:1–6—Who Is Coming from Edom?

Jer 23:5–6—A Righteous Branch for David

Jer 30—"David Their King"

Jer 31:15–17, 31–34—The New Covenant

Jer 33—The Lord Is Our Righteousness

Ezk 17:22–24—The Majestic Cedar

Ezk 34:11–31—The Shepherd

Ezk 37—Servant David as Prince

Dn 7:13–14—The Son of Man

Dn 9:24–27—The Coming Prince

Dn 10:5–11:1—A Man Dressed in Linen

Hos 3:4–5—David, Their King

Am 9:11–15—David's Fallen Booth

Ob 19–21—The Kingdom Will Be the Lord's

Mi 2:12–13—King of the Remnant of Israel

Mi 5:1–15—A Ruler from Bethlehem

Hg 2:6–9—The Temple Filled with Glory

Zec 3:8–10—My Servant, the Branch

Zec 9:9–13—The King on a Donkey

Zec 11:4–14—Thirty Pieces of Silver

Zec 12:10–14—Mourning for the One They Pierced

Zec 13:1–9—Strike the Shepherd

Mal 3:1–5—The Messenger of the Covenant

Mal 4:1–6—The Prophet Elijah